BUSKER

Stories from the Streets of Paris

A memoir by Nisha Coleman

HAGIOS PRESS

A CIP catalogue record for this book is available from Library and archives Canada.

ISBN: 978-1-926710-37-2

Edited by Harold Rhenisch
Designed and typeset by Donald Ward
Cover Art: collage created by the author
Cover design by Tania Wolk, Go Giraffe Go Inc.
Set in Adobe Garamond Pro
Printed and bound in Canada at Houghton Boston Printers and Lithographers, Saskatoon.

The publishers gratefully acknowledge the assistance of the Saskatchewan Arts Board, The Canada Council for the Arts and Creative Saskatchewan in the production of this book.

HAGIOS PRESS
Box 33024 Cathedral PO
Regina, SK, S4T 7X2
hagiospress@accesscom.ca
www.hagiospress.com

Pour Frédéric

If you don't know where you are going, any road will get you there.
— Lewis Carroll

There flowed in her veins some of the blood of the bohemian and the adventuress who runs barefoot.

— Victor Hugo

PRELUDIO

I've always wanted to live this way — sleeping when tired, eating when hungry, working when inspired. In other words, free. My dreams have time to resolve, because I wake when my body decides. I've grown accustomed to this tiny studio sublet. The bedroom is a narrow mattress on a thinly carpeted floor, next to a window. Roll off, and I enter the kitchen: a small sink, a hotplate, and a couple of cupboards. Turn around and I'm in the office: a small desk and an ailing café chair I found abandoned on the street. There are no plants, and for the first time in my life no animals. I'm the only thing breathing in here.

I eat my morning staple, Nutella toast, standing at the window with a coffee steaming on the sill. Below is the *Canal de l'Ourq,* where a group of kayakers circle in the shimmering ripples. They seem young and silly, high schoolers maybe, holding their paddles too high and splashing each other, squealing. The canal and the trees lining it are about as close to the elements as one can get here. In a city where even blades of grass are pruned and protected, where trees grow in lines, their shapes predetermined in blueprints, it's rare to open your eyes in the morning to wide green leaves flapping freely and the sun catching in the water. I'm horseshoe-in-the-ass lucky to live here.

I didn't come to Paris to live alone as a street musician. When I arrived at the Charles de Gaulle airport in early May, I was expecting to be whisked into the arms of the Parisian who invited me here, the handsome young journalist who had found me irresistible, charming and beautiful. The man who had made me believe in love at first sight.

"Come to see me in Paris," he wrote after we met in Canada. "Your life will be ten thousand times nicer than your best dreams."

A lover in Paris sounded pretty great to me, and it was ideal timing. I needed something to do after I finished my degree in psychology. Grad school wasn't seducing me. Adventure was. And love? Well, why not? Pierre seemed smitten and I let his enthusiasm grab hold. Grad school required decisions, direction, entrance exams and competition. Pierre *wanted* me. My Paris plan anchored me through my last year of university and didn't let go until I shuffled, bleary-eyed through the arrival gate.

"It didn't work out," is what I mostly tell people. I tend to stick to the short version.

I'VE BEEN LIVING ALONE NOW for almost three months, and I'm starting to get the hang of it. I'm learning to survive in this city. I make mistakes. Constantly. Take the wrong metro in the wrong direction. Find myself hopelessly lost in Paris' sinewy streets if I stray even briefly from a route I know. I'm learning French. Slowly. A language I thought I knew. I am lonely some of the time and scared much of the time, but I think that's the way adventure works. That's what I tell myself. My violin pays my rent, feeds me, takes me to new neighbourhoods and introduces me to people I wouldn't otherwise meet. It has cleared a path to the heart of the city, behind the scenes, beyond the cafés and the museums. My Paris is multi-layered and my violin is my access code to every tier. Music transcends social barriers, from the city's homeless to the elite.

"How long are you going to stay in France?" ask passers-by who stop to chat. Once they learn I'm a foreigner, they assume I'll eventually leave, but I only shrug. I try not to focus on the future. Paris has taught me not to have expectations.

I came here with only a backpack and a violin, so my wardrobe is modest — and most of it is in the dirty laundry pile. After a quick shower that converts the apartment into a steam bath, I put on a frayed mauve T-shirt and my handmade patchwork skirt, throw my long, increasingly unruly curls into a messy bun and tie a bright blue scarf over top. It's hot for Blundstones, but I've received enough disapproving glances at my Birkenstocks to gather that sandals are reserved for tourists and nuns. I don't dress like

Parisian women, in ballet slipper shoes or elegant summer dresses, but I'm careful to avoid anything that might associate me with tourists. Or nuns. No backpack, running shoes or camera. I'm somewhere in between — a resident, but not quite a local. I'm not even an *étrangère*. I'm a *sans papier*. It's complicated.

VIOLIN SLUNG OVER MY SHOULDER, I heave the thick blue door to the apartment shut and wind my way down the echoey stairwell. My street, *Quai de la Loire,* in the 19th Arrondissement, is a narrow cobblestone pocket of calm. In the daytime there are only stray tourists and a few strollers pushed by African nannies in colour-exploding dresses. Later, the quay will animate with picnickers and pétanque players. Wine will pour and steel balls will sail along the dirt strip between the bike path and the edge of the quay.

At the end of my street the scene shifts. Four avenues intersect, creating a diesel haze and a dissonance of car horns. I head toward it and plunge into the Metro through narrow, urine-scented tunnels, with grimy black floors and garish ads lining the white tiled walls. The pace quickens down here, as though commuters, once underground, are stricken with a sudden urgency to reach their destination. I speed walk with the rest of them.

The Metro car is quite full, but I manage to claim one of the last remaining pull-down seats. The buzzer sounds and a young Roma man with an accordion slips in just before the doors slam shut. In-car busking is illegal, and those who do it are rarely musically inclined — they halfheartedly churn out simple tunes on old, beat-up instruments — but this guy's different. He plays enhanced renditions of French folk songs with sophisticated runs and embellishments, swaying gracefully, eyes closed and smiling as his fingers whiz along the keys. The energy in the car lightens. He's probably played these tunes hundreds of times, yet he is handling each note with care. After three pieces, he swings his instrument behind him and winds his way through with a tattered paper cup. Some passengers scrunch their faces and turn away, but many open their wallets. When he passes by I have a euro ready, and as I drop it in the cup his dark eyes lift to meet mine. He nods at my violin and winks. When the doors open, he slides out and into the next car. For three stations I stare at the pale, stone-faced Parisians and listen to his muted melodies. At the *Hotel de Ville* exit I emerge into the pulsing city centre. The main street here, *Rue de Rivoli,* is among the busiest in Paris — a chain store mecca for both tourists and locals, their shopping itineraries traceable by the collection of bags they tote. Odours of baking bread and sweet pastries drift from a nearby bakery and mingle with the hot diesel air. I weave through the tightly packed crowd and cross the City Hall Plaza, *Place de Grève.* This was where public executions happened for centuries — criminals done in by swords, axes or guillotines, or else drawn and quartered, depending on the century and social status. With its temporary exhibit on plants, you wouldn't guess it now. Wooden boardwalks have been installed, leading to a variety of mini ecosystems. A man kneels before a group of small children and points to the lily pads in a tiny pond while explaining the importance of wetlands. Behind it, the Paris City Hall is palace-like, with intricate stonework, carvings and bronze statues. There are tour buses parked in front. I crouch slightly as I hurry past the groups lined up snapping photos. They don't want me in their frames. Not yet.

Along the Seine, the *bouquinistes* have opened their dark green metal bookstalls. Most of them are older, spectacled men smoking cigarettes in lawn chairs set up off to the sides of their booths. They sell old hardcover classics, *Le Petit Prince* and *Les Misérables,* or posters of *Le Moulin Rouge* and *Le Chat Noir Café.* A few offer Eiffel tower figurines, berets and baguette fridge magnets. Some of them nod to me as I pass. They've seen me around. They too are at the mercy of the elements and the tourists. But they are stationary and I am nimble and quick.

"*Bon courage!*" an old man with a pipe calls after me from his fold-up perch.

I cross the bridge to *Île Saint-Louis*, one of two small islands in the centre of the city. During the Middle Ages, it was a grazing area for market cattle, but now it's home to specialty boutiques, upscale restaurants, renowned ice cream and outrageously priced real estate. It's lunchtime, so the island is swarming with tourists in bright white running shoes or sandals, with cameras hanging around their necks like oversized pendants. They clutch guidebooks to their chests and traipse about in a happy daze with ice cream cones from the esteemed Berthillon wedged in their fists.

The *Saint-Louis* pedestrian bridge joins the two islands and is one of the hottest busking spots in the city. It's often taken, but not today, so I hurry to its centre and open my case. For the next while, the bridge belongs to me.

I tighten and rosin my bow, taking my time as I reacquaint myself to the space and assess today's energy. A performer in a concert hall does the same. There is a calm, lazy feel, far from the furious rush in the Metro. Tourist time reigns, which means moments can stretch and obligations are minimal. The people here are on a vacation high — blissfully free — the sun is in full force and the air is dry. I slip my shoulder rest onto my violin and raise it into position. As soon as I feel its firm body between my chest and chin I am grounded.

I don't look at the people passing by. Not yet. Instead, I lift my bow and begin to tune, taking my time with the open strings, letting their bright buzz break the ice. I feel the first eyes on me, waiting to see what I'll play. Two lovers pause, curious.

I decide to start with something bright and upbeat. A Handel sonata. The first movement is slow but in a cheerful F Major key to match the festive summer flavour. The two fast movements are fun and light-hearted, with playful string crossings and driving 16th notes. The sound is swallowed by the Seine, stolen by the wind, and its tone is rendered thin and dry by the sun, but sound quality isn't important here — it is the charm of the location that counts. Tourists grasp for their cameras. Some stop and lean against the bridge railing, others smile and flip a euro in my case on their way by. Parents from Italy, Spain, Japan and America — I can usually tell by the writing on their guide books — place coins in their kids' palms and nudge them toward my case. The little ones often stoop and take coins out of my case before their parents intervene. The older ones hesitate, transfixed and shy before dropping the coin. It's likely their first experience with a street performer — maybe even their first glimpse of a violin.

I was eight the first time I saw a busker — a young man playing classical guitar in the Toronto subway. At first I thought it was a recording, but when my mom and I came around the corner I saw that he was real: sitting against a pillar, swaying to the music with his head bent toward the strings. I was amazed that someone would do such a thing — *could* do such a thing: perform for random strangers. He seemed so vulnerable, at the mercy of all the people rushing by. And he was, but what you don't see when you yourself are the one rushing by is how generous anonymous people can be. As a busker, you learn to trust strangers. You have to.

When my bow comes off the string and the last notes fade into the sound of shuffling feet, the small gathering of people around me smile and applaud before turning to resume their agendas. I'm just a blip in their marathon tour of Paris, an element of surprise amidst the must-sees like the Louvre, the Eiffel Tower and a ride on the Bateau Mouche. Maybe one day they'll review their Paris photos and remember this afternoon in the sun, with the ice cream and the Handel.

An older French woman with pale skin and a white scarf tied around her head asks, "*Pouvez-vous jouer du Vivaldi?*" She has bourgeois confidence and reserved mannerisms — a refined, cultured woman with money. She might even be one of the island's exclusive residents. I begin the third movement of *Autumn* and she leans against the metal railing, eyes closed. Her thin lips form a smile, as if remembering something distant but pleasant. For a moment she is transported elsewhere.

I see it every day. Music is a powerful trigger. Last week, I was trying out a new spot on a narrow street in the Latin Quarter when a man approached, his cheeks wet with tears. "*Merci, mademoiselle*," he said as he placed a ten-euro bill in my case. Before I'd even finished the concerto, an old woman, face crumpled, waddled out onto her balcony and waved me away in disgust. While moving one person to tears, I had disturbed another. In one of the world's most densely populated cities, it's almost impossible to play anywhere without annoying *somebody*.

This bridge is different. It's too far away for nearby residents to detect even a whisper of melody. That's one of the reasons this location is among the most competitive: here you'll never get the boot. Already in the last hour, a guitarist, a flutist and a saxophonist have sauntered past, glancing at me briefly before continuing their search. Securing a good spot is a daily balance of chance and strategy.

On my right, a man strides toward me, smiling as if we know each other. He's wearing baggy jeans, a T-shirt, and a small canvas backpack slung on his right shoulder. Wispy grey hair sprouts in wild tufts from under his navy blue baseball cap. I figure he's either homeless or drunk. This line of work tends to attract the mentally unsound and those under the influence. Recently, for example, a bald, obese man approached, claimed he was my guardian angel and handed me two bottles of orange juice before trying to kiss me. A few days after that, a woman in tight jeans, her breath thick with liquor, began twirling and throwing her body wildly as I played a simple gavotte. It was entertaining at first, but her erratic moves were scaring away the tourists, so eventually I had to leave to find another afternoon playing spot.

This guy, though, doesn't have the signature drunken wobble, and up close I see that he's too clean and healthy to be homeless. He sits cross-legged in front of me, flips his bag upside down, and dozens of markers and ballpoint pens spill onto the pavement. He opens a small ringed notebook and begins to colour. His head is bent forward, but I can see he's grinning as he works. Half an hour later he hands me his masterpiece: an abstract psychedelia — a swirling blend of brown, yellow, blue and green. The paper is still wet with marker.

I thank him and tuck his drawing into my case. He smiles, loads his supplies back into his bag and continues on toward *Île Saint-Louis*, humming as he bobs away. He's not drunk after all — just part of the city.

It isn't good busking etiquette to play in one location for too long, especially one so coveted, so after two hours I move on. As I snap my bow in place, from behind I hear: "*Mademoiselle?*"

I turn to see a tall man leaning on a cane. He looks more like a Hell's Angel than a Frenchman. He is outfitted with a long black and white stranded ponytail, faded jeans and a grey button-up shirt. His dark moist eyes are sad but friendly.

"*Est-ce que vous voulez boire un café?*" he asks, gesturing to the cafe on the *Île de la Cité* side of the bridge.

I get a lot of invitations for coffee, at least one a day, and I usually accept. In Paris, I'll pretty much speak to anyone, at least for a short while. It's my way of learning French. The meetings are brief, require no long-term engagement and allow me a window into French society — always with a different view. Espressos can easily be consumed in three sips. Savoured, they can last for ten. If the conversation is particularly interesting, I'll order another. Of course, if anything goes awry, I can down it in one.

We take a seat on the terrace next to the immaculate *Notre-Dame* garden. He lights a cigarette and tells me his name is Martin. I let him lead the conversation, which begins with the usual inquiries: *Where are you from? How long have you been in France? How long have you played violin?* My pre-formulated answers give a false impression that my French is half decent: "*Je viens du Canada. Je suis en France depuis trois mois. Je joue le violon depuis 11 ans.*"

Once Martin launches into his story, though, things get considerably more complicated. His deep voice garbles his speech as he begins to tell me about a near-fatal motorcycle accident last year. Words drop into the abyss of incomprehension, but I'm able to piece together an overall gloomy picture. He underwent months of rehabilitation. His wife left him and he descended into depression. I listen sympathetically and nod a lot. As with many of the men I meet, Martin is lonely and needs to talk. After about half an hour, though, I tell him I have to get back to work. It's mid-afternoon — prime busking time. He nods with understanding. *"Bonne continuation, mademoiselle,"* he says as I toss my violin over my shoulder.

I like talking with people like Martin, older dudes with stories, life experience and minimal expectations. They have a paternal air about them. They correct my French, give me advice on places I could play or share historical facts about the city. *"Appartement* is masculine," an older man explained to me the other day. "But if you're using an adjective like *beau*, because of the vowel, you say *bel* instead. *Un bel appartement. Tu comprends?"* It's like being re-raised, which is reassuring for a girl who grew up with an emotionally distant father prone to depression. In Paris I have dads wherever I go. There is a lightness to these fleeting connections. They are pleasant but tiptoe along the surface. I remain unknowable. Untouchable. Free.

I grab a banana from a fruit stand along the *Rue de Rivoli* and devour it on a bench at *Place des Vosges* — my most recent discovery. It's the oldest square in Paris, dating back to the early sixteen hundreds. Its centre quadrant is divided into four identical grassy areas, each with an elegant two layered fountain and rows of immaculately pruned linden trees along limestone pathways. Ancient archways on all four sides add to the stark symmetry. Due to the flawless weather, the place is teeming with locals and tourists: sunbathing, picnicking, flirting on the grass and strolling under the archways, peering into the many art galleries. In the middle of the square, tourists snap pictures of a bronze Louis XIII perched on his horse. The original was melted during the Revolution, the plaque explains. This one's a reproduction, but no one seems to mind.

The east and west sides have restaurants with sprawling outside terraces. Waiters in bow ties and vests skirt gracefully around tables. Cork screws poke from the pockets of their crisp white aprons. The south end of the square features the Victor Hugo House, as well as a collection of homeless people under its archway. One is panhandling with a *"J'ai faim"* sign, but the rest doze, bundled in sweaters and sleeping bags despite the afternoon heat. I play on the north side, which has several art galleries, an antique shop and, halfway down, two painters, George and Maâmar.

Maâmar greets me with a shy wave and George kisses me on the cheeks, *les bises*, the customary greeting. When I first came to Paris, I found it shockingly intimate, but it has now become the norm. George is the extrovert of the pair; when potential buyers stop to admire their work, he does all talking. He wears a scarf and a beret, keeps a neatly trimmed beard, and his eyes gleam as if he's always sharing a joke. Maâmar is tall and quiet, with dark, kind eyes. He keeps to himself and is usually engaged in his latest sketch or painting. George and Maâmar have spread their prints out on two tables against the wall under the archways. Maâmar's are watercolours and George's are oils, but both depict scenes from the neighbourhood, *Place des Vosges* or the colourful wooden facades of nearby cafés. The pair have been selling their prints here for years.

A soprano's lament is pouring from behind the archway where I usually play. Monsieur Mystique. His voice timbre sounds like a woman's, so it's fun to watch people's expressions change when they peer into the archway and discover a large bald man in a cape. His voice is ethereal. Coming from a body like his is even more unusual, which is why he can attract large crowds. He's only practicing today and won't stay for long. On the weekends, though, *Place des Vosges* is his. All the buskers know that. When the piece ends, Monsieur Mystique packs up his stereo and sheet music and heads toward us, dragging his suitcase noisily behind him.

"Mystique!" he shouts with a gap-toothed grin that matches

my own. His black cape sweeps around his ample body. A top hat rests obediently on his hairless head. His red shoes have leather coils and spikes that poke out from under his long black pants. *"Joue, Nisha!"* he yells, shoving his fist to the sky.

Monsieur Mystique stays to chat with the painters, while I take over the archway. The acoustics are rich and generous here. I begin with a slow gypsy tune, bringing the bow slowly across the strings. The sustained notes blend as the sound swells, cloaking me in reverberating melody. The tourists are of a calmer sort here than in the area around *Notre-Dame*. They take more care framing their photos and stay longer, leaning on the ancient arches to listen.

After an hour or so, I notice a young man lingering longer than the others. He is short, with a striped, collared shirt and tight black pants. His blond hair is gelled straight up and his thumbs are hooked casually in the pockets of his jeans. A Parisian.

"Génial!" he spouts when I lower my violin, and he skips over with a two-euro coin.

"T'es musicien?" I ask.

He shakes his head wistfully. But he works for musicians, he says, as a sound engineer. He introduces himself as Cédric, then tells me about a Jazz Manouche concert he's attending later tonight with some friends. It's featuring a violinist.

"Tu veux venir?"

Pourquoi pas?

AFTER A CHANGE OF CLOTHES and a dinner of some olives, a carrot and crackers, I head back out to meet Cédric. I feel vulnerable walking the streets without my violin. It's as if I've been suddenly disarmed. I've grown dependent on it, I realize. I don't feel secure without its weight.

Cédric is waiting where the escalator deposits me onto the pavement. I follow him down the narrow Latin Quarter streets, which are packed with tourist families seeking places to eat. They zigzag slowly and stop frequently to peer in the windows. We veer around them. Several universities are also in this area, and groups of students are flooding the streets on a mission for a post-study drink. The street is popping with expectation. Energy fizzes around us like champagne.

THE VENUE IS CRAMMED with people and heavy with smoke. The walls are mediaeval, with thick dark wooden beams and abstract paintings of musicians playing saxophone, piano and trumpet. Cédric introduces me to his friends, who are jammed into the corner, smoking and drinking Belgian beer in round goblets. They stand as I approach and give me the *bises*. Between the first and second kiss, they shout their names over the roar of the bar, but by the time I sit down I've forgotten them all. Everyone speaks quickly between cigarette inhales, and with the music blasting and the surrounding shouts and laughter it's impossible to keep up with the conversation. The best I can do is follow each speaker with my eyes and smile when it seems appropriate. I'm relieved when the concert is announced and we descend the winding stone steps to the dim, smoke-filled basement.

I follow Cédric as he pushes his way to the front. Two guitars, an upright bass and a violin lie waiting on their stands. After a few minutes the musicians appear and walk to their instruments. My eyes are on the violinist, who brushes his curly blond hair out of the way and places his instrument under his chin.

They begin with *Sweet Georgia Brown*. From beneath his locks the violinist's face is contorted in concentration. His bottom lip twitches, while his thick fingers move with surprising dexterity and his left hand sails up and down the fingerboard. The solo travels from musician to musician like a shifting spark of inspiration, a moment of fury channelled through their fingers. The players are constantly catching each other's gaze and smiling, as if acknowledging that they are contained within the piece of music. It's like a moving vehicle they will not exit until it stops.

Before long, sweat has soaked through the violinist's white cotton shirt. As the group moves from one standard to another, I think of Stéphane Grapelli, the grandfather of jazz violin, who began his career busking on the streets of Paris and later played in smoky joints like this one before he started filling concert halls. I wish I could play like him, and like this guy, with this balance of abandonment and concentration. The violin seems like an extension of his body and he appears aware of little else. Smoke permeates the air, trapped in this ancient stone basement, and begins to make my eyes sting and water. I glance over at Cédéric. He is grinning up at the music, his head nodding as if in constant agreement.

AT THE END OF THE EVENING, I return to the cool air, flushed with inspiration. The sun has set, and the street lights have taken over, casting an orange glow over the cobblestones. The Latin Quarter is still heavy with tourists, tipsy on wine now, laughing and shouting.

Finally, we stop at the Metro entrance. I thank Cédric for inviting me, and he says, "*C'était un plaisir!*" as he kisses my cheeks. We exchange numbers, then I descend to catch the last Metro — but I won't hear from him. Nor will I call him. Contacts are easily made here, but deep lasting friendships are rare. Cédric is Parisian, busy with work and friends. He's a flash among many in this city of light.

The day has been eventful but not out of the ordinary. Tomorrow will bring much of the same: listeners and competitors; coffees with strangers; weirdoes, friendly locals and google-eyed tourists; unhappy shit disturbers and joyous lunatics. Tomorrow will also bring the unforeseeable. I am suspended in the present, at the mercy of haphazard events and strangers. It may not be the human love story I had envisioned, but it's a love story nonetheless. With a city. And the people in it.

LOURE

I DIDN'T KNOW PIERRE WELL. IT WAS LAST SUMMER. I'd grown tired of student jobs working retail or painting houses, so I decided on a whim to go to Halifax and busk. Playing on the street wasn't new to me. I'd been doing it off and on for years. It was fun and it paid well, but I'd always done it as a Saturday afternoon gig. This was the first summer I decided to try it full time.

Once I found the right busking spots, it quickly proved to be worthwhile. I found a cheap sublet and spent most of my days playing by the harbour or along one of the main streets, just outside the Visitor Centre — which is where Pierre discovered me one steamy July afternoon. I was playing Bach when I noticed him watching me in the distance, his arms folded casually. When the piece ended, he sauntered over with a confident smile.

"Would you like to have a coffee?" he asked. Just like that.

The invitation caught me off guard, but his accent was alluring, and no one had ever asked me out in this way, certainly not a stranger off the street. His dark eyes were calm and confident. I didn't think about it long. I was deeply flattered.

"Sure!" I said.

We had coffee at a nearby terrace. Pierre was a journalist from Paris, with a natural tendency to ask questions, which he did between cigarette inhales. But I preferred asking him questions because I liked hearing him speak in his sweet, singing accent. Everything he said sounded sensual and interesting. I urged him to tell me all about life in what I imagined was the most magical city on the planet.

"What can I say?" he shrugged, blowing a thin jet of smoke from the corner of his mouth. "Paris is a very beautiful city. But I've lived there my whole life."

Before we parted, we exchanged emails. A week later, Pierre wrote me.

"I'm thinking about you a lot," he confessed. "Why don't you come to see me in Paris? There is so much I want to show you." Then he added the bit about my life improving ten thousand times. He ended his letter with "*Je t'embrasse,*" which French people use frequently when addressing friends and family. But I didn't know that at the time. I took it very seriously.

I'd like to say that I thought about it long and hard. I'd like to say that I weighed the pros and cons of travelling to Paris over furthering my education. I'd like to say that I formulated a Plan B in case things didn't work out with Pierre. I didn't. As soon as I read Pierre's invitation, I knew I would go. It was exactly what I was looking for — a plan, an escape from the looming definition of a career path. I didn't want to have to *be* something. A psychologist? A sociologist? Another graduate with a social science degree working in a café? This was a way out, an invitation to the most romantic city in the world by a handsome Parisian who seemed head over heels for me. I was in my last year of my undergrad, and while most of my friends were planning their career moves, I began preparing for a departure. And by preparing I mean daydreaming. The only form of official planning was the open-ended ticket I bought with the last of my student loan money. I wasn't going to *live* with Pierre, I reassured people who told me I was crazy to move to another country for a man I hardly knew. I was going to *see* him. If things went well, I'd stay. If they didn't, I'd figure something out. When I called my mom to tell her about my plan, I was poised to defend my position. After all, she had taken off to California when she was just 21, and lived in a shack in Topanga Canyon with a tie-dying chemist from New Jersey. Even if she wasn't overjoyed, surely she would understand my need to experience things beyond text books. Par for the course, she didn't challenge my decision. Nor did she celebrate it. She took it in silence, save for a stifled sigh.

THE LAST FEW WEEKS OF UNIVERSITY were torture as my imminent arrival spun through my skull on video replay: *I'll walk through the airport doors, drop my luggage and jump into Pierre's arms. He'll swing me around, holding me close and laughing. Back at his place, there'll be chilled champagne. We'll drink it on his balcony, stealing kisses between sips. Later, we'll stroll hand in hand as he guides me through all his favourite places. We will go out for dinner — somewhere classically French — and spend the evening basking in each other's presence. Finally, back at his place, we'll make love and eventually fall asleep in each other's arms.* Sigh.

"Have fun in France," my dad said the day before I left. The fact that I was going to Paris neither distressed nor delighted him. He was indifferent. Of course, I was used to this, and had long ago given up trying to inspire reactions from him. The downside to the apathy was that I couldn't make him proud. The upside was that I couldn't disappoint him. I gave him a sideways hug good-bye while my mom waited in the car. They'd been divorced for five years. My dad had moved into town, while Mom still kept our house in the woods, ten kilometres out, even though my brother and sister and I had by now all moved away. "Keep in touch," my dad said, though we knew we probably wouldn't.

Mom drove me to the airport the next day. When we reached the security gate, she burst into tears and hugged me with a desperate force, clinging to me as if for the last time. My own eyes filled and I was consumed with guilt and fear. *Is it wrong to go?* I wondered. *Is this completely stupid?* But it was too late for that. The line was moving and uniformed men were shouting at passengers to get their passports ready. I looked back one last time to see my mother's red, tear-streaked face, and I felt awful.

Things got better on the plane — the meal was served, and the complimentary red wine made my thoughts sparkle again. The man beside me, who had a swirl of silver hair and a whistle in his nose, dozed on and off, while an action film played on the screen embedded in the seat in front of him. For me, the idea of sleep was preposterous. I was in an electric state. I didn't even have the attention span for a movie. I kept my screen locked on the animated airplane of the route-tracking program, and watched as the little icon slid almost imperceptibly across the Atlantic.

I'd brought my violin, though Pierre had warned me it was illegal to busk in Paris. That didn't worry me. I didn't care what I did. I would wait tables. I would hand out brochures, clean apartments, do dishes in the back of a café. Even the most menial tasks were appealing when associated with Paris, and Pierre. I had a few years of French behind me, and would surely be fluent in a couple of months. I would explore the city, discover its history, learn to navigate its streets and master the Metro. Along the way, I would meet the locals and eventually I would become *Parisienne* myself. I was up above the clouds. A god on cocaine. Invincible. Capable of anything. And I was absolutely fearless. I would make it all happen.

By the time we eased to the ground, I still hadn't closed my eyes — my second sleepless night. My eyes no longer retained focus and my body was humming. I stared in a daze at the rotating suitcases, until my heavy blue backpack came around the corner. I struggled to secure it on my back, then followed the "*Sortie*" signs. Finally the glass doors slid open and there was Pierre. He was standing motionless before me. Like a mirage. I had thought this moment would come naturally and in a blur of emotion. Now I teetered with uncertainty and my heart began to flail. I lunged forward and gave him an awkward hug, breathing in his tangles — they had grown long since the previous summer. He smelled like sandalwood, the beginnings of a beard had invaded the bottom half of his face, his eyes were not dark brown as I'd remembered them — they were hazel — and the friendly glister I remembered was absent. It was as if, well, as if he had changed his mind. Panic rattled within me and a bubble of clarity rose up from the bottom of my brain. *I don't fucking know this guy.*

"We'll take a taxi," said Pierre. He took my violin from me and headed for the door. I followed after him, stunned as if slapped.

The thin, Asian taxi driver smiled politely and said, "Bonjour,

bonjour," and put my backpack and violin into the trunk of his car. Pierre and I sat together in the back seat, then marinated in the thick silence. My heart was skittering and my shoulders tensed as I scrambled for something to say. We'd been chatting for months on the phone and Internet. It should have been easy. I tried to recall our last conversation, a common joke, something we'd shared. Nothing came. Not even everyday banalities. Not even the weather.

The taxi leapt onto the highway, picked up speed, then slipped into the fast lane, its tires gliding over the seamless pavement. I couldn't see the speedometer, but it felt as if we were going dangerously fast. The cars around us seemed like tiny insects, next to the monster SUVs I'd seen on the 401 heading to the Toronto airport just hours before. There were no minivans or pickup trucks. Seriousness permeated this road. There wasn't room for error at such speeds. No eating doughnuts or slurping to-go coffees or talking on cell phones. There were a few tractor-trailers, but they were European models, flat-nosed and stubby, with licence plates from Italy, Poland, Spain or Portugal. Back home, the trees had still been bare and there'd been patches of snow on the ground, but here the leaves were in full bloom. The chlorophyll was blinding.

"It's so green," I marvelled, pleased to have found something to say.

No one responded.

AFTER A HALF-HOUR OF SUBURBAN WAREHOUSES and tall grey buildings, the real Paris began to show itself. I put my face close to the window and peered at the rows of five-storey white stone buildings — surprisingly uniform — and the narrow sinuous streets that ran between them. The density was staggering. It was like three cities stacked on top of each other. Restaurants and cafés dominated almost every street, with tables spilling onto the sidewalks. Pedestrians darted out from everywhere, crossing the streets in the middle, without regard for crosswalks. Bikes and scooters wove in and out of stalled traffic, and the flashing green crosses of pharmacies gave the streets a festive feel. Everywhere, striped fruit stands displayed piles of oranges, bananas, figs and melons. Each stoplight brought together several new streets, which snaked away again, each iteration growing narrower and narrower the longer we drove. The traffic was at once chaotic and perfectly orchestrated, a Philip Glass overture on wheels. Our driver was quick and efficient, zipping on and off of roundabouts, speeding down a series of one-way streets. Life was all around me, yet all I could think was, "I can't believe people actually *live* here."

We finally stopped on a tiny cobblestone street and Pierre dug in his pocket for his wallet. The price on the digital counter was 54 Euros — about 75 dollars. That was more than I had planned to spend in my first week in the city, but I didn't want Pierre to pay. I found my wallet in my handbag and pulled out a crisp orange 50, a bill that looked too wide and bright to be real. Pierre shook his head and paid the driver himself. I pushed my money back into my wallet and said, "Thank you," but I don't think he heard.

We crossed the narrow one-way street to his building — stone, with symmetrical rectangles carved into it and lion head sculptures under wrought iron balconies. Pierre stopped at a solid red door and punched in his code.

Inside, the building was cool and smelled of old wood and oil paints. The red carpet lining the entry was worn quite thin, with only hints of a pattern lingering in its ancient fibres. A wooden staircase spiralled around and through each level, and soft green and yellow light poured in from stained glass windows. Pierre walked a couple of stairs ahead, with my violin slung over his shoulder. I trailed behind, clutching onto the polished banister as I pulled myself up the five flights. At this point, I probably should have offered to find somewhere else to stay, or at least acknowledged the awkwardness of the situation. It was obvious we had made a mistake and that I shouldn't have come, but I refused to admit defeat so soon. I was determined to regain Pierre's affection and resume my Paris dream. I just wasn't sure how. Then I remembered the gifts I'd brought, rolled up in pants and sweaters in my bag. It was premature, but it would at least ensure a positive exchange. I slid my bag off my shoulder in the hallway and dug the items out one by one.

Pierre blinked at the orange-scented shaving cream. When we'd met, he'd been clean-faced. Now his thick stubble suggested he'd given up the razor months before. He sniffed the bar of handmade soap I'd bought with what looked like suspicion. But to my relief he smiled at the maple syrup.

"This should go in the fridge," he said.

The kitchen was small yet functional. A collection of oils, herbs and tiny vials lined the shelf beside the fridge, and a row of wine bottles lay along the floor under the window. The fridge was tiny, and so were the things inside — little jams, little mustards, little cartons of milk and juice. The maple syrup towered above them all.

If I was feeling more confident, more myself, I might have said something like, "I'm so happy to finally be here." I might have commented on the things I saw: "That's a lot a wine! What are these herbs for? Your kitchen is really cute." I might have been bold enough to take a shower and change my clothes. I might have asked for a glass of water or explained that I hadn't slept in two nights and apologized if I seemed tired. I might have even kissed him. But all the gusto I had possessed earlier was gone. I just stood there, awkward and tongue-tied.

"I'll show you around," Pierre said finally.

I followed him into the dining room, which had a long wooden table in the centre and a buffet against the far wall for fancy dishes. Somehow I hadn't imagined he would be so *established*. Nothing was lacking or haphazard, the way all my student apartments had been, with a makeshift couch of pillows and cushions, a mattress on the floor, and batik fabric concealing holes in the drywall. Pierre was almost 30. He had a real job and a grown-up apartment. I was 23, fresh out of school, with nothing but a backpack and a violin. I don't know what he was expecting me to be, but I obviously wasn't it. He led me out onto a long narrow balcony lined with plants and began naming each one, doing his best to translate into English. This was the most he'd spoken to me yet, so I jumped on the opportunity for a comeback.

"The roses are beautiful!"

"No they aren't," he said. "I haven't watered them enough. They're basically dying."

Blood flowed loudly in my ears, as if my body were preparing to flee. I searched Pierre's eyes for any lingering affection, some indication that this was the man who not so long before had said he couldn't wait for my arrival, who had confessed he couldn't get me out of his mind, who had told me my life here was going to be better than in my best dreams. I studied his face. Aside from the stubble, it still had the rugged handsomeness I'd remembered, but its expression had changed. He was looking at me with indifference and an edge of annoyance, as if we'd just bumped shoulders on the street. The balcony was narrow and we were standing close enough that I could have kissed him then, but I didn't dare. If he recoiled, it would have been the end. Besides Pierre, I was alone in this city.

I turned and peered off the balcony at the narrow cobblestone street below. Fruit and flowers on display outside of boutiques dappled the sidewalks with bright reds, yellows and greens. I took a breath to say something about the impressive view, but it just came out as a shaky sigh.

Pierre continued through the door at the other end of the balcony. I followed him — into the living room. An oriental carpet covered a hardwood floor. Paper lanterns were strung along the ceiling. On the mantel sat framed photos of smiling strangers. There was a small couch in the corner.

Is this where I'll sleep? I wondered. *For how long?*

Then we entered a smaller room, more of a hallway really. A dresser took up the wall on the left. On the other side was a wide wooden desk with a computer and tapes and notebooks piled on top and spilling onto the floor.

"I was working on a documentary last night," Pierre said. He waved his arm at the disorder as he pushed past and into the bedroom.

The bedroom. There was only room for his bed. White Christmas lights lined the ceiling and a framed drawing of two lovers kissing sneered at me from the wall. Pierre opened the window — it overlooked a courtyard. Faint odours of cooking meat began to waft in, along with ghostly echoes of speech and laughter.

"You are tired," Pierre said.

I nodded. My fatigue was gaining ground. My limbs were limp, and it felt as if there was an opening in the back of my skull and air was blowing in.

"You can sleep here," said Pierre. He motioned to the bed. His bed. "I will, too. I was up working all night."

He pulled off his T-shirt and began to unzip his pants, so I ran to my bag, dug my pyjamas out and put them on in the bathroom. When I returned, Pierre was under the covers and setting the alarm on his cell phone. I crawled gingerly into his bed, painfully conscious of infringing on his most intimate space. We hadn't managed a conversation and now we were lying silently in bed like an old couple.

Despite my unease at lying beside a man I barely knew in a country I had just arrived in, once I was supine darkness reigned.

WHEN THE ALARM WENT OFF, I could barely move. My head was heavy and my muscles had turned to liquid. I stumbled to the bathroom and stared into my red-rimmed eyes.

No wonder Pierre isn't impressed, I thought. *I look like hell.*

Pierre announced through the door that we were going to a restaurant for dinner that night. His favourite Indian restaurant.

I inhaled deeply to provide a blast of cheer. "Great!"

This isn't just an opportunity to rekindle our fire, I thought, as I went back to my bag for some emergency mascara and eyeliner.

It's probably my last chance.

The restaurant was small and hot, and the air was thick with cumin and hot chilies. Only a few centimetres separated each table. The waiter nodded to us in greeting, pulled apart two tables, and motioned for us to take a seat. Pierre ordered for us both.

A few minutes later, the waiter returned with a pottery carafe of wine and a bottle of water. He lit a candle in the centre of the table and gave us a friendly wink. Pierre poured the wine in silence, and we lifted our glasses until they touched.

"*Santé*," he said.

I watched him bring the glass to his nose, inhale, then toss the liquid into his mouth and swallow in one fluid motion. Wine for me had always been mysterious and intimidating, with its invisible dimensions, the way people whirled it in the glass, the slightly differing shades, and the faint hints of wood and berries. I took a sip and tried to detect oak or fruit, but I only got red and dry.

"How can you tell a good wine?" I asked, hoping to ignite a compelling conversation.

"Your mouth tells you," Pierre said, and his dull gaze told me he wasn't kidding, and that he didn't care to elaborate.

For the remainder of the evening I scrambled to keep the conversation moving, but the subjects I launched plummeted like a kite in a dead wind.

"So, can you speak French?" Pierre asked.

"Oui, j'ai…apprends…quand je suis…enfant?"

Pierre winced and said, "You have a lot of work to do."

Neither of us mentioned the things we'd said in our emails, the picnics we'd planned, the exploring, the cuddling and the cooking, and neither of us mentioned the fondness we'd claimed to have for each other. Everything had dried up entirely. My stomach was tightening into a solid knot, and soon I couldn't eat any more. I felt my Paris dream slipping, and there seemed to be nothing I could do about it. I'd thought we would have sex the first night, but now I was less than sure. In fact, I was sure

I didn't want to. The distance between us was too vast. Nothing could bridge it. And from the way Pierre was behaving, it seemed his physical attraction to me had all but disintegrated.

I fell into bed that night with hopeless exhaustion and was taken off guard when Pierre's hands found me in the dark, gently kneading along my body. My muscles stiffened and I lay there in state of panic. My heart thrashed. By now the idea of such an intimate act was unthinkable.

"Do you want to make love?" he whispered.

I longed to rush out of there, to jump into a cab and forget the whole thing, chalk it up to a terrible misunderstanding. If I hadn't been across the ocean, I probably would have.

"Not yet," I said.

I held my breath and felt his hands retreat into the darkness, along with my last chance. It was over. I'd had one saving grace, and I'd blown it. There wouldn't be a next time.

Pierre turned his back to me, and his deep breathing soon morphed into a soft snore. I lay awake for hours, blinking into grey static, battling something worse than tears: emotional dry heave. A terrible voice rose from the shadows, saying, *Now what? Now what? Now what?*

FOR THE NEXT WEEK, I continued to sleep in Pierre's bed. He came home late most nights, and I made sure I was in bed before then. During the week, he got up early for work and I lay still, with my eyes closed, pretending to sleep. I heard the shower running, then a few minutes later his dresser drawers squealing. There was coffee grinding, the fridge opening and liquids being poured. Other sounds wafted up from the courtyard as the neighbours began to wake: voices, dishes, and faint music. I waited for Pierre to leave, then emerged and scuttled to the shower. For most of the morning, I sat on the balcony, sipping coffee from Pierre's Bodum and blinking at a scene that had been a mere fantasy a few days before. I had wanted Paris as much as I had wanted Pierre, I began to realize, but without the love story the dream was faltering. I wasn't feeling up to Paris. I lacked the energy to explore its streets the way other visitors did, with eyes wide with wonder. The city felt hostile, cold and uninviting.

In the afternoons I forced myself outside and wandered without a map from one narrow street to another, staring at the city as if it was projected onto a wall, beautiful but untouchable. It was all here, all the details I'd fantasized about while finishing my degree: white stone buildings with ornate wrought-iron balconies, cobblestone streets, little black lampposts, flower shops, bakeries with layered cakes and raspberry tarts displayed in the windows, brasseries with wide-open windows where men in aprons served coffee and beer on tiny round tables, fragrances clashing from the doors of perfume shops. And French! The language teased me on the lips of the locals as they walked quickly around me, graced with purpose.

I strolled through the Louvre gardens and looked sullenly at the statues — naked men and women with smooth bodies, in relaxed stances. I glowered at the meticulous rows of tulips and the purple blossoms exploding on the cherry trees. I wandered past majestic churches with thick carved columns, elaborate stained glass windows and tall arches, which cast round shadows that shifted with the sun. I stumbled upon the *Opéra Garnier*, with its intricate mouldings and golden angel statues. I only had to look at the open-mouthed tourists, snapping photos and traipsing the streets as if they were at an amusement park, to know that the rest of the world was ecstatic to be in such a city, but all its beauty only caused me pain, as if it was intended for others — anyone else but me.

I WALKED WITHOUT DIRECTION FOR HOURS. I didn't go into boutiques, museums or cafés, and bakeries, with all their warm smells of bread and pastries, only increased my gloom. I was supposed to be doing this stuff with Pierre. *He* was going to show me his beautiful city. Without him, I gazed bitterly at the many lovers, arm in arm or lip on lip, entwined on park benches, and

I mourned for the person I had thought Pierre was, though my memory of that guy was already fading. Once in a while I came across a busker: a saxophonist near Notre Dame; an accordionist on one of the bridges. I stared at them as I passed — until they caught my eye. Then I looked away. For me, playing on these streets felt impossible. The city was too hostile and seemed to vibrate at a frequency too hectic for my classical violin pieces. Also, the idea terrified me. I preferred lurking around the streets like an unseen ghost. It was safer that way.

Whenever I grew light-headed I went into a grocery store and bought an apple and a chocolate bar and ate in the nearest park, chewing slowly and staring at pigeons, children or flowers with an empty glaze. In the early evenings, I returned to Pierre's apartment and choked down a hunk of baguette with butter before going to bed. I was losing weight. I saw myself diminishing in the mirror, but the thought of a meal made my stomach tight.

I woke up when Pierre came home, usually late in the night. The door would slam, and a few minutes later he'd climb in beside me, smelling of wine and cigarettes. Then I lay awake, listening to his breathing, in and out, steady as waves.

ONE NIGHT I RETURNED TO PIERRE'S in the early evening and found him in the living room sipping wine with a woman. She was tall and elegant, with tiny freckles sprinkled over a perfect nose. Her hair had been nonchalantly swept up and held by a simple hairpin, yet it was immaculate, with every strand haphazardly perfect. She was wearing a green dress of silky material that wove around her breasts and swirled up to tie around her neck. I immediately felt grubby and childish in my standard getup: a faded grey hoodie and jeans. Unremarkable. That's what I was.

The woman stood to greet me when I entered the room. "I'm Elise," she said, leaning toward me for the greeting kisses.

I'd seen the locals doing this on the street. It was particularly striking to see two men come so close, their mouths in such proximity, just to say hello. Now I had to do it too. Carefully,

I leaned forward and planted my lips onto her soft, freckled cheeks, breathing in her scent of fruity shampoo and red wine, then I did the same on the other side.

As soon as I saw Elise and Pierre exchange glances, I understood that the kisses were intended to be virtual. Obviously. The lips don't touch the cheek at all. It's done in the *air*. I felt my face flush at the unintentional intimacy.

ELISE RETURNED TO HER SEAT BESIDE PIERRE, and I stood awkwardly, not sure what to do with myself. I wondered if Pierre had told Elise about why I was in Paris and staying in his apartment, and I wondered how long they'd been seeing each other, and if maybe Elise was the reason Pierre had changed his mind about me.

I couldn't blame him. She was an attractive woman with natural confidence and a hyper-feminine aura. Her movements were graceful, her voice spilled sensuality and her full lips begged to be kissed.

With nowhere else to go, I sat gingerly on the couch, painfully aware of my intrusion. Elise and Pierre switched to English for my benefit, but their conversation became slow and hesitant, and it didn't take long for French to creep its way back to their lips. I sat there staring at the floor, feeling boyish and dumb. I could never be like Elise — even if I did try.

When Elise got up to use the washroom, Pierre leaned toward me and whispered, "Elise will sleep with me tonight. You can sleep on the couch."

I nodded and kept my eyes lowered. My scalp prickled, and a coolness rushed across the surface of my skin. Pierre got up, and returned with sheets, a pillow and a blanket

"Thanks," I said, staring at the swirling pattern in the oriental carpet, trying to postpone imminent tears, at least until the lovers had gone to bed.

"Are you OK?" Pierre asked.

I nodded, but avoided his gaze. I didn't want him to see how

upset I was that we wouldn't be sleeping beside each other anymore, that our short history had come to a final end. I didn't
understand it myself. Maybe I still had a hope that he would
become infatuated with me again, that his ambivalence would
pass and the scenario I had imagined before coming to Paris
would magically come to fruition. I had secretly liked sleeping
beside him. I had cherished the closeness — the only closeness I
had with anyone here. Now I didn't even have that.

Pierre and Elise disappeared into the bedroom and shut the
door, I spread the sheet down on the couch and got under the
blanket, and suddenly, for the first time, real fear set in. I tast-
ed its electric buzz on my tongue. On the couch, alone in the
dark, it grabbed hold of me and crushed my lungs. I took quick
small breaths and curled into a tight ball, my muscles painfully
taut. I'd been cruising in a melancholy cloud all week, but now
desperation was moving in. Reality had revealed itself. Alone.
Broke. Don't speak French. No visa.

What. The. Fuck. Will. I. Do?

My heart beat against my rib cage and tears moved in like a
tide, spilling into the fresh pillowcase — indifferent in its steril-
ity. I cried for love that never was and for my current precarious-
ness in a vast and unfamiliar city. I had to get out of here. *And do
what? Go back to Canada? What would I do there? I couldn't live
with my mom — that was a classic failure move.* The thought was
unbearable. Not after travelling so far.

I hung onto one thought: I had come here for Paris, too, and
I had barely explored the city. I hadn't learned French. I hadn't
met any locals. I hadn't accomplished anything. I was in one of
the most beautiful cities in the world. A place I might never be
again. I had to stay in Paris. Somehow. I would stay.

The decision brought a whiff of relief, along with another
blast of anxiety. Now I would have to figure it all out.

Above all else, I needed money. Fast. And as far as I could
tell, there was only one way for me to make it here. There were
buskers in Paris. I'd seen them, on the bridges, in the Metro and

along the Seine. The next morning, I would take my violin and hit the streets.

PIERRE HAD SAID BUSKING WAS ILLEGAL, but he'd also said that rules were made for breaking. A fresh sense of purpose flickered as I stepped onto the street with the familiar weight of my violin in my hand. It lay dormant in the case, yet resonated with potential. Now I just needed to find a place to play. Somewhere in the centre, I knew from experience, where the tourists pulsate.

I WALKED FROM PIERRE'S in the 17th Arrondissement, all the way down to the Seine, then crossed a narrow bridge and took a left along the boulevard toward *Notre-Dame.* The air buzzed with the fury of excited visitors. I stopped in front of a florescent green tour bus stop with the cathedral as a backdrop. To my right was a bookstand, with comics, posters and figurines. Bodies continued to flutter past me.

Could I play here? I wondered.

It wasn't an intimate spot, but I needed only to know if busking was possible. It was as good a spot as any to try.

As I set my violin case on the sidewalk, my heart began to pick up speed. The transition from anonymous wanderer to street performer was suddenly unthinkable. I tried to open my case, but my hands wouldn't comply.

Now! OK, do it! Now! I urged. *You've busked before, damn it.*

Ignoring the quivering behind my ribs, I bent down and unzipped my case. I took out my bow, tightened it and slowly applied the rosin, running the solid pine resin along the horse hairs far longer than necessary, just to buy some time.

Like an old habit, there was comfort in this motion. Back and forth. Back and forth. Then, as if moving through water, I took out my violin and nudged the case forward. I felt people's stares, but I kept my eyes on my instrument as I slowly tuned the strings.

I decided to start with a simple Bach gavotte, a piece I knew so well I couldn't possibly screw it up. I brought my shaky bow to the strings and began to play.

Instantly, the familiarity of the tune relaxed me. I watched as my fingers navigated the piece naturally, moving along the strings as if independent from my brain. After the first repeat, I forced my gaze upwards. There were smiles. A young couple holding hands had stopped to listen. Someone snapped a photo. Children pointed and stared. The coins began to drop in my case.

I brought my bow off the string at the end of the piece and lingered for a moment in the sound of passing cars and shuffling feet. My lips stretched into a grin.

My next piece was Dvořák's *Humoresque*, a cheerful tune with playful rhythms and exaggerated pauses. I began it with my eyes upwards this time, connecting with anyone who was willing. Soon I had secured a workable balance of concentration and outward acknowledgement. When I spotted a police car approaching on the boulevard, my instinct was to stop and hide my violin, but if busking was truly illegal I had to know. I continued to play, despite the sudden tremor in my right hand as the car slowed and stopped at a red light directly in front of me. The windows were down. I watched as the sound of my violin reached the four officers' ears, and they turned toward me. The one in the passenger seat said something, perhaps a comment about my pale, panicked face, and they laughed heartily. The light changed and they waved to me, before disappearing into the rush of traffic.

So, it was as Pierre said. There were rules, but they could be broken.

"You make more than me," Pierre said, when he got home from work and saw the coins stacked on his living room floor.

"I'm going to start looking for a place to live," I said.

Pierre slumped onto the couch and shrugged. "Take your time. Stay as long as you want. But if you're going to live in France, you'd better get a cell phone."

His dark eyes once again gleamed with kindness, and he

smiled at my coins with what looked like pride. He asked to try my violin, so I put it under his chin and placed the bow in his right hand. After a few terrible screeches, he said, "It's too hard," and handed it back. I closed it in my case.

"I'm taking you out for pizza tonight," he said. "My treat."

That night, we shared a carafe of red wine and what Pierre assured me was Paris' finest margherita pizza. Finally our conversation expanded from our previous one-word exchanges to a flowing dialogue, punctuated with laughter, as Pierre told me about his upcoming work trip to Senegal, and suggested places in the city where I could play. His smile had returned to his lips, and as I gazed at him over the leaping candle flame, I realized I was looking at my first friend in Paris. This story, I knew then, was not a tragedy. It was a misunderstanding turned launching pad. I just didn't know where exactly it was pointed.

The next morning Pierre took me to a cell phone boutique to help me choose a phone and a cheap plan. The guy behind the counter's eyes bugged out when I asked if I could pay in coins. "*Ehhh, si vous voulez*," he said. Pierre laughed as I brought fistfuls of change onto the counter and arranged them in 10 euro piles. The phone was light and slim and fit perfectly in the front pocket of my jeans. It was a welcomed weight, a symbol of my permanency in France. Or at least a sign of my intention to stay.

For the rest of the week, I continued to play at my spot on the boulevard. It was noisy but comfortable. I felt secure, knowing that the police wouldn't bother me there. The pedestrian flow was constant and reliable, and while there wasn't much room to play on the sidewalk with all the people rushing by, I wasn't yet ready to venture farther.

ONE AFTERNOON A MIDDLE-AGED MAN on a bike stopped and stood with his head tilted and his eyes in a half squint. He wasn't much taller than me and had long thin hair that lapped wildly around his face and neck. The first few buttons of his yellow shirt were undone, revealing a fur-like chest. His eyebrows were long and shot out in several directions. He stayed to listen for several pieces, motionless in the jostling crowds. After a while I began to worry that he was a musician. Maybe he was a conductor, or worse, another violinist. There's nothing more intimidating than playing for another violinist's sensitive ears, ones trained to detect the slightest imprecision. Eventually my fingers ached too much to go on. As I lowered my violin, he said something that sounded like a question.

"*Je ne parle pas français,*" I said with an apologetic smile.

He continued in French, but slower. With his accompanying sign language, I managed to piece together a few facts. His name was Michel and he was a sculptor and a painter. He asked me if I wanted to see his work.

Thinking he meant in a nearby gallery, and pleased to finally have someone besides Pierre to talk to, I gave him an enthusiastic, "*Oui!*"

"*Suis-moi,*" he said, motioning for me to follow.

Michel walked quickly, pushing his bike by the handles. I trotted along beside him. We wove through the Latin Quarter and continued south into unfamiliar streets. He maintained his monologue, though most of what he said was lost on me.

I eventually surrendered to syntax and allowed the sound of the language to wash over me. I liked the Parisian rhythm. It was quick and articulate, with pauses filled with thoughtful euuuu's and words like *quand même* and *bon*. Statements often finished with *quoi*, like a verbal punctuation mark for added emphasis: *Je ne sais pas, quoi.*

Finally we turned right into a cobblestone courtyard. When I saw the stone building, I realized he wasn't taking me to a gallery. This is where he *lived*. On our right, just in front of the entrance, a statue of a Baroque man in a curly wig frowned down on me, as if to say: "Don't follow strangers home, fool." He was right, of course. It is unwise to enter a stranger's dwelling, particularly a stranger you can barely communicate with, but after a moment of hesitation I concluded that while Michel talked a great deal he was far from threatening. I disregarded the statue and followed Michael up a winding stairwell.

We turned down a dusty hallway at the top and were greeted by a potent waft of curry and incense. Many of the doors were open, allowing music from different apartments to mingle in gentle dissonance. Through one door, several people my age were drinking red wine and laughing at a kitchen table. In the next, two guys with dreads were jamming on a guitar and djembe. I deduced by the colourful clothing, relaxed demeanour and curry/Nag Champa blend that these were not average Parisians. They were artists, and this was an artists' residence.

Michel had to fiddle with his lock before the door finally scuffed open. Inside, there were canvasses, dozens of them sprawled along the floor and stacked against the walls. There wasn't even a walkable path to the living room. Michel grunted as if the state of his apartment surprised even him.

I stood in the entranceway, while he tossed trinkets into corners and pulled artwork off the floor. He cleared a stack of sketches from the couch and motioned for me to take a seat.

"*Je vais nous faire un café,*" he said, heading to the open kitchen.

Michel piled dirty dishes and pushed random utensils and art supplies out of the way until he had enough space to make coffee. I gazed around his living room at butterflies and moths pinned to a board, dozens of candles burned to various lengths, hanging plants with long tendrils spilling from their pots, a scattered collection of shells, rocks and bones, and several antique clocks. Sketches and notes on scraps of paper filled any extra space. I had expected abstract, avant-garde artwork, but most of Michel's paintings portrayed lush landscapes of the French countryside in a colourful impressionistic style.

A few minutes later, Michel joined me on the couch with two tiny black coffees. He grabbed a sketchpad and began to tell me about his life. When I didn't understand, he did a quick explanatory drawing. He was divorced, I learned, and had two young kids who lived in Texas with their mother. They rarely returned to visit and he didn't have the money to go to Texas. The last time he had talked to them on the phone they were losing their French.

"*Ils ont un accent américain maintenant,*" he said, shaking his head.

Michel explained that he was a night security guard at a museum and only managed to pay his rent because the building was subsidized for artists. Even so, he was struggling.

"I'm not rich," he said.

The more Michel talked, the more I understood, but when he started asking me questions I was limited by my impoverished vocabulary and appalling sentence structure. I tried to explain my situation with Pierre, but my words were too simple to convey anything more complicated than a toddler might say.

"I come to see a man. It don't work. I look for a house."

Michel listened patiently, squinting as he did his best to decode my speech. Then, without hesitation, he invited me to move in with him. He had an extra room, he explained. His kids' old bedroom. As I digested his offer, he leaned toward me, smiling.

I realized only at the last second what was happening and barely managed to dodge his lips. Dumbfounded, I slid over to the next couch cushion. Where the hell had that come from? There hadn't been any tender moments or romantic undertones. His outburst seemed to have come from nowhere, like a sneeze or a hiccup. I was too bewildered to speak.

Unfazed, Michel swooped in again, this time with his whole body, with his mouth puckered and eyes half closed. No one had ever tried to kiss to me like that before. *Didn't such things usually happen after a heart-felt declaration or some tender cuddling or at the very least a long held gaze?* I barely knew Michel and he was two decades older than me. The notion of attraction hadn't even occurred to me. Stupid. Why else would a man invite a young girl to his place? Even so, he seemed sensitive and harmless, and I didn't want to hurt his feelings. I couldn't think of what to say, so

I moved to the very edge of the couch, hoping he would understand and we could return to topics like his mother or his latest trip to Spain, but he reached over and began to gently massage my shoulders. I shrugged his hands away and stood.

"*Quoi?*" he asked. He looked surprised.

"*Je vais aller,*" I said, heading to the door. I didn't know what else to do. I wanted to say something like, 'I trusted you' or 'I thought we were friends,' but I couldn't think fast enough to find the right words.

"*Désolée,*" was the best I could do. I *was* sorry, too, sorry that he had tried to kiss me and sorry that my French was too poor to tell him not to. Now I just wanted out of there.

Michel followed me from the building, protesting and apologizing. I hurried down the Metro stairs, leaving him at the top.

"*Excuse-moi!*" was the last thing I heard as I turned the corner.

I returned to an empty apartment and collapsed onto the couch, hugging my knees to my chest in a ball of self-pity. I could never tell anyone about what had just happened. *You shouldn't have gone there*, my friends back home would say, with scorn evident even over the phone. And my mother. She would never stop worrying if she knew.

Promise me you won't do anything like that ever again, she would have pleaded.

Would it have been alright to go to Michel's as a young man? I wondered. *He wouldn't have asked a young man over to look at his paintings.* Obviously. A young woman alone in a big city — that's what I was. I'd have to act accordingly. *Be more careful.* But where was the balance between self-preservation and adventure? My whole life I'd been sheltered by school. The people I met were students, teachers, parents and professors. That context had provided a safe-zone, like the gates of a playground. I had always felt protected. *What was I supposed to do now that there was nothing standing between me and the rest of the world?*

I couldn't keep living at Pierre's. I needed my own space in the city. I needed to stop living out of a backpack and sleeping on his couch, I needed my own Paris, and Pierre needed his own back, to get on with his life of girlfriends and dinner parties.

I hadn't seen any For Rent signs in the city, so I used Pierre's computer one morning to search Craigslist and Kijiji for apartments. Based on my recent piles of coins, I calculated I could afford €300 a month for rent. I started to scroll.

After hours of searching, I found only small bachelor apartments, and nothing under €500, and every ad required a €1000 deposit as well as a guarantor. There were almost no shared accommodations and there was absolutely nothing remotely in my price range. My search became increasingly desperate. Finally, after I had scrolled back several weeks, I found an ad for a roommate. The price was €250. *Finally!* With the aid of an online dictionary, I carefully typed a reply, asking if it was still available. "When can I come to see it?" I asked.

That night I received a response. "Yes, it is still available. You can visit it in the morning."

Joy flooded my chest and relief tingled at my fingertips. Soon I would be in a space of my own. I jotted down directions, the phone number, and the name of my new roommate: Dominique.

The apartment was located in the suburbs. I didn't know much about the large suburban sections of Paris, only that there were contrasting neighbourhoods of affluence and immigrants. I really didn't know what to expect. Only that it required two metros and a regional train.

When I finally emerged onto the street, I saw that I had entered an immigrant suburb. The buildings were faded, grey and dirty, mostly brick and concrete, and the streets were asphalt lined with garbage — a shocking switch from the constantly scrubbed cobblestones downtown. There were no classy boutiques or cafés, only a Franprix grocery store and a telephone centre where people went to call overseas. The air held a mixture of sourness and spice. The passersby were several shades darker than the pasty Parisians of the *centre ville*. Some were even wearing traditional African dress, with coloured patterns and long flowing fabric.

I am not opposed to poverty. I had a modest upbringing and have certainly never sought extravagance. I can live on almost nothing and be perfectly happy, but a dreariness saturated the streets here — a hollow sadness that made my feet heavy and my heart sag as I followed the directions to a brick cube. The lobby was layered with dirt and dead flies. It looked like a cheap hotel, with a colour scheme offering nothing beyond a gamut of greys. As I walked up the concrete stairs, I was already missing Pierre's building, with its smooth wooden banister, soft red carpet, and gentle light sifting from stained glass windows. Here, a bare bulb illuminated each floor. When I reached the third level, the socket was empty, and I had to pass through a strip of darkness to reach the hallway.

I rapped lightly and the door opened. A person answered, with short blond hair in tight curls and albino white skin with piercing eyes. I stared hard, trying to assemble the details, but I absolutely could not tell if the person before me was a man or a woman. The baggy button-up collared shirt was too loose to detect the presence of breasts, and while the shape of the legs was clearly definable in tight white jeans, they offered no clues. I was stupefied.

"*Entrez,*" said Dominique, whose voice only increased the mystery. It was between registers, too high to be a man's and surely too low to be a woman's.

"*Merci,*" I said, and stepped inside.

I didn't need to advance any further to see the place. The kitchen had only a stove, a fridge and a tiny sink. There wasn't room for more than one person in there, let alone a table. Even a chair would have cluttered it. Patches of mould grew in the corner like neglected stubble. On the right was a room, only slightly bigger, with two narrow mattresses, one along each wall. The only other furniture was a rickety wooden table that supported an old television set.

"*Ton lit,*" said Dominique, motioning to the narrow mattress in front of the TV.

I knew that staring in horror was inappropriate, but I couldn't refrain. For an instant I projected myself into the scene. I imagined living there, imagined coming home every day to this place, having only a mattress to call my own, undressing under the covers, and falling asleep to the sound of Dominique watching television. A shudder ripped through my body.

"*La salle de bain*." Dominique motioned around the corner.

I wanted to make a run for it, to tear out and take refuge at Pierre's, but I had to see it through. I followed Dominique to the closet: a toilet, a miniscule sink and a narrow shower stall with a yellowing curtain.

"*Et voilà*," Dominique said, with a shrug. The tour was complete.

"OK," I said, as I backed toward the door. "*Merci beaucoup*."

I half expected a film crew to burst in, for Dominique to whip off the wig of curly locks and point to a hidden camera. We would laugh and shake our heads at the hilarious gag. I hesitated and gazed back at Dominique. No, it wasn't a joke.

"*Merci*," I said again and stepped out into the hall.

"*À bientôt*," Dominique said, then closed and locked the door.

I walked quickly back to the Metro and tried not to dwell on the obvious truth: I couldn't afford a place in Paris. What I had just seen was probably the best I could do.

I SPENT THE NEXT FEW MORNINGS at Pierre's computer, scanning pages of expensive housing ads. Hour by hour, my hope of finding a decent place was growing increasingly thin.

One night Pierre had a few work friends over for a drink and one of them asked how he had found such a rad apartment.

"It belongs to my dad's friend," Pierre admitted.

"Ahhhh," his friend said, in a way that told me that Pierre's apartment was exceptional in size and quality. I hadn't seen the insides of enough apartments to know that Pierre lived in a palace. I was getting the idea, though. Parisians, I now understood, often go through agencies to rent apartments — a procedure that requires a bank account, a real job, a guarantor, and of course a visa. Even with these, the competition for apartments is fierce. The laws are so favourable for tenants once a lease is signed that landlords are known to be ruthless in their selection process. Subletting would have been the natural solution, but it was illegal in France. If I was ever going to find a place, it would not be through the traditional route.

I continued to do the only thing I could: play music. I went for long walks with my violin, even ventured into new neighbourhoods. Whenever I found a place that felt right, with enough people to be profitable but not enough to lose the sense of intimacy, I stopped and gave it a try. I played on bridges, pedestrian streets and boulevards. Sometimes I returned to a spot, like a little market square that Pierre suggested near his place. Sometimes I gave up within half an hour. The coins accumulated daily, but I continued to sleep on Pierre's couch.

I still wasn't eating much. Despite all the steaming crêpe and panini stands on almost every corner in the tourist districts, I didn't indulge. The sweet sugary steam was intoxicating, but I was too anxious to eat. My stomach had a constant undertone of nausea, as if it was full of stones. Besides, I didn't want to spend money on ready-made meals when I'd need every centime to pay my expensive rent if I ever found a place. I lived on bananas and granola bars that I got from the health food store around the corner from Pierre's. I also bought a jar of peanut butter, and in the evenings I'd spread it on a piece of baguette for supper. I kept the jar hidden at the bottom of my back pack. I was ashamed of it. It represented my failure to adapt to French culture. I continued to lose weight, and though I'd never been great at cooking for myself or eating at regular meal intervals, I promised myself I'd eat better once I was settled, just as soon as I found a place to live.

PIERRE CONTINUED TO COME HOME LATE. Sometimes he didn't come home at all. When I told him I was having trouble finding an apartment he simply shrugged and said, "No hurry." And I believed him. He was too absorbed in his busy life to even notice me.

I decided to try playing on one of the small bridges between *Saint Michel* and *Notre-Dame,* not far from my original spot in front of the bus stop. The tourists were plentiful and the setting was more intimate than the boulevard. As soon as I began, I was a target for cameras. Photographers could fit both me and *Notre-Dame* in the frame, and many lingered to capture the scene from various angles. I gazed obligingly into their lenses, smiling, and most tossed me a coin before moving on to the next attraction.

After awhile, I noticed a young man approaching in the distance with a saxophone case slung over his shoulder. He was remarkably tanned, with sun-bleached curls that bounced as he walked. He stopped and leaned against the railing of the bridge to listen. If I was in his spot, he didn't seem to mind.

"*Bonjour,*" he said when the piece ended. He said something in French. I understood: "Play. Street. Often?"

I nodded, and asked in broken French whether he was also a street musician.

"Yeah," he said in perfect English. "Where y'all from?"

"Canada, you?"

"L.A."

California had once been as foreign to me as France, but now that I was across the ocean, I felt sudden solidarity with this guy's casual demeanour, and I was relieved that with him I would not have to stumble through fractured phrases to be understood. For a few minutes, I would be able to speak unhindered.

"You know, there are better places for you," he said. "You should try the *Île Saint-Louis* bridge. It's pedestrian. There'll be less noise."

"I saw an accordion player there," I said. I'd been trying to avoid taking other buskers' spots. I wasn't sure how they'd react, and preferred to avoid confrontation until my French improved.

"Yeah," he said, and shrugged. "Lots of people play there, but it's no one's spot. You gotta get there early, that's all."

"Where do you play?" I asked.

"At the Pompidou," he said. "Every day except Mondays. And

only my own compositions," he added with a satisfied smile. "I've been searching for a long time for the perfect city — one that will receive and accept my music. I think I've found it here in Paris."

"What's the Pompidou?" I asked.

His eyebrows leapt in surprise.

"I haven't been in Paris very long," I admitted.

"It's the modern art museum," he said. "It's the only place in the city designated for musicians and artists by the Minister of Culture."

"So it's illegal everywhere else?"

"Officially, sure, but no one will bother you here," he said, waving his brown arm close to his body so as not to smack the passing tourists

"Where do you live?" I asked, wondering how a busker had managed to find a place in Paris.

"I live in the area," he said, "My place is *super* small. It doesn't have a bathroom or a kitchen. I have to bathe in a sink in the hallway." He laughed. "But, it's better than the squat I lived in for four months. That was awful. I spend most of my time outside anyway."

That sounded like something I could afford. "How much do you pay?" I asked.

"400 Euros. Why, you looking for a place?"

I nodded. "But I can't afford anything over that."

"Well, I've got a guy for you," he said. He fished his cell phone from the pocket of his jeans. "His name is José. He's slimy, but his places are cheap, and he rents to illegal foreigners like us."

Illegal foreigner. It had a dangerous air to it, suggesting a life of suspense and pursuit. I recited my number and he texted me José's information.

"Now you have my number too." He slipped his phone back into his pocket and reached toward me for a handshake. "Name's Taylor, by the way," he said. "Well, I'm off to play now. See ya."

I watched him walk briskly along the crowded sidewalk,

weaving confidently around the shuffling bodies. He wasn't exactly integrated here, but neither was he a tourist. He was somewhere in between, comfortable in his own realm on the fringe of French society. I longed to take ownership of the city that way. Ever since I arrived, I had felt at the mercy of the city, scrambling to learn the rules, to push my way in. *Maybe this number holds the solution,* I thought. I packed up and walked to a quiet street. Then I dialled.

"*Allo!*" The voice was deep and hoarse, with an edge of impatience.

"Hi, is this José?" I asked, hoping he spoke a little English.

"Yeah."

"I got your number from Taylor, one of your tenants. I'm wondering if you have any rooms for rent."

"How much you can pay?" he asked.

I swallowed. "No more than four hundred?"

There was a pause. "Yeah, I got one," he sighed — as though he was making an exception. He told me an address. I jotted it in my notebook. We would meet in front of the building the next afternoon.

Keep your hopes deflated this time, I told myself. *A pleasant surprise will be better than stark disappointment, and for 400 Euros, you can't expect extravagance.*

JOSÉ WAS WEARING a red collared shirt, and his long hair was slicked back with gel. He was only slightly taller than me, but was bulky with muscle. In one meaty hand he carried a briefcase and with the other he pulled open the elevator door and motioned for me to enter. There was only room for one, but he followed in after me. I had to lean up against the wall to prevent our bodies from touching. His spicy cologne filled the tiny space.

We rode the five floors in silence. I felt his glances, quick but carrying the heat of judgement. I looked much younger than 23. Many people who stopped to talk on the street thought I was still in high school. I probably looked like a runaway teenager, though he didn't ask me any questions at all. This was the underground, I realized. And not asking questions was part of the business.

Upstairs, José rapped his thick knuckles against one of the doors. A tall guy and with blond curly locks and a round face answered.

"*Bonjour,*" José said and explained that I'd come to see the place. The young man nodded and turned awkwardly. There was nowhere for him to go.

No matter. I didn't need to enter. The room was no bigger than nine square metres, the legal minimum. Squished in there was a bed and a desk, along with a sink, a hot plate and a tiny shower stall. The guy's few possessions cluttered the space. The air inside had a tropical humidity to it and it smelled of sour laundry. The thought of entering made my chest hurt, as if someone was stitching my lungs together. I would have preferred a tent. I'd seen a few around, along the Seine and set up along some of the boulevards. *Maybe,* I thought, *it wouldn't be so bad. Urban camping. Risky maybe. But at least it would be free.*

"Four hundred euros," José said, as if announcing a bargain. That was over $600 — double the rent I'd paid as a student, with a bedroom five times the size of this apartment. "The bathroom's down the hall." José's fat index finger pointed the direction.

"*Merci,*" I said. I nodded to the tenant who still hadn't said a word. I would have liked to ask him how he survived in there, but not with José hovering.

We took the stairs. The wood cracked loudly as we spiralled down the five floors without speaking. When we reached the street, José turned to me with a serious face. "Well?"

"I . . . the apartment . . . it's really small," I began.

He rolled his eyes. "You got a visa to be here?"

"No," I admitted.

"You got the money for a deposit?"

I shook my head.

"You got a French guarantor?"

I didn't answer.

"You won't be able to rent *anywhere* in Paris," he said. "No *way*. That's why I help people like you. You don't need any of that with me. You leave when you want." He shrugged.

I knew he was right. Deposits and guarantors were on every housing ad I'd seen.

"I'll be in touch," I said.

My heart skittered as I marched up the boulevard. True panic was setting in. I had expected more from Paris. I thought she would open her arms to me, make things easy, accept me among her streets and keep me safe. I'd thought anything was possible here. I wasn't sure how much longer I could impose myself on her before I broke down and called the airline for a flight home.

I dodged into an Indiana Café and picked up a Fusac, Paris's free Anglophone magazine. I scanned the listings, but they were all for rich tourists, with prices per week and ranging from 600 to 1000 Euros. Suddenly, a heading caught my eye: "Free rent for young female artist in exchange for light housework." *Yes! This is what I have been looking for! It all made sense now.* The ad had been placed there just for me. I called the number immediately. An older sounding British woman answered.

"Hi, I'm calling about your ad in the Fusac," I began, voice trembling with desperation.

"Are you an artist?" she asked.

"Yes. Well, actually I'm a violinist."

"Oh," her voice lowered in disappointment. "I'm looking for an *artist*," she said.

I wondered if insisting would be fruitful, if begging would get through to her. Would she take pity if she knew my situation? Did she realize how impossible it was to find a place in this city? After a few seconds of silence she said, "Sorry dear. Good luck. Bye now."

Rage tingled in my fingers and I stumbled, exasperated, toward the Metro. The streets were animated with young Parisians heading home from work or going out for an *apéro* with friends. I longed to call out, to tell someone about my situation. "Isn't this unbelievable?" I wanted to shout, and they would nod their heads in sympathy. We'd sit out on a terrace with a beer and bowl of peanuts and brainstorm solutions. Maybe we could even laugh about my latest encounters, or else I could have a good cry and they would pat my shoulder and reassure me that it was OK, that this city wasn't as impossible as it seemed, that I shouldn't give up. Instead, I ducked into the Metro and returned to Pierre's in a deflated state.

Pierre was sitting at his computer in the office when I came in and nodded to me as I walked by.

"How was your day?" he asked.

"*Ça va*," I said.

I didn't tell him about my meeting with José.

THOUGH PIERRE WASN'T PUTTING any pressure on me to leave, I was desperate to find something. I was tired of imposing on his life, and I wanted a space of my own. One thing had become clear to me: if I ever did find a suitable living space, I would need a great deal of money to pay for it, so I started putting in longer days. I played until my body ached and the coins began to pile up. After two weeks I had saved almost 1000 euros, mostly in the form of one and two euro coins. They began to dominate the corner of Pierre's living room. I spent almost no money at all — just Metro passes and enough food to keep me from fainting. I was so flustered in the mornings that I didn't think about food when I left Pierre's, so I often found myself dizzy by the afternoon. Then I'd slip into the nearest fruit stand for an apple or some tangerines, enough to make it through another playing session. On my way back after I finished for the day I would grab a baguette and fill it with peanut butter or cheese. I bought spiced gouda or compte, cheeses that were mega-treats back home but here were commonplace and inexpensive. Pierre was an excellent cook, and on the rare occasions that he was home he usually made something: spinach pasta or homemade pizza or gazpacho. He always served me some. Most of the nutrients I consumed during this time were thanks to Pierre.

I continued to try new spots. One afternoon I went to the Pompidou, where Taylor had said he busked, but it was saturated with eccentric performers: unicycle riders, fire throwers and magicians. I tried to play on a pedestrian street around the corner, but the police showed up after five minutes.

"You've got to stop," they said. "You'll bother the residents here."

So I started playing on *Boulevard Saint-Michel,* where the sidewalks were wide and crowded. It was noisy and impersonal, but the pedestrian flow was always abundant and a stable hourly wage was guaranteed. I tried different spots along the boulevard: first, opposite the giant fountain with a sculpture of Saint Michel wielding a sword and kicking a demon's ass while two small dragons spit water, then up the street, outside a Paul bakery, where there was always a line-up, so there was always an audience. One early afternoon I ventured even farther, not far from the Sorbonne. The feeling on the street was calmer there — less bustling. That's where I noticed a guy my age standing off to the side, listening intently as I played. He was wearing a white cotton shirt and blue striped pants. His short hair had the sharpness of a recent cut and his face was smooth and pale. His eyes had the signature clarity of a musician. As I played through my repertoire, he remained motionless, calmly watching. Normally this sort of attention would have made me nervous, but I was feeling confident that day and was playing better than usual. When I finally stopped to pack up, he still hadn't moved.

"*Bonjour,*" I said.

He gave me a shy smile.

"*Tu es musicien?*" I asked, conscious of my accent, which immediately gave away my foreigner status.

"*Pianiste classique,*" he said, and added that he was also a musicology student at the Sorbonne. He gestured up the boulevard toward his school. I nodded. I had seen the university several times. People were always stopped in front of the courtyard to snap pictures of the building's façade, with its perfectly smooth columns and sculptures and the round chapel towering above. People lap up symmetry and backdrops. I'd have played there, but I knew I'd be kicked out in seconds. You're not even allowed inside without a student card.

After I packed up my violin, we sat cross-legged on the sidewalk. The musician's gaze was steady and reassuring. He spoke slowly, using simple words. It was the first time I felt like I was having a conversation in French. I wasn't stuttering, and he seemed to understand what I was saying. Our speech had a natural rhythm that propelled forward with minimal effort. It was like riding a bike for the first time.

"Where do you live?" he asked.

As I described my housing woes, he listened thoughtfully and nodded with so much empathy I nearly wept. Then he told me he was leaving soon for an internship in the Middle East.

"Would you want to sublet my apartment?" he asked.

I stared at him for a moment, wondering if I had understood correctly. Then a "*Oui!*" shot from my mouth. I agreed to see it the next afternoon, but I was sure I would take it, no matter how many hours a day I would have to play.

We introduced ourselves. Jérémie wrote his phone number and the Metro closest to the apartment into my notebook, then glanced at the time on his cell phone and leapt to his feet.

"*À demain!*" he said with a wave and hurried up the boulevard. The traffic was starting to thicken and angry motorists were honking at no one in particular. Pedestrians were jay walking between the unmoving traffic, and scooters were speeding along the bike lane, veering around the cyclists.

As I made my way to the Metro, my shoulders ached from the long day of playing, but the air felt light, and when my stomach protested its emptiness with a sharp jab I stopped at one of the many crepe stands in the Latin Quarter. A few moments later, as I bit through the soft, thin crepe layers and the gruyère filled my mouth with its delicious salty oil, I knew that things were going to start tasting better now. They already did.

At six o'clock the next day, Jérémie met me at the *Jean-Jaures* Metro station in the 19th Arrondissement and lead me toward his apartment. The neighbourhood was like a new city altogether, different from any other version of Paris I'd seen before. The buildings weren't the white stone ones from Pierre's neighbourhood, or the grey ones from the suburbs. Most were made of brick or concrete and exceeded the city's five-storey limit. Some were simple cubes. Others were slick, with glass walls at avantgarde angles. Jérémie lived along a canal, which had a festive air to it. People had set up picnics and were sipping on cups of beer from a nearby café. On the opposite side of the canal was a movie theatre, with a long terrace facing the quay, where houseboats were tied to thick metal cleats.

Jérémie's building was modern, with a white concrete exterior. The hallway had the feel of a relaxed hotel, with gold and white wallpaper, a plush red carpet and motion sensor lights that shut on and off automatically. At the end of the hall, we stopped at a wide blue door.

"*Et voilà!*" he said, swinging it open.

The apartment was just one small room with a narrow mattress in the far right corner by the window. There was a bookshelf on the wall to the right and a desk along the other. The kitchen was a sink and a hotplate beside the bookshelf. On the right, just as you walked in the door, was a tiny bathroom. I knew enough now to recognise this place as luxury. In fact, I was almost sure I wouldn't be able to afford it. "*Et…c'est combien?*" I asked.

Jérémie paused thoughtfully. He explained that the rent was 620 but he received a government subsidy, so could offer it for 300. He eyed me apologetically.

"*Vraiment?*" I asked. After weeks of free fall, a parachute had burst open above me.

"*C'est trop?*" he asked.

"*Non!*" I had to hold back an urge to hug him. "*C'est parfait!*

Merci! Merci tellement!"

"*Merci à toi,*" he laughed. He said he was happy to find someone — someone he could trust.

I asked him how long he would be gone. He shrugged and said several months at least. Maybe longer, if things went well. He didn't seem in a hurry to return to Paris. I looked around, revelling at the tiny space that would soon be mine.

Jérémie looked at the time on his cell phone and said he had to go. He was meeting friends for a picnic on the *Pont des Arts,* the wooden pedestrian bridge that stretches out over the Seine.

"Come with me," he said, as if to overwhelm my already bursting heart.

We bought cheese and a baguette and some fruit at a corner store by his place, then took the Metro to the Louvre Station. I followed Jérémie to the bridge. It was exploding with picnics — hundreds of people joined in what looked like one massive feast. Within this sea were smaller groups and Jérémie weaved between them — and I weaved behind Jérémie — until at last, three quarters along the bridge, he spotted his friends. As we sat down with them, we were subsumed into the vibrant, humming mass. Strumming guitars melded with the jumble of languages and laughter. As I looked out over the Seine, I saw the Eiffel tower glowing orange in the distance. Tourist boats slid out from under the bridge as they charged along the river, illuminating more groups of picnics down below along the quay. The fist that had been clenching my stomach released, and I was suddenly ravenous as I stared at the bounty of cheese, bread and fruit before us. A few girls had made salads and passed around some paper plates. Wine was in a perpetual pour. Everywhere I looked were smiles. Paris had accepted me. Or would at least tolerate my presence. That was good enough.

GAVOTTE EN RONDEAU

IT'S EVENING AND I AM AT HOME, IN JÉRÉMIE'S APARTMENT. I have lived here for the three months now. I'm not surfing the Internet these days. I don't have a connection. I'm not talking on the phone. I only use my cell for texting. I'm not hanging out with anyone. I talk to people all day, but making *friends* in this city of light has proven difficult. Tonight I am sitting on my narrow mattress, with my back against the wall and one of Jérémie's comics on my lap. *Astérix*. The language is simple enough for me to understand most of it, complicated enough that I have to look some things up, and amusing enough that it doesn't feel like a dry French lesson. Reading through Jérémie's comic collection is one of the ways I've been trying to force French into my neurons for the last three months. Why did I expect the language to come so easily? Maybe because people speak about "picking up a language" like grabbing bread at a corner store. I thought French would just sift into my brain through an osmosis-like process. I thought I'd start to dream in French by the end of the first week and think in French by the second, and near the end of the month my *English* would begin to fade.

These fantasies were quickly deflated. When I first arrived, I was appalled to discover that my French level was little more than rudimentary. I had taken the obligatory French classes all through public school, and two years in high school, so I had a stash of vocabulary, but I couldn't do much with it. I could ask to use the washroom or name the fruits on display in the grocery store, but I couldn't ask a sales person what to do with those raw, yellow dates on display, or how to get one of those membership cards everybody else had. Or, I *could* ask these questions, but it would require a great deal of time and patience from the employee, as well as those waiting in line. But unexpected events are always coming up in grocery store lines. A product won't scan, for example, and the cashier will say something, too quickly. I'll stare at her, startled and dumbfounded. *"Pardon?"* I'll ask, and she'll repeat the incomprehensible phrase. My heart will start to pound, because I don't know what she has said and because there are people waiting behind me and I can tell by the cashier's frown she's already annoyed. I don't want to ask pardon again, when chances are I still won't understand, so I give a blank smile, to which I receive a scowl and a shake of the head, while the people in line roll their eyes and sigh. Busking requires a certain amount of nerve, but approaching a checkout counter is the scariest part of any day. On the street, when people stop to chat, they *want* to talk to me. They have time on their hands. They ask questions, first about me and, when they find out I'm Canadian, about winter or caribou, or they'll tell me about their cousin who went to live in Montreal a few years ago. I can relax during these conversations, because there are no time constraints and no expectations. There is nothing to lose.

These first few months of learning French has been in many ways like being reborn. I began with an infant phase — my speech was no more advanced than a two-year-old's. My accent was strong, and my sentence structure all over the place. People either found it enraging or cute. There were funny moments when simple mistakes ended up sounding weird or sexual. There was an element of safety and naivety, as if bad things couldn't happen as long as I didn't have the words for them.

It has been a constant battle. The genders. The complicated conjugations. The impossible pronunciation of *tu*. Despite my efforts wrestling French, kicking and screaming into my mouth, French always seems to be running away, evading my lips and forsaking my tongue. Phrases enter my ear canal, dance gracefully through my brain, but will often not allow for any *meaning*. It's as if the language takes pleasure in being a gorgeous but untouchable entity, admired but not possessed. It sticks its slender tongue out at me as it skips away, too light and delicate for my brutish mouth.

And English always seems to want to trickle back. It's constantly at the tip of my tongue, waiting to contaminate my sentences. I have tried shutting down my English brain altogether, but things in my surroundings are constantly activating it: store names, advertisements, posters and songs. Americans speak it loudly in the Metro and on the streets: *What stop are we getting off? I'm hungry! Are you? What do you wanna do tonight?* I wish my native language was something obscure like Icelandic or Norwegian, one that no one speaks and that won't come back to haunt me as I tackle this new one.

Now I'm entering my fourth month in France and transitioning into a new phase, a sort of adolescence, in which I can begin to explore the language and take more risks. My French is now functional. I can carry on real conversations, and while people don't mistake me for a native speaker, they frown less and treat me more like an adult. Of course I make mistakes, lots of them, all the time, and I'm still terrified of talking to sales people, but I am learning to relax into the language. It's like realizing for the first time that you can tread water and don't have to try so hard not to drown. As I think less about the rules and syntax, the music of the language takes over, and I find I can actually swim.

While my communication has improved, my nutrition has not. Despite my intention to eat better once I was settled, my habits have remained unimpressive. French culture is centred on food and French food is centred on meat, so when I tell people here that I am a vegetarian I get either looks of a) confusion, as if they're not sure what I mean, b) pity, as if I'm suffering from an unfortunate illness, or c) discomfort, as if I've admitted to belonging to a radical cult. Mostly, though, the reason I haven't been eating well is that food isn't the religious experience for me that it is for others. People flock to this country like pilgrims to savour its culinary finesse. I am not a participant in this scene. All those *steak frites* and sausages and mussels I see people scarfing on terraces are out of the question for me. To be fair, my food habits have *always* been lacking. Eating has always felt like an inconvenience, something that takes up far too much time and energy. If we only needed to eat twice a week I might feel differently, but thrcc timcs a day strikcs me as excessive and exhausting. Since coming to France, though, I've been eating like a nomadic gatherer: snacking on pickles, bananas, apples, bread, carrots and nuts. I eat cheese now, though I haven't tried anything exotic — nothing stinky or mouldy or expensive. Just familiar ones like Baby Bell. And Nutella has become a daily necessity — my beloved hazelnut chocolate spread that can give even a terrible day a shade of OK. I make salads sometimes, but meal preparation remains near the bottom of my priorities. I buy my groceries at the little supermarket down the street, *Franprix,* where the floor is dirty but the prices are low. It's just a way to fuel the machine, really, as I concentrate on other things. Like busking. And finding my way through this city. Even if that means reading Astérix comics on a Friday night, with my only company a warm night breeze sneaking off the canal and through my open window.

FOR OVER A DECADE, weekends at *Place des Vosges* have belonged to Monsieur Mystique. He comes early, brings food and water, and performs all day long. Monsieur Mystique is a gifted countertenor. He is a natural singer, but not a natural performer. His voice is strong and pure, yet when he sings he keeps his head lowered and avoids eye contact with his listeners. He couldn't command an opera house with his presence, just as I could never lead a symphony orchestra as a concertmaster. That's why the street is an ideal venue for both of us. The pressure is off, the audience is ever-changing, and there are no expectations. We aren't waiting to be "discovered," no one has bought a ticket to hear us, and no one has to give us anything. Our music is more a gift than a commodity.

I need my own weekend busking haven, though — a place with the same magic combination of intimacy and tourist abundance. Popular spots like *Île Saint-Louis* or *Pompidou* are taken early and are often oversaturated, so it's usually a waste of time to go there. I'm better off exploring for new, untapped locations. That's why this afternoon, I've headed to the Latin Quarter in search of an unclaimed nook. I'm crossing the street beside *Notre-Dame* when there is a sharp tug on my violin strap. I turn and yelp at the sight of a hideous hunchback glowering up at me, with warts covering his deformed face, straight out of Victor Hugo's pages. I jump back to free myself from his grip, and a chorus of laughter erupts. Dozens of people lined-up waiting for guided tours of the *Notre-Dame* towers are staring at me with wide grins. I feel my face burn and force a smile as I hurry from the limelight.

Once I'm sure no one is watching me anymore, I turn back and watch Quasimodo creep up behind an unwitting Japanese couple. He taps the woman's shoulder. She turns, screams and sprints away, followed by her husband. The crowd doubles over and I can't help smiling as I continue toward the cathedral.

Miraculously, the bridge beside *Notre-Dame* is musician free. This place is better than the Latin Quarter — there are no residents to disturb. The sound won't be so good, but the tourists are in swarms, so financially it will make up for it.

I wade through the thick swarms and lay my case against a black lamppost just before the bridge. The cathedral towers behind me. It will be an irresistible shot for those with cameras. I open my case and take out my bow. As I apply the rosin, a curious crowd is already starting to form — they're probably only in Paris for a couple of days and are hungry for entertainment. Some, I notice as I bring my violin to my chin, already have change in their hand, just waiting to hear a couple of notes so they can drop it in my case, snap a picture and move on to the next spectacle. It won't matter what or how well I play here. It's the act of playing that counts.

I begin with Dvorak's *Humoresque*, an easy piece to start the day and one that most people recognize. My violin is lost in the open air, but the coin yield proves prosperous. The scene is more irresistible for photographers than I had thought, and they are not shy to approach for close-ups, either. A few actually pose beside me, as if I'm a monument. One woman even risks getting her eye bowed as she approaches on my left and puts her arm around me while her friend snaps our portrait. I've become an inanimate thing, like a wind-up toy or a blow-up doll — pure entertainment, barely even breathing. This, too, is part of the job, so I play on.

The initial small crowd begins to attract more passers-by. Soon there's a healthy gathering of about a dozen. Some sit cross-legged on the ground and stare at me as if at a TV. Others nod to the tune, and one older man makes conducting motions in the air as he drops a euro in my case on his way past. I'm not playing anything virtuosic, just my usual repertoire of Bach and Handel, with a few *Four Seasons* movements as an occasional crowd pleaser, but after two hours without pause, my back, neck and shoulders are aching and my fingers are stiff and beginning to cramp. I lower my violin and nod to my larger-than-usual audience. They applaud louder than I deserve and reward me with a flurry of coins before dispersing. This, I declare, is my new weekend haven. Just as long as it remains competition free.

I return the next afternoon, and to my delight the bridge is still vacant. I'm just unpacking my violin when a short man with wispy hair and wide blue eyes approaches and shouts, "*Bonjour!*" He's wearing jeans and a white T-shirt faded nearly to transparency. His thinning hair and eye crinkles suggest he's a couple of decades older than me, but he radiates with playful energy. He's looking at me as if he knows me, but I'm sure I've never seen him before.

"*Je m'appelle Franck,*" he says. "*Je fais aussi des spectacles.*" He pulls a rubber mask from his back pocket, slips it over his head, and I immediately recognize the grotesque face. "I work over there," he says, pointing to the intersection by *Notre-Dame*.

He leans toward me, puts his hand on my shoulder and whispers in French, "It's hard being street artist, but you must never get discouraged." He gives me a wink, and I watch him rush away toward *Notre-Dame* for an afternoon of terrorizing tourists.

Less than an hour later, I spot a police officer with a shaggy moustache and an upside down smile strutting my way. I pull my bow off the string and shrink before his humourless glare.

"Mademoiselle," he says in a low grumble. *"Il est interdit de jouer à Notre-Dame."* Forbidden to play at *Notre-Dame. Shit.* No wonder the spot was free.

The officer watches me put my violin in its case, then turns and disappears into the crowd in search of other infractions. I've never seen so many cops in one city. They roller blade and cycle in groups. They strut the streets or drive around in motorcycles and tiny cop cars. If this guy says it's forbidden, there is no point in trying not to get caught. Yesterday was a mere fluke.

This is what I hate most about busking: getting kicked out of places, especially good ones. My vulnerability gets suddenly exposed and my life as a busker in Paris is thrown into question. I can't help but take it personally. These are the times I long to call a friend, to feel like someone is on my side and have them say, "Stupid cops!" or "Don't worry. Try somewhere else," but with no friends to call, a pang of loneliness swells in my chest, acute and sore like a pulled muscle. Almost instinctually, I wander over to Franck's intersection and find him taking an unsuspecting woman's hand, while her young son stands helplessly to the side. Thinking it's her child's, the woman squeezes Franck's hand, but after a few paces she turns to see that her son has been replaced by a beast and lets out a wild cry. The crowd hoots with laughter. Even the son smiles at his mother's expense. Two police officers standing off to the side chuckle to each other. Street performing must be equally as forbidden here, but they have no intention of asking Franck to leave. They are enjoying themselves too much.

After terrorizing a few more tourists, Franck tears off the mask and bows dramatically, while the crowd whoops and cheers. He makes his way through the spectators, mask in hand, and bit-by-bit it fills with money. When he's collected his loot, he hurries away from the crowd, in my direction.

"*Salut*," I say as he's about to pass me.

He looks up and his face glows with delight. He empties the coins from his mask into the pocket of his jeans, then motions for me to follow. He takes off down the street, clinking with every step. I hurry after him, struggling to keep up without breaking into a run. The trauma of the police incident is already starting to fade. Suddenly he dodges into a café. "*Tu veux quoi?*" he asks when I join him at the counter. I hesitate, bewildered, unable to match his terrifying speed.

"*Deux cafés*," he says to the waiter before I can answer. Even indoors his blue eyes radiate as if with an internal light source.

I follow Franck and our two espressos to a table in the corner. He launches immediately into a lengthy monologue, speaking quickly and leaping from one subject to another. At one point, his rhythm changes and his words begin to rhyme. He must have broken out into poetry, but I only manage to catch a stray word. Just maintaining eye contact requires concentration.

When I tip the last of espresso into my mouth, Franck rises, tosses a handful of change from his pockets to the waiter and hurries back out onto the street, eyes blazing.

"*Je veux te montrer quelque chose*," he says. He wants to show me something. *Ah. OK.*

I haven't played much today, and normally I would head back to work, but the police encounter is still too fresh. I don't have the energy to go out looking for another spot, and I'm curious about Franck. He's inhuman, like an elf or a leprechaun. He takes off down the sidewalk, and I hurry along beside him until we reach the archways across from the Louvre. Franck grins and holds open the door.

Inside are vast antique galleries with a collections of museum-aged sculptures, paintings and furniture, all with price tags that cause my heartbeat to falter. I can't even believe this stuff is for sale. I touch nothing and hold my violin case close to my side as we wander from gallery to gallery. The employees are conservatively dressed — suits or slim black dresses. They frown and give us sideways glances over their bifocals. We're obviously not here to make a purchase. Not even worth a "hello." Franck's coins continue to chime as he moves quickly about with wild spontaneous hand gestures that make me flinch. I wonder what happens to people like us who break artefacts like this. I hope we won't find out. I clutch my violin even tighter.

Franck drags me onward through the shops, providing ongoing commentary, pointing out sculpting techniques and identifying the period in which each work was made. When I ask how he knows so much he laughs. "I'm a sculptor," he says. "I studied fine art at university. I have a studio outside of Paris."

I stare at him, confused. The thought of Franck completing a work is a paradox. He doesn't seem able to focus on anything for more than a few fleeting moments.

He laughs again and hurries on. He only pauses when we reach the street again, and even then only for a second. "*Suis-moi!*" he shouts as he darts down a narrow street to our left.

I follow behind him. The city feels light and playful in his presence, completely at our disposal. We soon slow and meander through a maze of tiny streets until suddenly he stops at the door of a tiny restaurant.

"*Tu aimes le couscous?*" he asks, eyebrows raised.

I admit that I've never actually tried couscous, and mention that I'm vegetarian. Franck considers this solemnly for a moment, then his eyes flicker.

"*Pas de problème!*" he says, and the bell on the door clangs our arrival.

The place is small and empty. Arabic music is blasting from the back. As we take a seat at the table by the window, I notice a man peering at us from around the corner. He turns down the radio and emerges with a welcoming smile. He is tall and bald, save for some short black curls on either side of his head, and he's dressed in a clean white chef's jacket. Frank does the ordering.

A few minutes later, the man sets two steaming plates before us.

"*Bon appétit!*" the chef says with a curt nod, and then disappears back into the kitchen.

I stare at a heap of cooked potatoes, carrots, onions, tomatoes and chickpeas in a spicy tomato-based sauce poured over a fluffy canvas of couscous. This is the first real meal I've had in a long time and the size of it is intimidating.

"*Mange!*" says Franck, as he plunges his fork into the mix.

I take a bite and my mouth alights with spicy pleasure. It's like discovering a new colour: strong, solid and rich, almost florescent, and speckled red with peppers. We eat for a while in silence, chewing blissfully. A blanket of comfort permeates me: the comfort of a decent meal. Before this, I never made the connection between a full stomach and the feeling of being loved, but now it's obvious. I look up at Franck in wonder. His body suggests 50-something, but his spirit is somewhere between five and fifteen years old. Yet he possesses an element of wisdom that suggests antiquity and a signature calm twinkle that says *I know enough not to take life too seriously.*

"Do you only perform at *Notre-Dame?*" I ask.

He shakes his head. "I go somewhere new every year," he explains. "This year I went to Sweden and Norway. I drove, camping in my van along the way. I performed my act to pay the bills."

I nod and chew.

"*Une pierre qui roule n'amasse pas de mousse,*" he says. A rolling stone gathers no moss.

The adage could be taken two ways, I think. *Depending on whether you consider moss to be desirable or not.*

Franck obviously doesn't. He wants to remain untouched by societal expectations and immune to the judgement of others. He's happiness in the flesh. I watch as he opens his mouth wide, takes a big forkful, and grins at me with his mouth full. He eats the same way he walks and talks, with a mix of urgency and amusement, as if he's striving to squeeze the most enjoyment out of every second and every morsel.

Suddenly he puts his fork down and gives me a solemn stare.

"I can tell you're lonely," he says.

I stop mid chew and stare up at him in surprise. He nods with such understanding that my eyes suddenly fill, as if he has just uncovered a hidden tear reservoir. A jolt of longing rocks my chest. I *have* been lonely. So lonely. I've just avoided feeling it by staying constantly active, keeping my mind occupied with music and learning French, but after almost four months in Paris I miss so many things. Little things. Inside jokes. Splitting a pitcher of cheap beer with old friends. Chatting all night long. My family — their absence is suddenly gaping. Pierre was the only stable connection I had in Paris, and I haven't seen him since I left his apartment three months ago. I've been on my own all this time.

I blink away the tears and ease the knot in my throat by swallowing a bite of potato. *Breathe. No meltdowns.* I finish my glass of water and focus on the rest of my meal. I won't be able to finish it all, so I will have to be strategic with my last bites. *You've chosen to live in Paris and must accept your status as étrangère and your lack of close connections. Foreigners often group together to minimize this sense of estrangement, and you could too, if you wanted. You could join the Canadian Club and chug maple syrup on their monthly hiking trips. You could go to hostel bars and meet young foreigners on the road — lonely backpackers looking for a friendly ear.* But I'm not seeking to be a transient expat. I want desperately to fit in here, to participate in the culture, to live it, to become it.

"You just have to live the way you want to live," says Franck, as he leans close to his plate and scoops the last of his meal into his mouth.

I have reached my capacity and lay my fork down in defeat. Franck jumps up and approaches the counter. I take out a pile of coins from my bag, but Franck pushed them away with such determination I put them back without protest and watch as he pulls fistfuls of coins from his pocket and slams them on the counter.

The owner frowns with exasperation, but Franck doesn't seem to notice.

"*Merci!*" he says to the man. And to me he shouts, "*On y va!*"

Back out on the street, Franck is walk-running again. He steers us right, then left, then right again and suddenly stops in front of a tiny white Peugeot. He winks, produces a key from his pocket and unlocks the passenger door, then runs around to the other side and hops behind the wheel.

"*On va voir la Tour Eiffel!*" he shouts.

Still in a mist of delayed reactions, I get in, shut the door and reach for the seatbelt. Franck lets out a whoop as we blast onto the street. Other than the taxi ride from the airport, this is the first time I've been in a car in Paris. Franck weaves in and out of traffic like a true Parisian, speeding and paying minimal heed to traffic signals. I've always witnessed the chaotic race of Parisian traffic from the sidewalk. It's strange to be part of it now: adrenalin-laced speeds and abrupt lane changes. And the light! By now the sun has mostly set and the buildings and monuments are illuminated. The entire city is glowing. Franck guides us past *Notre-Dame,* the *Pantheon,* the *Champs Elysée,* and finally the *Arc de Triumph* and the *Etoile,* the 12-avenue roundabout. He circles around it a second time and I gaze out the window, enthralled by the vortex of streaming car lights. After two loops, he speeds off onto another avenue.

"*La tour Eiffel!*" he announces as we whip around a corner. We are at the base of the tower. One of its iron legs, a giant radiating arch, stretches sublimely across the windshield.

Franck slows to inspect an impossibly tiny parking space. I almost laugh, until I realize that he's seriously considering it. He backs the car as far as he can into the space, then we jerk forward and backward, nudging the cars on either side several times.

"*Un bisou,*" he calls it.

If you gave "kisses" like that in most North American cities you'd have a chorus of car alarms to deal with, but here the cars are jostled about in silence. After several minutes edging back and forward and many bumper kisses, Franck finally yells, "*Voilà!*" and we get out to inspect. Mere centimetres separate the cars.

Frank laughs with satisfaction, while I stare in awe. I failed my first driving test because of a botched parallel park and I didn't even have a car behind me.

"*This way!*" Frank shouts, as he heads off toward the tower.

I lurch after him.

As we weave our way around the stationary bodies, the tower begins to sparkle like a thousand tiny strobe lights, and a sea of tourists cheer and applaud. The night air fills with camera flashes. Several Indian and African vendors circulate with flashing Eiffel tower key chains and figurines. "*Cinq euros!*" they sing. The Indian sellers draw it out: "*Ciiiiiinq euros!,*" while the African ones shout it quickly, as if the words were hot on their tongues. Vendors are selling ice cream, waffles and cotton candy in booths blaring out circus music. The smell of hot sugar sweetens the night air.

"*Regarde ça,*" Franck says, and leads me by the elbow to a small metal square that marks the very centre of the tower. I gaze up and stand unblinking, hypnotized by the random flashes of light and complicated, converging angles. In Canada, most of the country's splendour involves natural beauty, like waterfalls, mountains and forests, but Paris is a dense display of human invention. Everything is premeditated, the trees are carefully pruned and each blade of grass is accounted for, even the residential buildings are works of art, and this tower is the epitome of all this innovation. It glows, it sparkles, it lifts its skirt and says, "Look at me!" It's the perfect icon for Paris. The pretty girl who knows she's pretty. I'm in love with Paris, I realize. Despite my loneliness, I can't help it. She's too damn gorgeous.

When I finally pry myself away I see that Franck is over at one of the white booths. He's left another pile of coins on the counter and is holding two tricoloured ice cream cones.

"*Tiens!*" he says. He hands me one and motions with his head for me to follow him across the street. He leads me over the bridge across the Seine, past a fountain the size of a swimming pool and onto the steps of a huge white building that he tells me is the *Palais de Chaillot.*

We stand there in silence, licking our ice creams and watching the Eiffel sparkle in the distance. Franck tells me that at first Parisians considered it to be an eyesore and the plan was to tear it down after the 1889 World's Fair for which it was built. *"Mais, c'est normal,"* he laughs. "Parisians complain about everything. They don't know how to be happy. But I do!"

That much is obvious. Even moreso when he breaks into a tap dance routine, twirling around and around with his half-eaten cone held out to the side. After a complicated sequence, muted by the rubber soles of his running shoes, he ends dramatically on one knee, ice cream thrust victoriously to the sky. I laugh out loud for the first time in so long that I can actually feel a surge of serotonin begin to circulate.

Who is Franck? Does he have family or friends? He hasn't mentioned anyone. He appears completely alone in life yet in a state of constant ecstasy, as if the world itself were his family, his playground — his paradise.

To my relief, when Franck drops me off at home that night, he doesn't try to kiss me. He doesn't even ask for my phone number. A simple *bises* good night and I'm back in my apartment, my brain buzzing in the aftermath. I get out my violin and practice the harder sections of the Gigue movement of the D Minor Partita. The notes that usually give me trouble come easier tonight, as my left hand shifts smoothly up and down the fingerboard. I play loudly, happy for the soundproof cement construction of the building, which allows me to practice late if I feel like it. The notes sound good ricocheting off my little studio walls. Despite the minor key, they sound, well, happy.

I PASS *NOTRE-DAME* several times in the weeks that follow, but Franck isn't there. The usual line-up of tourists waiting to visit the towers extends into the stark sun. Their expressions reveal boredom and discomfort.

Much like a superhero, Franck appeared when I needed him most, when the cops had booted me from my new spot and my loneliness was starting to pull me under. Franck didn't just fill my stomach and my heart, he provided an ideal model of this most unorthodox lifestyle — the busker lifestyle, at once free and dependent on strangers, precarious but exhilarating. Franck does what he wants. I imagine him zipping throughout the city, rescuing lonely souls, jingling with every stride, mask poking out from his back pocket.

Live the way you want to live, he told me. And I am. I'm a busker by choice, after all. A rolling stone. I don't have much moss, but I don't desire it either. I traded moss for freedom when I decided to stay in Paris.

Boulevard St. Michel. The afternoon swelter has succumbed to a cooler evening breeze. Hordes of hungry tourists are heading to the narrow Latin Quarter streets in search of a restaurant, and the buskers are all about. When it's this hot, it's best to play later in the day, after the heat breaks like a temper tantrum and everyone is breathing easier.

A young, dark-haired guy carrying a guitar case glances at me as he brushes by. He hesitates after a few paces, reaches into his pocket and comes back to toss a euro in my case. I give him a blink of thanks and my confidence twirls with delight. Unlike tourists, who tend to give because they like the *idea* of street music, musicians are more likely to give out of musical appreciation. The ultimate compliment.

Later, on my way to the Metro, I notice the guitarist at a table on an outside terrace. He has his instrument out and is quietly fingerpicking beside a half-drunk beer and a package of rolling tobacco. His head is lowered, but as I pass him on the sidewalk he glances up, smiles with recognition, and motions for me to sit. I have no plans, so I pull up the wicker chair. Immediately, a waiter dashes over to take my order.

The guitarist is from Italy and his name is Antonio. He has light brown skin, a short layer of dark stubble, and long chest hairs that poke out from under his T-shirt. He shrugs when he speaks, as if everything he says is light and obvious.

I live in the area (shrug). I study guitar at the conservatory (shrug). I'm also learning composition (shrug).

It gives him a certain nonchalance, as if he's completely unconcerned about life — not indifferent exactly, just worry-free.

When my beer arrives, and before I can get at the coins in my case, Antonio slides a five-euro bill onto the table and shrugs again.

"*Santé,*" we say, raising our slender glasses.

His hands soon return to his guitar and he begins to pluck a soft tango. His fingers move gently, taking their time as they spread to form each chord and glide gracefully up and down the neck. The melody is soft, but audible for anyone on the terrace and it provides a soundtrack for our conversation.

"So you are not from French speaking Canada?" he asks. Antonio's accent is strong, but his French is much smoother than mine.

"No, I've been learning French here. I never thought it would be so difficult!"

Antonio nods sympathetically.

"Yes," he says. "French is complicated. Many many rules. I also have trouble eating here because I am vegetarian."

"*Ah bon!*"

I'm thrilled to find another vegetarian and we launch right into a discussion on meat substitutes. After a few minutes I notice that Antonio hasn't blinked in some time and his eyes are wide with an odd glazed quality.

"*Ça va?*" I ask.

"*Je veux t'embrasser!*" he says as he lunges from his chair. Before I can dodge, his gaping mouth is upon me. I pull away and jump to my feet. My heart is tripping and I'm too flustered to speak. As with Michel, there was no forewarning, no tender moments, and no ambiguity. His lust manifested so suddenly that I was unable to avoid collision. My head spins as I gather my things to go.

"*Désolé*," he says, as if he'd merely elbowed me accidentally.

Much like when Michel tried to kiss me on his couch, I find myself too dumbfounded to speak. And my solution is the same. I don't know what else to do but flee the scene. I'm not just surprised. I'm outraged. It's a violation to be kissed in such a manner, as if I were an object at a man's disposal and my own attraction was irrelevant. As far as I can tell, our conversation was flirt-free, with no signature smiles or eye sparkles, which would have at least provided a hint. We were *talking*. Surely I haven't become irresistibly gorgeous, so what is this epidemical libido that strikes so suddenly? Am I expected to go along with it, to behave as if I'm consumed by overpowering passion? Are the women here also seized by this sudden subsuming force?

I drop my violin at home and go for a stroll along the quay. I walk slowly, careful not to step on any picnickers' fingers. For once, I don't wish that someone will invite me to join their clan. I feel safest when I'm alone, and right now I need to feel safe. Lust can strike at any moment, and until I figure out what to do about it I'd rather be isolated than violated.

LATER THAT WEEK, I'm on my way to the Metro after a day of playing when I see Taylor, the sax player from L.A. who tried to help me find an apartment. He's playing on one of the bridges near *Notre-Dame* and I stand at the edge to listen. He's improvising. The notes are wild, with sporadic jumps and no hint of a melody. The passers-by don't seem enchanted. Most hurry past without a glance. I am the only one who has stopped to listen, but Taylor doesn't seem to care.

After a few minutes he looks up, sees me, and stops playing. He is sweating and exhausted. "Wanna go to the park?" he asks.

We sit in the grass at the *Jardin de Luxembourg* and I tell Taylor about the unfortunate kiss with the Italian.

"I know exactly what you're talking about," he says and shakes his head. "I have trouble meeting women here because they assume I'm *that* kind of guy. As soon as I catch their eye, they look away."

"I guess I should stop making eye contact with people too," I say.

Taylor laughs. "Well it's pretty much an open invitation for a guy to approach. But don't you *want* a boyfriend?" He raises his eyebrows.

"No," I say quickly. Taylor frowns, confused. "I guess I just don't trust their feelings," I add. "I was invited to Paris in the first place by a guy who heard me playing violin and thought he was in love with me. Turns out he wasn't."

Taylor nods. "Music is the most powerful aphrodisiac there is. People easily confuse love with the emotions they experience listening to someone play. I have gay men falling in love with me. One guy got obsessive and stalked me for a week. It was terrible."

"But the feeling isn't genuine and it doesn't last," I say with an edge of bitterness. "I won't fall for that again. And anyway I don't want to be dependent on anyone here. I think I'm better off alone."

I'm aware that in telling Taylor my tale I am also giving him a warning. *Stay away. Or at least keep your lips away from mine.*

He gets the message. When we get up to leave he says, "Let's drink some wine sometime. I mean, as friends, of course."

"Sure," I say. "As friends."

A couple of days later, I see him sitting in front of the Pompidou, surrounded by a group of young women. I stop and observe from a distance. Taylor is obviously the main attraction. The girls are laughing at something he said and one of them is touching his arm.

Are they under his musical spell? I wonder. He didn't mention girls falling in love with him when he plays, but he doesn't seem to have a problem with it. Maybe he didn't want to admit how he benefits from the musical aphrodisiac phenomenon. Annoyance flickers in my chest with a splash of jealousy. I want friends of my own. Women. I want into their world. My wish is in vain, though. They never approach me. They don't ask me out for coffee. They are beautiful, mysterious, and untouchable.

Taylor notices me watching and waves. I wave back, but don't approach.

He's occupied with his harem, a place I don't belong. Obviously.

THE LAST FEW MONTHS, I've been alternating between the same three pairs of pants, which are now faded and as thin as summer pyjamas. I've reached my shabby threshhold, so today on my way home I wander into a used clothing store, expecting Parisian thrift stores to be a cut above the ones back home, but, no. This place has the same musty smell of clothes that have been stored in garbage bags, and the racks have a familiar collection of hideous wool sweaters, frilly T-shirts and tight, tapered jeans. The cash desk is overrun by shoes, boots and plaid old man slippers. Beige nylon curtains take up the entire front wall. The back has been invaded by pastel flower-print blouses. *Quelle horreur.*

After some rummaging, I manage to find a pair of jeans that fit relatively well, and at the back of the store I discover a spewing pile of roller blades. *Aha.*

I've been wanting a pair for a couple of weeks now, ever since I saw a few hundred roller bladers whiz by right in the centre of Paris. The whole street was closed down for the evening event. Most of the bladers were young and they whooped and laughed as they passed. It happens every Friday night, I learned. Since then, I've been wondering if this is something I could belong to. *This is my chance,* I think. *It might offer a small amount of regularity to my otherwise random days, and maybe I'd meet some locals my age.* The only problem is that I've never roller bladed.

No problem now. After some digging I find a size 36 for €10. They're bulky, with big yellow plastic clips, not like the slim modern ones I've seen people wearing, but they'll do. I bring them up to the counter and pay for my stuff with 50 centime coins, which I arrange neatly on the counter. The woman grunts in annoyance, but she can't do much. Money is money.

Before I join the Friday night roller blading clan, I will need to practice on my own.

Fuelled by the prospect, I put them on as soon as I get home. It's hard to advance on the thick carpet in the hallways and I nearly perish in the staircase as my feet roll off every step. Finally, I exit the building and stumble across the cobblestone street to the paved bike path, where the strides will be smoother. I see people roller blading here all the time.

The motion is similar to Nordic skiing, which I did in high school, so it doesn't take long for me to grasp the rhythm, but the pavement is uneven, with bumps and holes and I keep stumbling and nearly falling. The path is thick with bikers and joggers, which I try to ignore as they slow and whirl around me. I keep my head down and focus on lengthening my strides, determined to make it to the end of the path. On my way back, confidence is setting in. My strides are smooth, my spine is straight and my arms are loose. But then one of the wheels catches on a ridge and throws me off balance. I thrust my arms out, trying desperately to avoid a spectacle, but my legs roll out from under me and I veer backwards, topple, and land hard on my ass.

Nearby pedestrians glance over in concern, or perhaps amusement. A group of teenagers whoop and laugh as they speed by in a car.

I sit for a moment, disoriented, trying to decide if I'm injured. No, nothing hurts, but I'm close to tears. Falling is only funny when you're with someone else. Alone, there is only stark embarrassment.

With my confidence snuffed, I don't want to roller blade anymore, but I'm still ten minutes from home. I drag myself to my feet and slowly glide back, feeling ridiculous. I'll probably never rollerblade again.

Back in my apartment, I ache for company. A simple Internet connection would be enough to ease this throbbing solitude. In university I was online at all hours, procrastinating at finishing my essays by emailing, chatting and Skyping with friends. Some of them were across the country and others were just down the street, but the Internet made everybody feel close. Just being online gave me reassurance that I was connected to a social community. Which I've now lost. *And it's entirely my fault,* I think, steeping in my own misery. I've neglected my friends and family ever since I moved here. At first I didn't want to tell them that things hadn't worked out with Pierre, especially the ones who thought the idea was crazy to begin with, but now, even though I'm settled in this apartment, I still feel the need to remain at a distance. If I really want to absorb this culture, to become a part of it and grow as a person, I can't have old versions of myself getting in the way, old versions that are etched in the minds of the people I know. The only way I know to become something new is to distance myself from them. All of them.

One thing I've learned in Paris is that when I play my violin on the street I can safely exist — I am untouchable. Unknowable. The tourists take me for a Parisian. Why wouldn't they? Perhaps they imagine me packing up my violin and meeting with my Parisian boyfriend, having a drink and smoke at a terrace before making love into the night. But I don't fool any Parisian. Not in my scuffed Blundstones. Not in my faded, ripped jeans and the striped scarf wrapped around my head. Parisians can't place me, though. Romania, some guess, thinking I'm of the gypsy sort. Eastern European, others wonder — something to do with my almond eyes. If I speak enough they'll catch an anglo tang and assume American or British. Almost never Canadian.

Oh Canada. I see the maple leaves plastered on suitcases and backpacks and baseball caps in a desperate attempt not to be mistaken for Americans. I used to cringe at the sight, but now when Canadians pass me I find myself following them with my eyes. I sit next to them in the Metro, eavesdrop on their conversations, wishing I could engage in a chat, longing for the ease that comes with one's own country folk.

Once, I couldn't resist. A young couple dragging suitcases with Air Canada tags walked passed me and I said, "*Vous êtes du Canada?*"

They stopped and looked at me. "Oui," the guy said in an anglo accent that I suddenly found charming and sweet.

"Me too!" I cried, my joy unfiltered. I could have hugged them.

The guy's face fell. "Oh," he said. "That's cool."

And there was nothing else to say. Of course they hadn't come to Paris to meet another Canadian. They wanted French. They wanted exotic. Different. I turned away, hot-faced and angry at myself. For showing them what I really was: a boring old Canadian, when they needed me to be a cute little Parisian. I won't do that again.

So, I'm only visible when my violin is audible. Otherwise, I blend into the mass of traipsing bodies. Then I slip off to my tiny room and disappear completely. Everybody back home seems far away now, vague and dreamy, as if they belonged to another lifetime. They do. Sometimes I worry that when I resurface I will have faded from everyone's lives.

Yeah, I knew Nisha, they'll say. *She went busking in Paris and we didn't hear much from her after that. She just kind of disappeared.*

With no internet connection and a phone that never rings, I'm living a century ago, in some sort of self-inflicted time-warped exile. I could die in here and no one would know for days. Weeks maybe. Who would notice if I didn't show up to play on a bridge or under the archways of the *Place des Vosges?* I have no paper proof of my existence, either. No bank account. No lease. No bills. In my darker moments, like right now, I realize with a jolt of panic that in Paris I have managed to erase myself completely.

And yet there is also something comforting about this. Because I cannot fail, I cannot be rejected, I cannot lose and I can never be wrong. Still, this freedom comes at a price. The loneliness. And tonight it is chewing away at my heart like a school of bottom feeders. I stagger into bed and cry fat tears that spill everywhere. My nose runs and my face becomes a wet mess.

Twenty years ago I was four and in my bed choking on sobs just like this. I had been spanked by my father and when he returned to my room I thought I was in trouble again. But no. He lay down beside me and started stroking my hair. Then he began to sing: *If I had a donkey and he wouldn't go, would I whip him? Oh! No! No! I'd put him in a stable and keep him nice and warm. The best little donkey that ever was born.*

The irony of the lyrics didn't register, of course. I was just basking in the warmth of this new sensation, of being loved by my father. It didn't even matter that he was the instigator of my tears. This moment of head stroking and soft singing remains my fondest memory of him. It didn't happen again.

The donkey song taught patience, something he had little of, but it's something, I now know, he *wanted* to possess. His persistent depression and self-loathing just got in the way. *C'est tout.*

Of his three children, I was most like him: a self-deprecating perfectionist, painfully shy and outrageously sensitive. Perhaps because of the mirror I held up to him, he was toughest on me. "Don't be yourself," he said to me one afternoon, when my brother and I weren't getting along. In hindsight, the advice must have come from his own self-hatred — of the elements of himself he recognised in me. But I was five, and I took it to heart. Maybe what he should have said was, "Don't be like me."

Now I know what I am in Paris. A ghost. I make apparitions. Under archways and on windswept bridges. Then I disappear again, back to the safety of my homemade purgatory. Maybe I have finally found a way to do what my father advised all those years ago. *Don't be yourself.* The only way to do that, really, is to not exist at all.

Cantabile

I PEER IN DISBELIEF OVER THE SIDE OF THE STONE WALL that overlooks the Seine. A few days ago there was a busy highway here, with cars whipping by. Irate commuters were honking and cursing as they raced to the exit ramps. Now there is only sand, beach chairs, and big blue umbrellas. Vehicles have been replaced by near-naked bodies sprawled on the sand, with exposed, oiled skin. *Paris Plage* is written on the many coloured flags that line the metal railing of the Seine. *Paris Beach.*

I hurry down. The nearest access is an exit ramp, with a misty spray blasting from an overhead length of metal tubing. Sunlight illuminates the tiny droplets in the wet, hazy zone beneath it, creating a shimmering rainbow. Children linger, twirling and giggling, while adults take micro-showers on their way through, temporarily relieved from what is turning into a hot, humid afternoon.

The walkway is jammed with pedestrians, but without the frustrated vibe of other crowded places in Paris. There are families, groups of friends, and couples. Men and women strut in bikinis and tight Speedos. Gay couples stroll hand in hand. A homeless guy staggers along in a winter coat. Groups of teenage girls keep a cool stride, speak quickly and shriek at each other's jokes. Young couples walk with their arms around each other's waist or kiss in the sand under the wide umbrellas. Two African families sit in the shade of some palm trees, the women dressed in vibrant robes and headscarves. Children are everywhere, in strollers, on shoulders or clutching their parents' hands. Some people are licking ice cream or sipping pale beer in plastic cups. No one in the slowly moving crowd seems to mind edging along the path between the sand and the Seine. They are under some sort of beachside spell.

I step into the percolating mass and adopt the collective casual pace. Tall palm trees line the side of the walkway. Bike rentals are free, and so are a pool and a climbing wall. Bliss-faced men and women are getting their neck and shoulders kneaded at a complimentary massage booth. Farther east, the sand gives way to a long stretch of grass and a wooden walkway with more chairs and umbrellas. People are sitting in the shade with a book. Others are lying completely still with their eyes closed. There's a small open café by the water — the source of all the beer. A man with a guitar is serenading the terrace with gentle jazz chords.

Then I see what I was looking for. Buskers. They are under the bridges. I find a lone echoing clarinet in one, a small jazz Manouche ensemble in the next. Then I come across a young guy dancing with a crystal ball, with a large crowd around him. The way he moves, the ball seems to be a separate entity with its own free will. It's as if they're waltzing together. Police and security are casually patrolling the area, and the usual severe glare is softened to that of near-amusement. They look like they could go for a beer themselves.

They don't seem to have a problem with buskers, I notice, so performing must be permitted. So I wander back west until I find a bridge that is unoccupied. *Pont Neuf.* From here I can see the lapping Seine, as well as the top of the Eiffel tower peering from behind a row of buildings.

I open my case and unpack my violin. Some passers-by turn and slow their stride. I tighten my bow, wondering what I could start with. I'm always nervous in a new location. *I need something uncomplicated and reassuring.*

Kreisler's *Liebesleid*, I decide. It's a fun, expressive piece, playful at times but with an undertone of sorrow, and thanks to the bridge's generous acoustics, the sound moves gently and curls around me like smoke before dissipating in the afternoon heat. A curious crowd begins to form. It grows steadily as I play. Before long I count a total of forty-five listeners, the most I've ever had on the street. Normally an audience of this size would cause me to fumble and my bow hand to shake, but I'm surprisingly relaxed. The flawless weather, the amplified acoustics and positive vibes have allowed me enter the Zone, a rare state for musicians, where mistakes are impossible and the music flows without effort. As if dipped in butter, my bow glides across the strings, making them quiver and hum. I play continuously, starting the next piece just as the last notes fade into silence. I move on to a Sonata with two slower movements, so I can truly exploit the echo.

My listeners are calm and attentive. They're not wearing backpacks or shorts or carrying guidebooks. These are, I realize, Parisians on vacation. August is a special month in France. Nearly the entire country is on holiday and many businesses are understaffed. People have warned me not to expect much from banks or the post, and many establishments, unless they are cafés or bars or hotels, shut down completely. *Paris Plage* is part of that, a playground for Parisians on vacation, an urban paradise. So. My month of August is secured. *Place des Vosges* and *Île Saint-Louis* will always be there, but *Paris Plage* is a fleeting haven for buskers, and I must play here as often as I can.

I arrive at my bridge, *Pont Neuf,* every day around noon. Even in the rain this spot works: people take shelter under the bridges and I provide the entertainment while they wait the weather out. I couldn't possibly bother anyone here, except maybe the clown who arrives in the early afternoon. He twists balloons into shapes: animals for children and male genitalia for select gay couples. He has a wide red smile painted on his face but he never laughs, and when no kids are around he turns his back and lights up a smoke.

The crowd on the Plage is ever-changing, with one exception: a moustached man. At first, he didn't strike me as odd. He stood in the back to listen a few days ago, and was so physically unremarkable that he blended into the crowd. Average height. Average build. Short grey hair. Blue eyes. The only thing notable about him was his flourishing moustache.

Now I can't ignore it. The moustache, that is. It is constantly in motion, twitching and flitting as if it were a separate entity with thoughts and desires of its own. His face is so dominated by its presence, I've come to think of the man simply as The Moustache.

Lately he's been edging closer, out of the background, standing only a couple of metres away, with his right foot forward, arms folded across his chest and his head in a tilted daze. His eyes are vacant, as if he's in a trance. I can't tell if he's a weirdo or a classical music enthusiast.

TODAY IS A SOLIDLY DISMAL DAY, with heavy clouds and little hope for sunshine. The coins are scarce and the damp air soon penetrates my clothes and begins to seep into my bones. The sound of my violin falls dead in the thick wall of humidity. After an hour, shivering too violently to hold my bow steady, I decide to take refuge somewhere for a *café au lait* — the closest I can get to a large, North American style body-warming coffee without resorting to Starbucks. *Café au laits* are pricey, so I don't indulge often, but in dampness like this they are a necessity. I'm snapping my bow in place when The Moustache scuttles over and with a wide grin and says, "*Coucou!*"

His moustache slides back and forth with glee, and he blinks rapidly as if he's got dust in his eyes. "*Tu joues tellement bien!*" he says, then clasps his hands together and shakes his head as if in wonder.

"*Merci,*" I say as I zip my case closed.

He tells me he is a doctor and also a piano player. I try to picture him in a hospital setting, dressed in green scrubs, with a stethoscope round his neck. Doctors, in my mind, are calm, serious people, but the moustache is skittish and goofy. I could imagine him at the piano, but only playing jumpy ragtime stuff.

We walk together along *Paris Plage,* then up the ramp to the street. He's on holiday for the whole month of August, he tells me. Instead of going to the ocean like many Parisians he prefers to stay and wander the streets. "I even have a Bateau Bus membership!" he exclaims, and pulls the card out from his wallet to prove it. The image of the moustache sitting at the front of the water bus, gazing at the passing scenery with no destination in mind is the most congruent yet.

I turn and head over to St. Martin Street. The moustache continues to tag along. He doesn't seem to have an agenda of his own, and I wonder how far he's planning to walk with me. I've been heading to *L'imprévu* in the 4th Arrondissement, a colourful, hip spot run by two young Americans. The ambiance there is more relaxed than in the more normal fast-paced brasseries, so I can stay for a while without feeling like I have to place an order every time a server passes. I go there about once a week to write. I don't want The Moustache to know my usual hangout, so I stop at the next place, a smoky café with tourists and card-playing older men inside. I tell him I'm going to have a coffee.

"*Bonne idée!*" he says and skips over to hold the door. I hesitate. My French isn't perfect, and it's possible I have unwittingly invited him. Still shivering from the dampness, and not sure how to backtrack, I enter. Giddy now, the Moustache rushes ahead and chooses a table by the window. I have a flicker of regret as I take a seat across from him. His eyes are now glowing. My intuition tells me that this man is kind, annoying, obsessive and unstable, but not dangerous. I decide to wait it out. Maybe I'll learn something.

The Moustache is uncomfortable with silence. He is a practiced rambler and doesn't leave room for me to speak. My lack of participation only increases his nervousness, making him talk faster, spewing facts and anecdotes.

"You know, Mozart composed his first symphony when he was only five. Imagine that! Hilary Hahn always has the same expression when she plays violin. Have you noticed that?"

He bursts frequently into unprompted laughter, slapping the table as if a joke has been told, while his moustache twirls and flicks. Someone watching us from outside could easily mistake our conversation for a captivating one, but it couldn't be more ordinary. The Moustache is not unpleasant. He has a great deal of energy and a positive tone, but his words are trite and uninspiring. If he spoke English he would say things like, *Okie dokie, Yeppers* and *You bettcha!* He's the kind of guy who would annoy the hell out of you if he were your dad, and constantly embarrass you in public. Some of my friends' dads were like that, though it never bothered me. I found them friendly and funny, but with The Moustache, we've only been here a few minutes and I already find myself losing patience.

"*Je joue du piano*," he reminds me, and begins to tap his fingers on the table while he hums. Then he leans forward to tell me I have very supple wrists, and moves his hand back and forth to simulate vibrato. "And never the same expression when you play!" He chuckles to himself.

I gaze into my coffee cup. It has been empty for a while now, but I haven't managed to find a second of silence to suggest we leave. Annoyance is beginning to fester near my sternum. Miraculously, the Nokia ring sounds from inside my pocket.

It's a photographer I met at *Paris Plage*. He took a few shots of me and said he'd call once they were developed.

"The photos are ready," he says.

Relieved to have an excuse to part with the Moustache, I agree to meet at the *Châtelet* Metro entrance.

"I have to meet someone," I say.

The Moustache nods. He is disappointed but understanding, insists on paying the bill, then gallantly holds the door. Then, instead of saying goodbye, he follows me to my meeting place, chattering about some restaurant in Montmartre where he sometimes performs.

To save myself, I wave at the photographer in the distance. He's wearing a scooter helmet, and from here his dark stubble under it looks like black soot smeared across his face. The Moustache asks if he's my boyfriend, and I hesitate only a microsecond before nodding. I barely know the photographer, but he'll do for a pseudo boyfriend.

I thank the Moustache for the coffee. Smiling, he leans toward me and his clammy bristles press against my cheeks. A current of revulsion shoots up my spine.

"*C'était un plaisir,*" the Moustache says. "*À demain!*" he adds.

The photographer's name is Harold, and when I approach him I try to appear as friendly as I can for the Moustache's benefit, putting my hand on his shoulder as I linger with the *bises.*

"Who's that?" Harold asks, nodding toward the Moustache, who keeps turning back to look at us. Harold pulls off his bike helmet, and his dark static-ridden hair splays.

"That's the Moustache," I say. "I don't know him very well. He listens to me play at *Paris Plage.* He says he's a doctor."

"Hmmm," Harold scratches his dark curls "He seems weird."

Harold is French, but insists on speaking English. His accent is unapologetically heavy, but I like listening to him talk about zees and zaat, and it's a relief to speak English. I welcome the ease and relaxation that slipping into my mother tongue allows.

The previously heavy clouds have thinned from an achromatic dark grey to eggshell and it's not raining anymore, so Harold and I walk to the *Marais,* a trendy area with tiny designer boutiques, cafés and narrow streets. It's also the gay district, and the rainbows adorning the shops and restaurants give it a festive feel. We stop for a beer at a café with tiny round tables perched on the sidewalk. There is barely room for pedestrians to brush past. We have to protect our drinks from handbags, ample hips and strollers.

Harold spreads his photos of me on the table. From the looks of his fancy camera I had thought he was a professional, but these are amateur at best. They are taken at awkward angles and the lighting is weird, too dark in some and overexposed in others. I ask if he's a photographer, and he laughs.

"Not at all!" he says. "I was just trying out this vintage camera."

He tells me about his plans to work on a kibbutz in Israel next year. He's been planning the trip for a while and the details are finally coming together. It's only after he tells me this that I notice the tiny gold star hanging around his neck, nearly buried in his chest hair.

He pulls out the rest of his photos. The first is of a stunning woman with long jet hair that tumbles perfectly off her shoulders. She has high cheekbones and a wide smile, which reveals an immaculate row of teeth, and is wearing a little white summer dress with a delicate embroidered pattern. In the next photo, Harold and the woman are lying in the grass together. She is on her side smiling at Harold and he's on his back, gazing cooly into the lens and holding the camera above them to take the picture. They look like newlyweds.

"Who's that?" I ask.

"That's a girl I met yesterday," he says. "In this picture, we had only known each other for an hour! Incredible, non?" he shakes his head and smiles.

Since he's being candid, I ask if they made love.

"Yes," he shrugs.

"But she's not your girlfriend?"

"Girlfriend? No, why?"

"I mean, will you ever see her again?'

"I have her number. Maybe. I don't know."

I ask Harold if he's in love with anyone.

"In love?" he laughs. "You mean like, *le grand amour?*"

"Yeah, I guess."

He thinks about it for a moment, then shakes his head.

I pause to allow the revelation to seep in, then I ask, "How many…how many women have you slept with?"

"What do you mean?" he asks.

"Like. . . I mean…had sex with."

"In my *entire* life?" he roars and smacks the table. "Nisha, I'm thirty-four years old!"

I'm beginning to understand. Harold is part of a dance, an ongoing dance that can happen right on the street when two people look at each other for more than a microsecond and something in that held gaze says, "I want to fuck you." Sometimes it ends there, but sometimes the two parties strike up a conversation, then have a drink and talk about surface things, when really their bodies are aching to be in bed together, so, later, they'll make the transition elsewhere, somewhere private where they can really get down to business. Or something like that. I dunno. This game exists in Canada too, but it's much more prominent in France. A national sport, it sometimes seems.

Since we're on the topic, I tell Harold about the lustful outbursts from Michel, the artist, and Antonio, the Italian, and he nods in understanding.

"*C'est normal!* You need to simply say that you're not looking for a man. *Je ne cherche pas un mec.*"

I try out the phrase. Harold laughs and says, "*Voilà. C'est ça!*"

I laugh too. Harold is the most laid back Parisian I've met so far and his honesty is enlightening. I can see why girls like him. If I *was* looking for a one-night stand, Harold would be a promising candidate. He is handsome in a rugged way, with a thin layer of dark stubble, a tan complexion and thick dark hair. His brown eyes are kind and he has a sweet, genuine smile. He is silly and fun, but there is a serious charm about him. He has a way of looking at women, not with the I-want-to-fuck-you gaze that I find so distasteful, but as if he's transfixed by their majestic beauty, and it doesn't go unnoticed. I've seen him do it several times in the last half hour, and witnessed the prolonged gaze that most of the women reciprocate, ever so slightly, like a momentarily shared secret. It is confirmation, that she finds him attractive, that if she wasn't with her boyfriend or mother, then maybe. . . .

Harold isn't a typical working Parisian. Besides the odd modelling gig, he makes his money by getting up before dawn and taking his scooter to the best of the vintage markets in Paris — and there are a lot of them. He has an eye for value, and after some serious scouring will come home with T-shirts, shoes, hats, lamps, and army wear that he'll put on eBay. It's tough work, he tells me, and he's often tired from his early morning hustles.

"I don't have much money, but I also don't have a boss. I work when I want," he says. "I like it that way." He shrugs.

When we finally get up to leave, Harold gives me his number. "Call me soon," he says.

While I'm sure he'd make a fine bed-friend, I am confident he'll make an even better friend-friend, and I need some of those here. Having a solid friend-friend is a development that makes the city appear considerably brighter as I walk to the Metro. I barely notice the swiftly returning rain clouds.

I ARRIVE AT *PARIS PLAGE* in the early afternoon and start with the Largo from Bach's C Major violin Sonata. It's more difficult to play than it sounds. When it comes to Bach, the slow, melodic movements require considerable concentration. The bow must remain fluid and the rhythm calculated, but maybe the most challenging is the intonation. It's not just where the finger is placed that determines whether you're in tune but the angle of the finger, too. In Bach's solo pieces, the notes are especially exposed. The movement I'm playing now, for example, contains double stops — two notes played at once — which are even harder to get in tune. I keep my eyes on my violin for the first half, wishing I hadn't started with something so challenging.

When I look up again, the Moustache is there. He smiles and skips over, so that he's directly in front of me, then starts moving his head from side to side, as if he's tapping along to a campfire song. When people drop coins in my case, he gives them an approving nod, but if they take my picture his shoulders tense and he frowns fiercely in their direction. When a round-bellied man with a long-lensed camera starts shooting from several different angles, the Moustache scowls and throws himself into the frame to thwart the picture. When the man approaches for a close-up, the Moustache, yells, red-faced, "*Arrêtez! Vous dérangez la violoniste!*"

Startled, the man looks to me and I raise my eyebrows helplessly, as if to say, *Don't worry, you aren't really bothering me,* but the photographer fishes a coin from his pocket, drops it in my case, then disappears into the crowd of passers-by in search of simpler subjects.

I don't feel much like talking to the Moustache, not after his bristles touched my cheeks yesterday, and certainly not after this display of unwarranted jealousy, so I keep playing, hoping he'll eventually have some obligation and take his leave, but he remains standing about a metre away, smiling and unblinking.

Eventually, my left hand starts to cramp. The strings have turned my fingertips black and my left shoulder is throbbing, but still the Moustache appears alert, joyful and with no intention of leaving. I keep going. This is the longest I have ever played without pause. My muscles are beginning to burn and beg for a rest, but the Moustache shows no signs of parting. Finally, dizzy and sore, I lower my violin, and the Moustache yells, "*Bravo!*"

As I kneel to collect my coins and put my instrument away, my neck muscles suddenly seize. My eyes squeeze shut and my hand instinctively clutches the back of my neck. The pain is immobilizing and I must wait where I am for it to pass. Suddenly I feel the Moustache's hands on me, massaging, hard and with an air of authority, digging his fingers into my cramping muscles. I struggle to my feet, forcing his hands away, disoriented by the pain and awkward at the unwanted intimacy.

As I leave, he follows me to the Metro again, asking questions about my family medical history. I don't say much. I don't want to encourage him. When we reach the entrance I duck from his puckered bristles and skip away down the stairs.

THE NEXT MORNING, the thought of seeing the Moustache fills me with the sort of unease I used to get before going to school or a job I didn't like. For the first time since I became a full time busker, I dread going to work. *I could simply avoid Paris Plage,* I think. But no, I can't. It's the only place I can play for long periods of time without disturbing residents, and I need to accrue savings before the cold rainy months arrive. I must keep playing there.

In the end, I decide to go early and find a spot on the other side of *Paris Plage.* Hopefully the Moustache will see that I'm not at my usual spot, then carry on with his day.

I manage to find a bridge at the far east end of *Paris Plage*. It's wider and has a bend in it. The acoustics are OK but it's darker under here, and not so inviting for passers-by. I start to play anyway. Though my wage is reduced, I'm at least moustache-free.

Less than an hour later, my heart sinks when I catch sight of the Moustache grinning in the distance. He waves and skips toward me like a child who has just spotted an ice cream truck. Annoyance sears like acid in my gut.

I look down and try to concentrate on my Bach A Minor concerto. I'm entering the fast section, with its intricate bowing, and my left hand is scrambling to keep up, when the moustache distracts me with his darting eyes and flicking moustache. He pulls a small disposable camera from his breast pocket and without looking through the lens, he points it in my direction and snaps a picture. He goes for a few more angles, snapping and glancing around guiltily as if the authorities might leap out and reprimand him.

I've been photographed hundreds of times this summer, but now that it's the Moustache behind the lens, I feel violated, as if he's trying to take permanent possession of me.

When I finish the concerto, I stop to pack up. I'm done here. I'll take refuge at *Place des Vosges* — if it's unoccupied.

His moustache droops in disappointment. "*Tu t'arrêtes déjà?*" he asks.

"*Oui, je suis fatiguée.*"

He asks if I'll play tomorrow.

"*Je ne sais pas.*" I can hear my annoyance surging audibly in my voice.

Place des Vosges is only two stations away. I could easily walk, but I don't want the Moustache to discover my other locations. My regular busking spots are sacred.

As usual, the Moustache follows me to the Metro, and as I turn to descend the stairs he flits his fingers in a wave. "*Adieu, chère amie,*" he says with melodramatic longing.

I shudder and slink down the stairs. His obsession is tightening around me like a sloth's grip: gentle at first, barely noticeable, but before you realize it, it has become fiercely relentless.

"Do you think the Moustache is dangerous?" asks Harold one evening, as we devour monstrous falafels from L'As de Falafel in a square in the Jewish quarter. A strudel and a cheesecake that Harold got at the Florence Finkelsztajn bakery wait beside us in a paper bag, though I don't know how we'll have room. The falafels come in pita capsules busting with hot falafel balls, cabbage, eggplant, hummus and cucumbers. They're too wide to bite, and the plastic forks they gave us can barely support the weight of the contents.

"No, not dangerous" I say, with my mouth half-full. "Just really annoying."

"Maybe you should tell him to leave you alone," Harold suggests. "You'll probably see him again, even after *Paris Plage*. Paris is a small city, you know."

He's probably right. I had always seen Paris as huge and complicated, until Harold took me for a ride on his scooter a few days ago. The city simplified as we slipped from one neighbourhood to another in a matter of minutes. I'd been mostly taking the Metro to get around, so the city had maintained a sense of monstrosity. Since the scooter tour, Paris has become much more manageable in my mind.

"Well, he seems really fragile," I explain. "I don't want to hurt him. Hurting him would hurt me too. I would feel terrible. He would be crushed."

"Well, you have my number," says Harold. "You know you can call if you ever need me, *mon ami*."

We call each other that. *Mon ami*, after the direct way our friendship was declared. Harold would have slept with me the day he gave me the photos, but since I explicitly announced that I wasn't looking for romance, he decided to commit to a friendship. This demands significantly more effort than an occasional bed buddy. There is an emotional engagement. A friend must "be there" for the other. A friend is a listener, someone you care about, someone you can call when you're in trouble. You do things with them. Show them things. Tell them things. And Harold is becoming all of this. A true friend in this not-so-big but very dense city.

FOR THE NEXT TWO WEEKS, the Moustache doesn't miss a day. He is always standing before me, grinning and clapping enthusiastically after every piece, and sometimes shouting *Bravo!* I try to ignore him the best I can, but if I stop to stretch he rushes over to see if I need anything, and more than once he has offered to massage my shoulders. Outsiders must think he's my very overprotective father. Or maybe they see him for what he is: a lonely, obsessive man. When I finish playing for the day he invites me out for coffee or dinners, which I deflect with excuses of rehearsals or soirées with friends. He waits until I pack up my violin, then follows me, talking incessantly all the way to the Metro. At the entrance I duck away with a wave good-bye, though a couple of times I'm not quick enough and he smushes his moustache against my cheeks in the parting *bises*.

But I'm becoming less annoyed with him. He is just a work hazard, an inconvenience that comes with the job. There are others, too. The weather. The police. Competition. Obnoxious drunks. Business professionals have to endure difficult clients, abusive bosses or lazy co-workers, right? I just have to try to deal with the Moustache with tolerance and patience. I can't prevent him from standing in front of me while I'm playing, but I *can* limit our discussion, and I can refuse his invitations.

I manage this technique successfully until the last day of *Paris Plage*. That day, the Moustache doesn't have his usual dreamy expression on his face. Wistful longing soaks his dreary blue eyes. His moustache droops at the corners and is completely motionless. He watches me play for two and a half hours, and when I finally lower my violin he hangs his head.

"Well that's it," he says. "*C'est fini.*"

We walk along the beach together, but now he's dragging his feet and exhaling in long, painful sighs. As we pass the Plage's outside café, he stops and begs me to have a drink with him, his face twisted with urgency. He looks like a child pleading for candy at the checkout. Much like the exasperated mother who sighs and tosses the item in the cart, I find myself veering to one of the outside tables.

What the hell? I think. *I'll never see him again. Probably.*

The Moustache's face brightens. A waiter arrives and we order beers, the pale golden ones I'd seen everyone drinking for the last month.

"Dear friend, oh dear friend," the Moustache laments. "I am losing you today." He takes a sip of his beer. Tiny white bubbles linger along his moustache bristles. I offer him a sympathetic smile. He *will* be losing me today. I have neglected to disclose my other playing locations, and not just for my sake. It's in his best interest, too. He needs to move on.

The Moustache leans forward. "I have a garden," he whispers. He is barely audible. "I have a secret garden in my head that no one else can access. Not even my wife and kids."

I try to maintain a gaze as if he has merely told me that he has a pet cat at home. *Oh yeah? That's nice.* This is the first I've heard of a secret garden, a wife *or* kids. For a moment I imagine an Eden with vines and flowers and… naked women. I quickly shove the image aside. The Moustache meets my eyes with insistence, as if pleading with me to understand.

At a loss for words, I nod and stare at the sticky beer rings that plaster the table.

"You remind me of someone," he says. "You have the same eyes."

The Moustache goes on, but his voice is so low I can barely make out what he's saying. I lean forward to catch a few words and realize he's talking about the girl he lost his virginity to.

"I was seventeen," he whispers, "on a family vacation."

I pull back, nod occasionally, but avoid the details. I retain only that he was profoundly affected and thinks of her often. I cringe at the thought of me frolicking in the Moustache's garden without my consent. And I hate to think of what I might have *done* in this garden of his. When he sighs and shakes his head in a moment of silent nostalgia, I tell him I should be going. My glass is empty, while his has barely been touched. He nods but remains motionless, so I stand and collect my things.

"*Chère chère amie*," he says under his breath. "*Adieu, adieu, adieu.*"

"*Bon courage avec tout*," I say. In English I might have said, *Have a nice life.*

I turn to go, but he holds up a finger for me to wait. He pulls out his wallet and hands me something. His business card.

"Call me if you need anything, medical or otherwise," he says.

I stare at the card. It's white with a simple design: his name in blue, his phone number in black, followed by his profession — physician. In the top right corner is a hospital logo. I look up, astonished. So he's a doctor after all.

I LEAVE DR. MOUSTACHE staring at the beer bubbles rising in his glass, walk up the ramp and around the corner, then peer back over the wall at the sand, grass and palm trees. Soon this oasis will be an abrasive highway again. Many of the amenities, including the climbing wall and the pool are already being dismantled. The moustache is alone at his table, head lowered in a mournful daze. He looks small from here and terribly frail. Despite the annoyance he has caused this month, I feel only pity. Though he is well into his 50s, he has probably never played the dating game, at least not the one Harold is actively involved in, or if he has played the game, it has been a while. He had a magical experience years ago, and seems unable to move forward. For the month of August he stops working and resides in his garden full time, a frolicking seventeen year old, reliving an old fantasy — a fantasy for which I had provided the soundtrack, and one that has reached its end.

At least until next year.

Fortissimo

MY MOM CALLS ONE MORNING TO TELL ME ABOUT A DREAM SHE had. Her voice is muffled.

"You had a match and were about to light yourself on fire," she says. "I screamed for you to stop and you laughed and lit the match. You burst into flames." Then she starts to cry.

The dream stays with me all day. It is chilling, emphasizes my vulnerability, and reminds me that something could go wrong — that I am not protected. I could get sick or hurt, or beaten or killed. I don't even have health insurance here.

And the very next day, I almost do get killed. An old lady is dangling change out of a taxi window. There is a line-up of cars behind her and people are starting to honk. I look up from my violin and see her there, waving her clutched fist impatiently for me to approach. I stop playing, run toward her, and fail to see the oncoming motorcycle. The force of it pushes against me, ripples my clothes, and causes my bow to strike against my violin with a dull hum. I can feel the hardness of the metal and the indifference of speed. I think I sense the driver recoil, at least mentally, but it happens too fast for muscle action. The motorcycle rushes on, and I'm on the other side of the bike lane, whole and untouched. There is a collective gasp on the sidewalk and the old woman is looking at me with wide, horrified eyes.

"*Faîtes attention!*" she scolds.

That is what my mom was trying to tell me when she described her dream and wept into the receiver. You are not invincible. You are not immune. *Faîtes attention!*

LATER, I'M PACKING AWAY MY VIOLIN for the day when I hear, "*Bonjour!*"

I look up to see a young woman, my age, with dark hair that flows to her shoulders in gleaming waves. I get men of all ages and backgrounds stopping to chat, and sometimes little girls or older women, but never young, beautiful women like this. She's wearing a long red dress with several layers that wrap around her slender body. Her dark eyes are caring and curious. She introduces herself as Céline, and to my astonishment she invites me out for a drink.

I had nearly dismissed the idea of befriending a real Parisian woman. I've had coffee with a German woman, split a carton of tropical juice with a Chinese woman, and ate an ice cream cone with an American one, but Parisian women were out of my league. I thought.

Céline and I start down the street, walking aimlessly in search of a bar. Before long I ease into the rhythm of her speech. She's an actor, and is taking cello lessons, she tells me. She has just finished writing a musical, and is looking for musicians to perform in the jazz ensemble. She works a call centre job, but hopes to have her *intermittent du spectacle* status next year.

"*C'est quoi?*" I ask.

Céline explains that if an artist does a certain number of performances a year, the government provides a modest salary to make up for the lull between jobs. "It's not much," she says with a shrug, "but it will allow me to quit the call centre and focus on theatre." Her dark hair shines like a shampoo commercial and she struts with nonchalance, her gaze cool behind red framed sun glasses. I suddenly feel as if I'm walking beside a movie star and my spine uncurls. I'm at least two centimetres taller.

WE STOP IN FRONT OF A LARGE busy terrace. The tables are small and round and close together, and the wicker chairs all face forward as if they're in a theatre. It's early evening and many young professionals are winding down from a day of work with a beer or glass of wine. Céline and I take a seat near the front, gazing out at the traffic and the busy sidewalk. Locals on the street are rushing home from work or to fetch their kids from day care. Cars fly by in a constant stream.

A waiter brings us two beers and a small bowl of green olives. We nurse our drinks and take turns asking each other questions, everything from our ancestors to future goals. Céline's mother is French, I learn, and her father Algerian. She's never been to Algeria, but she knows how to make a killer couscous, which I tell her is my new favourite meal.

"I'll make it for you!" she says, which strengthens my growing hope that we'll become friends. The more we talk, the more the artist spirit stiches together our scattered, patchwork lives. We share a necessity to live around art, no matter how difficult it might get.

"So tell me about where you grew up," Céline says.

I explain that the majority of Canadians live in cities, but I am a classic Canadian stereotype. I grew up among hundreds of acres of forest. There *were* metres of snow in the winter. My neighbour *was* a lumberjack, maple syrup producer, and hunter. There *were* moose and bears. A beaver even lives in my mom's backyard pond. The swamp where I grew up, I realize as Céline's eyes light up, has taken on a new exotic air.

"I'd love to see these landscapes, the wild nature and the animals," she says.

A waiter approaches and asks us if we plan on eating. What he really means, of course, is *what* do we plan on ordering. I look around. People have moved on to steaks and salads now. The man puts his hand on his hip, waiting. I look to Céline for help. She shrugs, as if to say, *Why not?* so we order salads and the man dashes away with our empty beer glasses.

Our meal arrives, with three quarters of a bottle of rosé that we didn't order. The waiter tells us that the wine is from the gentlemen over there, and points to a young guy with curly blond hair on the other side of the terrace.

The guy waves and shouts, "I couldn't finish it!" in a strong American accent.

Céline allows him a reserved smile and a nod of approval, but her glance does not last more than a second. It is not an invitation for him to join us. He clearly wants to approach, but smiles and stays where he is. Céline is in control.

I can see the American in my peripheral vision as we eat. He glances frequently in our direction, but Céline is busy telling me about her play. It's about a young woman, a struggling jazz singer who works as a server in a bar but who dreams of success. Céline waves her hands and her eyes flash as she visualizes the scene, then she pulls the script from her bag and begins to read the first section. It's a dialogue, between the protagonist and her father, about her choice to be an artist.

"But you'll eat pasta for the rest of your life," says the dad.

"But I like pasta!" the protagonist retorts.

Suddenly, from behind, a deep voice says, "Have a good evening, ladies."

Céline and I look up. It's the American. He has come over to say good-bye. Up close, he is extremely tall but his face is baby-like, with round dimpled cheeks.

I watch as Céline gives him a quick assessment, then offers a carefully controlled smile before she says, "Sit down if you want," in perfect English.

I snap my head toward her in amazement. "You didn't tell me you spoke English!"

She smiles. "My degree is in English," she says. "But you said you wanted to learn French."

"*C'est vrai*," I laugh.

The American grabs a chair from a neighbouring table and slumps into it. Céline takes charge.

"So, what are you doing in Paris?" she asks.

"I'm here for a golf tournament," he says. "I'm on the university team." He speaks slowly and his voice has a grogginess to it, as if he's just woken up from a long nap.

"What are you studying?"

"Well, I mostly play golf."

"But you take classes, no?"

He yawns. "Not really. Well sometimes, I guess. When I'm around. But I'm off playing golf a lot. That's what got me into the school. I'm a good golfer," he says with a wink.

Céline and I exchange glances. Perhaps she's wondering the same thing, how an intellectual institution could be unconcerned about academic achievement. How do they pass exams? How do they write papers? How do they *graduate*? I gaze at the tall, sleepy giant. It's hard to imagine him exerting any energy at all. Just speaking seems to exhaust him, but maybe he's saving it all for tomorrow. *This guy's life seems to involve little else than golf*, I think, *a sport that neither of us know anything about. Or care to.*

Before long, Céline has had enough, too.

"Well, good luck with the tournament," she says.

The cue is unmistakable. He takes it, and slowly rises from his chair.

"Thanks," he says. "I think I'm gonna get going now. Big day tomorrow."

He lumbers into the street and disappears into the evening crowd. Céline raises her glass and finishes the last of her rosé.

I'm impressed by her cool demeanour, the way she controlled the conversation and kept the golfer at a safe and comfortable distance. I could learn a lot just from watching her.

As we're leaving the café she tells me she's having a soirée at her place next week. "*T'es invitée*," she says.

"Wow. *Merci. Avec plaisir.*"

It's as if a secret vault has just opened up: the lair of a *Parisienne*. Finally.

ON THE DAY OF THE SOIRÉE, I can't decide between my green cowboy shirt, my colourful tunic, or my handmade patchwork skirt. The guests will probably be well-dressed, so I should muster as much class as I can. I put on the skirt. Too rustic. I hold up the cowboy shirt. Not feminine enough. I settle for the tunic and jeans. I lean toward the mirror and glare at my round face. *When will I stop looking like a kid and more like a woman?* I wonder. Even when I do put on mascara or eye-liner, it ends up looking more like dress-up than make-up.

Now for my hair. It has always been an issue — somewhere between wavy and straight but far enough from both that it often ends up resorting to frizz, especially in humid weather like today. Braids are too juvenile, so I throw it up in a bun. That looks too plain, so I split my hair into two sections and put it up in mini buns on either side of my head. Now I look like a half-classy Japanimation character. It will have to do.

When I'd asked Céline what I should bring, she said *"une bouteille,"* so I head to the grocery store, and then spend way too long pacing the wine aisle, staring at bottle after bottle of red and white with varying dates, locations of origin and prices. Finally a young guy in a collared shirt and shiny leather shoes brushes down the aisle, humming, and after a quick sweep with his eyes stoops to pick up a bottle of red. I wait for him to turn down the next aisle before I grab the same. It's 9 Euros, has a castle on it and is from 2003, which I hope is old enough to be decent. I bring it to the cash desk.

My stomach swirls with nervousness as I get off the Metro and walk toward Céline's. The sick sensation gets stronger as I make my way into the courtyard of her building. Tension grips my stomach and scrapes along my chest. I wish I knew more what to expect. *Will I be the only foreigner? Do the others know each other already? Who will I talk to and what about? Am I dressed appropriately?* I can hear laughter, and as I head down the hallway I realize it's coming from Céline's place.

"Nisha!" she cries when she opens the door. *"Entre!"*

Her apartment is almost as small as mine, but there is a separate room for the kitchen and her bed is a mezzanine, high up on the wall, with a closet and a tiny desk underneath. There are about a dozen people, standing in groups of two or three, chatting and holding little plastic glasses of red wine. A few glance over, but most remain engaged in their conversations. Many of the women are wearing tiny dresses, some with little shoes that look like ballet slippers, others with tall leather boots. These women are virtually make-up free but seem to glitter all on their own. They are relaxed and glow with confidence. A few of them have cigarettes nestled between their slender fingers. The guys are dressed in jeans, T-shirts and Adidas running shoes. Casual class.

Céline introduces me to her friends. Most are artists who also work at the call centre. Conversation is surprisingly smooth and I'm quickly able to relax. No one flinches or gasps when I tell them I'm a street musician. Many of them are musicians themselves and grill me with questions. *Where do you play? You make enough to live in Paris? What kind of music?* They hear my accent and ask where I am from. I don't hesitate to mention my swamp origins. It may not be classy, but it's different and exotic to Parisians. I also hope it will excuse any lack of sophistication they might already have picked up on.

Soon my nervousness is gone and I'm absorbed in the joyful chaos. There are frequent changes of discussion partners as people go to and from the table to replenish their glass or grab a handful of snacks. The drinking is moderate, and the tone doesn't have the wild, out of control feeling of some of the university parties I'd attended in Waterloo. There is no slurring of words, no glossy eyes, no hysterical laughter and no roughhousing. Everyone is in complete control of their faculties, and it appears they intend to remain that way. The glasses are so tiny, it would take dozens of refills to reach any level of significant inebriation.

After awhile, Céline announces that it's time to play "the game." The others nod and sit on the floor in a circle — a bit difficult in such a tiny space. Someone puts the wine bottles in the middle for easy access. A new surge of uneasiness begins to ripple in my stomach. I dislike games in general, but it wouldn't be right to abandon the party so abruptly. Besides, slipping away unnoticed would be impossible in such close quarters. I take a spot close to the door and nervously await instructions.

Céline explains the game. Everyone will write questions on slips of paper and place them in the hat. Then we'll go around the circle and take turns answering the questions aloud. This is not what I had expected from a Parisian soirée, but I nod that I've understood and take the pen and slips of paper that are handed to me.

Maybe it'll be bonding, I think, a way of getting to know these people beyond the usual *what do you do?* and *where are you from?* I make my questions anecdote-based. *What is your worst disaster in the kitchen?* and *How did you discover that Santa wasn't real?* And *Have you ever pulled the legs off of flies?*

"*Nisha commence!*" Céline says, once all the questions have been submitted. She approaches, beaming, shaking the hat into which we've all thrown our questions. All eyes are on me as I reach my hand in and pull out my first slip.

What is your preferred sexual position?

I feel my face and neck flush. My larynx tightens as I stare at the words. I can't talk. If I tried to say anything, my voice would come out as a whine or squeak. I continue to stare helplessly at the question. Céline laughs and asks me what it says, so I hand it to her. She smiles and announces that since I don't know anyone I can refuse to answer. She gladly takes the question herself and says that she enjoys mounting the man like a horse. The others chuckle and someone emits a "yee-haw!" Céline throws her head back in laughter and suddenly I get an image of her in the act, bouncing up and down in ecstasy with her head back and hair flying wildly. I glance at the mezzanine. It would never allow for such a position. They'd have to do it on the floor. Maybe she has a roll-up mat for such occasions.

To my relief, I get to skip my turn. A tall curly-haired girl on my left reaches into the hat and reads her question out loud: *Do you prefer to dominate or be dominated?* After my question, I know it's not referring to the workplace. She is so confident and commanding, with her big curls and tall black boots, I expect her to say dominate, but without hesitation she admits that she would rather be dominated.

Céline continues around the room with her hat. Her friends

disclose intimate details, which delight the other guests, but I'm too anxious about my next question to pay much attention. My heart is slamming now and my mouth feels full of dust.

Finally the looming hat returns. Miraculously, I pick my Santa Claus question. I take a deep breathe, then explain to the room how when I was four I noticed price tags on some hair barrettes in my stocking.

Céline's friends smile politely, but my story is ridiculous next to their sex-in-a-closet, triple orgasm, and six-times-in-one-night accounts. I can't help wrapping my arms around my knees and rocking a little. Everyone else here is so confident and sexy.

As the game continues, I'm amazed, not only at how candid Céline's friends are but how experienced. I refuse to answer most of my questions. Even if I were comfortable talking about this stuff, I wouldn't have much to contribute. These guys are sexual veterans, and they speak about having sex as casually as if describing trying on a pair of shoes.

When I'm finally leaving her place later that night, Céline apologizes for the game. "I hope you weren't uncomfortable," she says, leaning in for the *bises*. "I'll call you soon."

The night air is damp and the city streets are nearly barren. I glance at the time on my cell phone and rush to catch the last Metro of the night. It roars into the station as I reach the top of the stairs, and I barrel down, two at a time, making it in just before the doors slam.

The car is silent except for the grinding wheels, and I am alone with my thoughts. I didn't enjoy Céline's game, but I feel enlightened after the openness and nonchalance of her friends as they recounted their most intimate experiences. They allowed a graphic glimpse into their sex-lives. I always thought it was better to solidify a strong emotional connection before delving into the physical, but Céline's friends seem to do the opposite: they test the body chemistry first and the emotional after. *Have I been doing things backwards?* I wonder. *B before A? Should I be letting my body guide my heart and my head?* Céline and her friends would probably think so. Harold would too. They would say that *le grand amour* is rare, and in the meantime life is to be enjoyed. Have fun.

I think back to the women tonight and their genuine, natural beauty. I can do pretty, but I've never been able to pull off sexy. Not like the *Parisiennes*. Sexy, I'm now convinced, is less in the clothes and more in the head. It's a mind-set. An attitude. A way of holding oneself up to the world.

Maybe if I hang around Céline and her friends, I think, *I'll pick up some of their energy. Maybe I'll learn to hold myself differently and eventually feel comfortable in more feminine clothing.* Or maybe I'll never shake my tomboy tendencies.

I don't have the money for a change of wardrobe anyway, so for now I'm stuck with my jeans, T-shirts, hoodies and hats.

It's POURING RAIN, but I've finally memorized Veracini's e Minor Sonata and am looking forward to trying it on the street, and since museums are the only sure place tourists go in weather like this, I head to the Louvre. Music is strictly forbidden here during the day, but I can usually get away with it under one of the archways that lines the busy *Rue de Rivoli*. There I'm able to spot the security man coming for his rounds and can vacate before he arrives.

The passers-by are scarcer than I had hoped. Those who have braved the rain are crouched under umbrellas and scurrying to their destinations. I don't mind. I'm here for the Veracini. I play it once through, with only a couple of memory lapses. The first movement fits the weather particularly well. It's slow, and ranges from high pleading laments to low heaves and a ringing G string. The faster movements are lively and have an almost frantic feel. They're fun to play, with the bow leaping off the strings and dozens of neurotic trills. I'm on my second time through when a man with blond wavy curls and a young woman, also blond, stop to listen, arms wrapped around each other's waist. They exchange words before the man steps forward and says, "*Est-ce que vous faîtes des inaugurations?"*

I stop and look up at him. "*Bien sûr,*" I say.

"*C'est quoi votre tarif?*"

He speaks quickly with a touch of impatience, like an important professional with not a moment to spare, not even on a rainy Sunday afternoon. I hesitate. I haven't played any gigs in Paris yet and have no idea what the going rate is.

"*Vingt cinq,*" I say, then instantly regret it. Twenty-five Euros an hour is a bargain. I make a better wage on the street.

"*D'accord,*" he says. He hands me his business card from his wallet and tells me to come at 6 p.m. on Tuesday. Then the two of them turn, open their large black umbrella and dash out into the heavy rain.

"Coiffirst" is written in gold on the card. It's a hair salon. The name is a play on words with *coiffeur* (hairdresser) and an anglicism, *first* written as first. The address is in *Saint-Germain-des-prés*, one of the poshest neighbourhoods in all of Paris.

I ALWAYS LEAVE DETAILS until the last minute, so the hour before I have to leave for the gig I find myself in a frantic fluster. The only black I own is a faded button up shirt that looks grey next to my black polyester pants. I get the iron from the back of the closet and press the shirt on the floor over a towel. With no time to spare, I give my teeth a quick brush, throw my hair up in a bun and head straight to the salon.

My hair only becomes an issue when I catch a glimpse of my reflection in a store window. It hasn't been cut in so long that it flows up and out of the elastic, leaping over the top of my head in wild, chaotic curls. But I'm approaching the salon, now. There isn't much I can do.

With my neglected, unbrushed hair, I edge along the stone walkway that has glowing chandeliers and tiny, vertically strung golden lights, until I reach the double glass doors. They are tall and framed in brass. Inside, the salon has a calm lightness, as if I've entered an eerie dream. It spans two floors and stretches around a large courtyard. The mirrors at each station are made of gold and lined with tiny bright bulbs, which lends them a movie star effect. All accessories are stored out of sight, leaving the wide counters empty and immaculate. The place smells of soft, expensive chemicals. No outrageous fruit scents. I inhale deeply. More of a subdued sweetness. I'm a few minutes early, so I head upstairs to explore. It's the VIP floor, for really *really* rich people. Up here, the wide coiffure chairs look like La-Z-boys. The shampoos, conditioners and serums are colour coded and sit in rows along white counters. Each station is private, divided by curtains in varying styles. One is of shimmering pearls. Another has delicate white tendrils hanging from the ceiling. And on it goes. The deco is modern in a sparse, empty way — large spaces with a few glowing blue cubes and bright illuminated columns. Mosaics adorn sections of the floors and walls of each hair station. The first one is made of little pebbles for a nature-inspired look. The next one is futuristic-themed, with iridescent white glass. I pass another with blue stones in the shape of water droplets.

Finally, I'm looking down through the window overlooking the courtyard. Down below a jazz band is setting up next to tables of champagne flutes and hors d'oeuvres. Elegance infiltrates everything, from the polished wood floors to the intricate cornice mouldings. I am reminded of Bach and Mozart, hired to play for royalty, permitted among the rich — but only temporarily. My violin is my backstage pass, a glimpse into this exclusive world. Like Beethoven and Mozart, I could never belong here. *And I wouldn't want to,* I think. *It would require too much effort to care about things like hair and clothes and maintain control of my speech and behaviour.* Just being here is stifling, as if the oxygen is being slowly siphoned out.

I return to the reception area, to find the man who hired me. He is frantically zipping about, designating tasks to his employees. When he catches sight of me he rushes over, then hesitates as his eyes narrow at my hair. He asks if he could do something with it. *Une petite coiffure.* It is more of a demand than an offer, and I regret fussing over my shirt instead of my hair. Curious as to how anyone could remedy the sad state of my strands, and hoping to learn a few tips on hair management, I accept his proposal for a quick fix.

He sits me in a chair near the entrance. In the mirror I see the first guests starting to file in behind me. I should already be playing. The owner summons one of his male employees and tells him to take care of me. From his hand motions, it seems that his plan is to get my hair up and out of sight.

In my stylist's eyes, I detect annoyance with a touch of disgust. "*Pas de problème,*" he says to his boss. "*Tout de suite.*"

He sighs loudly as he removes my cheap elastic, which releases a tangled nest of hair that falls as a solid mass to my shoulders in a complicated network of knots.

"*Désolée,*" I mumble, but he doesn't seem to hear.

Suddenly he does something I haven't dared to do in years. He gets out a brush and begins working out the tangles with quick aggressive strokes. My hair is very thick and best left alone unless it is wet and heavily conditioned. A dry brushing promises disaster. It separates the strands and, much like whipping a soufflé, increases the volume tenfold. As I feared, my hair is not taking well to this treatment. I watch in the mirror as it becomes a large, cloud-like puff. A group of guests file in and eye me curiously. When it's clear that the knots are too advanced for the stylist's delicate brush, he abandons his initial plan, grabs my hair in a fist and pulls fiercely. I wince and try not to cry out, and wonder if he's being rough as punishment for my poor hair-care. He twists the handful of strands tightly against my scalp and ties it in a ponytail with a sturdy hooked elastic.

Some visibly important clients enter the salon, and my stylist, who has been silent and solemn-faced until now, abandons me to give them a loud enthusiastic greeting. I remain in the chair and avoid eye contact with the guests, who continue to enter and mingle as they admire the renovations. In the mirror I can see the billowing puffy mass of my ponytail. I am on display, as if part of a "hair disaster" campaign.

In the reflection, I study the hair of the other women. It's not so much the style but the *quality* of their hair that strikes me. They must invest in the best products and technology treatments to have such gently flowing, silky strands. Their hair is how I imagine their lives to be: orderly and calm, unlike my chaotic, messy display. *Could my hair be so pleasant?* I wonder. *So silken? So obedient? So flowing? If only I took better care of it?* Hmmm.

After ten minutes of waiting, I'm starting to get anxious. My stylist is nowhere in sight. He seems to have forgotten me, and I am certain a puffy ponytail wasn't what the boss had intended. I can't play classical violin with this frightful mass behind my head. Finally, after several minutes, I catch sight of the stylist, coming my way. He hurries by with determination.

"*Excusez-moi!*" I plead.

"*Je reviens,*" he says, maintaining his brisk pace.

After five more excruciating minutes, he's back in position with special sprays and pins. Before long he has plastered the hair around my scalp and created a thick, solid bun at the back of my head, which he traps in a small net, pinning it aggressively to my now fully congealed hair. I look like a ballet dancer, minus the grace.

"*Voilà,*" he says triumphantly.

I slide out of the chair, set up quickly and begin to play. I work through my street repertoire, which I know so well I don't need to concentrate.

My eyes scan the guests. They stand rigid and upright, as if their confidence is an air current running up their spines, and they frequently burst out in hearty laughter, exposing white rows of teeth. Besides physical attractiveness and expensive clothes, these invitees possess a carefree lightness as they move about, conglomerate, split, mix, and join again. Somehow, they all seem to know each other intimately. Or maybe, they consider themselves a part of the same club — the wealthy club — that they don't have to know each other personally to presume they have things in common. *Just as they get their hair done in the same place, they probably vacation on the same islands, eat in the same establishments, enjoy the same vintages and smoke the same cigars. No matter who they talk to, they can be sure they won't have to meet anyone poor.* Unless they stopped to talk to the musicians, of course.

A freakishly tall woman with spiky blond hair passes by, pursued by a gaggle of male photographers. One of them suggests she pose in front of the violinist. We exchange glances. Her blue eyes are large but vacant, as if made of glass. It's like trying to connect with a doll. She stands beside me and smiles carefully into the lenses. It's not a happy smile. It's a complicated one, calculated, as if trying to show secrets, a sad story, and barely contained sexual urges. There is a flurry of flashes as the photographers capture the scene from several angles, before she continues on. Her wispy body moves with smooth grace, while the photographers scramble in pursuit.

After an hour I take a break and help myself to a glass of champagne and a leftover sandwich quarter. Entering into one of the closed social circles is unthinkable, so I make my way to a vacant window on the second floor and gaze down into the courtyard, where the jazz musicians are playing. Three guitars and a saxophone bop together to the tune while the drummer moves his head back and forth with his eyes closed.

Before long, an elderly woman joins me. She's not here to listen to the music. She's here to talk to me. She is tiny and brittle, but her hair is thick and healthy looking, cut just below the ears and looks as though it has been plucked from a schoolgirl. Though she may boast the same social status as the other guests here, she doesn't have the youthful dynamism of the others. She lives in the countryside, she tells me, but is a regular client at Coiffirst. She also has a chalet in the *Pyrenées*. She opens her purse, takes out a small notebook and writes her name and number.

"Call me," she says, handing me the slip of paper. "You can

come and visit me at my chalet."

I have a vision of a massive stone manor house, the two of us sitting by a raging fire and servants coming by with tea and treats. We talk for a few more minutes before I tell her I have to play again, and she clasps my hands in hers. Her fingers are bony and freezing but her gaze is warm.

"*Merci pour la belle musique,*" she whispers.

The next hour goes by quickly, and soon the guests begin to file out. They leave in groups, laughing and walking with purpose, not as if the night is winding down but as if it's just begun. They'll likely continue their evenings elsewhere, in clubs or high-end bars. *Who knows where they go?* Not me. I put my violin away while the last group leaves, and as I fold up my stand, there is only silence.

The boss comes in from the courtyard and says, "*Ah, vous voilà!*" He shakes my hand, pays me double my given rate and writes my phone number into his big black leather book for future events. Then he takes a white gift bag off the counter and hands it to me. "*Un petit cadeau,*" he says.

As soon as I've turned the corner and am out of sight, I open the bag. There is a small white box inside. It's hair treatment for "dry, frizzy and unmanageable hair." *Did the jazz musicians receive this gift,* I wonder, or *is it a suggestion from my personal stylist after battling the savage state of my strands?*

No matter. When I return to my small abode, I head straight for the shower. I release my hair from its nylon shackles and let the hot water wash the sticky products away. Once my hair has been towel dried, I open my gift and gently massage the cool white cream into my long and wild strands. Then I hit the pillow and hope for the best.

Staccato

I REACH IN MY BAG FOR MY KEY AND MY HEART SURGES IN MY chest when I realize the pouch I keep it in is empty. I check all the other compartments, frantically, but I know exactly where it is: inside the apartment, just a couple metres away. Instead of returning it to my bag like I usually do, I must have tossed it on the desk when I came home last night. Jérémie had warned me. This is a self-locking door, this is the only key that exists, and if I leave it inside or lose it, I'll be *dans la merde*.

Well I'm in it now. I retreat to one of the benches along the canal to think. It's early evening and people are starting to make their way to the quay for picnics and pétanque. In a couple of hours, it will be dark. I need to find a solution, soon. A locksmith will be expensive, and I'd have to prove that I live here. Technically I don't. I'm not on the lease and subletting is illegal. The mere sight of my mountains of coins on the floor would elicit suspicion. You never know who might call the authorities on a *sans papier*. I've heard of it happening. There is only one person I can think to call: Harold. *Mon ami*. Maybe he'll have an idea.

In less than five minutes, Harold arrives on his scooter, beeping the horn and grinning as he pulls up onto the sidewalk outside the apartment.

When we reach the door, he opens his backpack and takes out a large rolled up chest X-ray.

"What's that for?" I ask.

"Haven't you ever broken in anywhere?" he asks.

I watch as he eases the X-ray between the door and the frame. I knew he would know what to do.

"I've done this many times," he says. He moves the X-ray up and down, slow at first and when that doesn't seem to work, with vigorous jerks. After about ten minutes of this he's sweating and out of breath. "OK, I don't think it's going to work," he says, scratching his dark, messy curls. "Is the window locked?"

"I don't think so," I say, following his train of thought. It would be a dangerous feat and we'd need a very tall ladder.

We head back outside and examine the building. Although it's only on the first floor, the window ledge is quite high, even with a ladder. To the right of the ledge are four cement ridges a half metre apart, one above the other. They stick out about 20 centimetres. Someone tall enough might be able to climb them, but I don't want Harold to risk his life for my key.

"I think I should call a locksmith," I say.

"I'll be right back," Harold says. He turns and jogs up the sidewalk.

"Where are you going?" I call after him.

"To borrow a ladder!" he yells.

Harold returns with a long ladder from a nearby café and sets it under the ridges.

"This is too dangerous," I plead. I'm already imagining the worst. Harold could die if he fell the wrong way.

"Don't worry," he says. "I'm a good climber." He smiles but his lips don't turn up all the way and I catch a glint of fear as his eyes shift up toward my window.

Harold approaches the ladder, marches quickly up the rungs, then hesitates. To get onto the cement ridges, he'll have to pull himself up. He takes a deep preparatory breath, then launches himself against the wall, grasping tightly onto the second ridge. He tries to walk his feet up, but his soles are worn and slippery. After hanging suspended for a minute, he swings his legs up onto the first ridge with a grunt of exertion and grabs onto the third one with his hands. A few pedestrians stop to watch as he prepares his next move.

A young blond woman stops and gazes up with concern. "What you're doing is extremely dangerous!" she calls.

"I think you should come down," I shout, with a tremble in my voice. A bitter taste of panic reaches the back of my throat, and I hug my arms into my chest. I'd rather pay a couple hundred Euros than have Harold in the hospital, or worse. He's starting to stiffen with apprehension. I wonder if the crowd is adding an element of pressure — like when I performed on stage and my hands lost their dexterity. Every movement is harder with people watching.

"Come down!" I yell again.

Ignoring our comments, Harold takes another deep breath and focuses on the ledge. A few more passers-by have stopped to form a small crowd. Slowly Harold makes his way closer, until he is on the very edge of the second ridge. But the window ledge is at his chest level — still too high. He'll have to climb higher. Someone in the crowd mutters that Harold must be crazy. Carefully he reaches up, grabs the fourth ridge and with a wheeze pulls his body up one more level, then crouches, waiting for a few moments to catch his breath.

I dig my teeth into my knuckles and my heart is pounding against my ribcage, when, slowly, Harold reaches across and touches the outside of the window frame. The crowd is growing bigger, but no one speaks. The tension is tight in the air, and I am rattled with regret. I was a fool to leave the key inside, and I should never have involved Harold.

He takes a few more breaths, then lifts a shaky leg up and across the divide. Now he's on the ledge. With a gasp, he lunges to the left, bringing both feet in front of the window, and clutches the top of the frame. The audience makes a sound of breathless wonder, like when an acrobat does a wild flip at the top of a circus tent. It's too horrifying to watch and yet no one can look away. Harold is providing a spectacle for the neighbourhood, an out-of-the ordinary event that people will tell their families about when they get home. I could almost pass around a hat for people to drop coins in. It's entertainment after all. Isn't that what people pay for?

Cautiously, Harold shimmies along the ledge. A metre left to go. Finally, he reaches my window and pulls it open. The crowd below bursts into applause. They are delighted with the performance. Watching a man climb up the side of a wall is not unlike watching a man play a Paganini Caprice. It is the possibility for error that provides excitement. That's probably why I prefer busking over the stage. No one is waiting for a specific outcome or to hear a specific piece. I play what I want, and without a real audience there cannot be mistakes.

Harold lifts his arm triumphantly before diving head first into the apartment. Trembling, I bound upstairs and throw my arms around him. "Thank you!" I cry, close to tears.

"I saved my princess," Harold says. He is smiling, but I can tell he's shaken. He's soaked with sweat and still breathing heavily. I pour him a tall glass of water and he downs it in seconds. I refill it and he sits on my mattress until he catches his breath. After a few minutes he stands and grins. "Want to go for a scooter ride?"

The apartment key is lying innocently on the desk. I grab it and we return to the street, where the crowd is now gone. We return the ladder, then head to the scooter. Harold pulls an extra helmet from inside the seat compartment and slides it onto my head. We hop on, and I wrap my arms around his stomach. It's still damp with perspiration. The engine snarls, and we shoot onto the street.

The breeze against my skin is soothing as we glide through the city, weaving around traffic and careening over cobblestones, riding for the sake of movement. The setting sun casts a warm glow on the white stone buildings, making the city seem to radiate from within. We wind on an undefined trajectory, embracing the delight of pure aimlessness. I hold on tighter to *mon ami* and smile under my helmet.

TODAY, THE WEATHER IS WARNING me to stay home. The air is unbearably humid, so heavy it enters the fine pathways of my lungs with resistance. Clouds the colour of asphalt hang low in the sky. On the street there is a feeling of suspense, as if everyone knows the sky is going to crack. They just don't know when.

As I set up at *Place des Vosges*, the clouds are already beginning to leak. The painters are there, as usual, under the archways, selling their work. Maâmar is sketching and George is sipping coffee from his thermos. The place is nearly vacant, but I don't mind. It's a good day for introducing a new piece. There aren't too many listeners. I've been working on the Giga from Bach's D Minor Partita. I played it years ago in high school for a recital and just started practising it again two weeks ago. As soon as I have even one spectator, a piece changes, becomes more difficult — perhaps because part of my brain power becomes focused on my listener. Even today on the street, with just the painters and a few straggling tourists, the notes are harder to pin down than they were when I was alone at home. I am getting lost in their labyrinth, sometimes uncertain which passage comes next. My left hand is growing stiff and my bow is bouncing slightly, making precision more difficult, but since there is no one around, I can play it several times through.

By the third time, the stiffness subsides and the music comes alive — it's now more than just the sum of the notes. My fingers slip into their places naturally and the melody flows with little mental effort. Near the second half, a woman and her young daughter stop to listen. "*Génial!*" she exclaims when I finish, and hands me a five Euro bill. The piece has passed the initiation phase. It is now ready for a full street performance.

Most of the pieces I play on the street I would never play for a concert audience. The performance itself is not the point here, not for me. It's about creating an atmosphere, using the music to connect with strangers and adapting the piece to my surroundings. I exaggerate everything: the pauses are longer, the ritardandoes extreme, and I am not worried about making mistakes or forgetting my place. Sometimes I do play a wrong note or lose where I am, but then I simply incorporate this into the mood of the piece. Sometimes I'll play a repeat four times. Sometimes I play things at twice the speed. Sometimes I blend two pieces together. The pieces stretch out and meld to the street. You would never hear them played this way on stage. There is room to explore. There are no rules.

Satisfied now, I set the piece aside and begin a Handel Sonata, but I've barely reached the first repeat when a saxophone
suddenly blasts from an adjacent archway — only a few metres
away. Enraged, I lay my violin in its open case and head over to
investigate, shoulders back in preparation for a confrontation.

I discover an elderly man with a long grey beard, swaying
on a tiny stool. He's wearing tattered, mismatched clothes and
a Breton sailors' cap. Dozens of abstract drawings, crayon on
construction paper, are sprawled out on the ground in front of
him. It looks like the hallway outside a kindergarten classroom.
By his feet is an empty wooden bowl and a pink sign with *Merci*
scrawled on a slant. He's not playing a saxophone — it's a comb
with a plastic bag around it, but the timbre is strikingly similar.
When he notices me standing there, he squints and rocks wildly
to his improvised honks.

"*Excusez-moi*," I shout, but he has closed his eyes now and is
making enough noise to drown out an entire orchestra.

"*T'inquiète pas*," Maâmar consoles me when I pack up and
join him and George. "He's crazy, but he's harmless. We call him
le gentil fou." The Kind Fool. *Right.*

I'm not afraid of him, but I worry that he is going to in-
fringe on my livelihood by making this place a regular spot for
his street gallery and performance hall. *Place des Vosges* is one of
the few places I can count on all year round.

Maâmar is working on a watercolour sketch of a man with
wild grey curls and piercing emerald eyes. The expression on the
man's face is dark but distant. Under his chin is a violin.

"Who's that?" I ask.

Maâmar looks up in disbelief. "*Mais, tu ne connais pas Tim?*"

I shake my head. I'd definitely remember someone like this.
Maâmar tells me that Tim plays at *Place des Vosges* almost every
morning. Bach from memory.

I peer at the drawing more closely. The green and grey shadows around Tim's cloaked body portray a dark but sprightly aura.

Maâmar has captured the movement of his spearing bow arm so well, I can almost hear the sorrowful opening of the D Minor Partita. It seems impossible that Tim and I have both been playing in the same spot for months and never crossed paths.

Maâmar teases me that it's because I sleep in too late. "Come earlier," he says. "You've got to meet Tim."

The rain is thrashing from the sky now and the Kind Fool is wailing even louder, in high, frantic shrieks. He has no intention of stopping.

By now I've learned that when enough setbacks strike, it's best not to insist. Forcing music into the air is like trying to make someone be friends with you, so with my case light and nearly empty I head home and change out of my soaked clothes. As the rain smashes against the window, I boil a pot of water on the hotplate and throw in a bag of mint tea. Then I hide under the covers with *The Bone People*, a novel about a reclusive artist living in an isolated tower on a beach in New Zealand. Though the landscape couldn't be more different, I feel as holed up as the protagonist, shielded from the rest of the world by my soft blanket. I should have listened to the clouds in the first place. Today is not a playing day. It's a cocooning day. I wish everyone in the city could experience this, being wrapped in a blanket mid-afternoon on a day the clouds just will not stop weeping.

Diminuendo

*If, as you learn a new language you lose the characteristics
that once defined you, are the traits that appear in the new language
genuine aspects of yourself? As my French improves, am I becoming
myself again? Or am I developing a new version of myself?*

At first, my French was so poor that I couldn't recognize myself
in the stutters and broken phrases, but things are different now.
French is coming into focus and I can articulate my thoughts
and feelings. A personality is forming, pushing through the layers of language. It's shadowy, though, and only partly formed.
Some of the qualities I thought defined me seem not to have
survived the voyage. My sarcasm, for example, has perished en
route. As a result, my sense of humour has taken a hit and my
way of interacting with people is different. I am more of a passive
participant than I used to be, just trying to keep afloat. When I
do speak, my voice surprises me. It's higher pitched, cheerier and
with a slightly childish air. I wonder if this is a new quality, or
if it will dissipate and shift as my French continues to improve.

For now, I have become a voracious listener, which allows my
ego some respite. It can take a rest from its usual preoccupation
of entertaining and impressing. Here, I can just be.

It's mid-September now. The locals are back at work, but the
tourist population is still flourishing. People from around the
globe are strolling about, carefree, exploring the galleries and
boutiques at *Place des Vosges* as I play through the first movement
of the Bach D Minor Partita. Many lean against the ancient
walls to listen. *Merci*, some say, as they drop a coin in my case.
It's one of the few words most of them have learned for their trip
to France, and every nationality pronounces it differently. Some
roll the R, some scratch it from the back of their throats, and
when the Anglos say it, it sounds more like *Mercy*.

"*Vous jouez très bien*," an Asian man says to me between pieces. He speaks slowly, pronouncing each word with deliberation.

I smile and ask where he's from.

"*Je viens du Japon,*" he replies. "*Et vous?*"

"Canada."

"Oh, then you must speak English," he says, his accent disappearing almost completely. "I speak it much better than French."

"Where did you learn?" I ask.

"I studied architecture in the States," he says. "I live here now, in Paris, on a little street just over there." He motions to the other side of *Place des Vosges*.

We chat for a few minutes more, before he says, "Would you. . . like to have dinner with me? At a restaurant?" His eyes drop to the ground as he awaits my answer.

It might be his kindness or his sharp air of intelligence, or the fact that he seems lonely, but something about him compels me to say yes, and his face brightens.

"Are you free tonight at eight?"

"Sure," I say.

"Wonderful," he says. "I have a place in mind. I'll print off the directions and be back."

He hurries away, and returns a few minutes later with a cream coloured envelope. Inside is a carefully folded map with highlighted streets. A black star marks the establishment, not far from the Louvre: *Le Grand Colbert.*

"I'll see you tonight, then," he says. "Oh, by the way, my name is Nobuaki."

"Nisha," I say, and out of reflex I reach out and shake his hand.

BUSKING IN PARIS would be simple if I could play at *Place des Vosges* all day every day, but the residents would start to complain, so after two hours I pack up, say good-bye to the painters, and go off to find another location for the rest of the afternoon. I head toward the centre of the city, stopping for bananas at a health food store along the way.

I walk along *Rue de Rivoli*, then take a left down a little street toward the Seine. I notice that my usual spot on the *Île Saint-Louis* bridge is taken by a group of American Jazz musicians. They're often here and they play for hours, so there's no point hanging around. I cross the two bridges to the Rive Gauche and check my spot in the Latin Quarter, but it is also occupied — a banjo/fiddle duet. Tourists are everywhere, but I can't find a decent place and my chest is beginning flutter with panic. Time is passing.

Finally I resort to one of the wider bridges near *Notre-Dame.* My violin is drowned out by cars and scooters, the diesel fumes are overpowering, and most of the people passing by are locals in a hurry. They have no desire to turn their heads, let alone stop to listen. Many are already being serenaded by MP3 players or shouting into cell phones and are not even aware of my presence. I'm just another distraction among many.

I will need to spend some time finding new spots: intimate, undiscovered locations hidden from the noise and rush. After a disheartening hour and a half of playing, I stop and pull out Nobuaki's map. It's already seven. No time to go home to change, but the Metro will get me there too early, so I decide to walk. I take my time along *Rue de Rivoli,* which is heavy with shoppers and traffic and thick with Parisians rushing home. A group of teenagers takes up the whole sidewalk, laughing and stuffing slender French fries into their mouths. Every hundred metres or so there is a homeless guy passed out in a sleeping bag that I must gingerly step around.

At the Louvre, I take a right. On the other side of the five-star *Hotel du Louvre,* I discover the *Comédie Française.* I've heard about this place. Some locals stopped recently to tell me I should play here.

I like what I see. The building is tall and grandiose, with smooth, round columns supporting its archways and a balcony that stretches across the front, with French flags arranged in equal intervals. I'm standing in *Place Colette,* an open cobbled area with a sprinkle of benches, trees, and black lampposts. To the right is the sprawling terrace of the Café Nemours where people are sitting at tiny round tables, with their wicker chairs all facing outward. And at one of the far left tables, is Nobuaki. He's sipping an espresso and watching the passing pedestrians. I notice he has changed his clothes — he's wearing a stiff white collared shirt, black pants and dress shoes. I now regret not going home to change, but I'm stuck with my faded purple T-shirt and frayed patchwork skirt. It's authentic, at least.

When he spots me, Nobuaki tosses the last of his coffee into his mouth and hurries over. He shakes my hand again and to my relief, doesn't seem bothered by my informal attire.

"You should play here in front of the theatre," he says. "Especially weekends. Lots of people go to the matinees."

"Here too," he says as we pass through a narrow archway leading to an open area with rows of fluted columns accented with vertical black and white stripes. Kids are clambering and playing on the shorter ones, while adults are leaning against the tall ones for a rest and a guidebook consultation.

"This is *Palais-Royal*," Nobuaki announces. "It was a royal palace for many years, but before that it was home to Cardinal Richelieu." Nobuaki is on a roll. I don't even have to ask for clarification. "Richelieu was a very powerful political and religious figure. He founded the *Académie Française*, the official body of authority on the French language."

I picture the Cardinal roaming the premises, his long red robe trailing out behind him.

"And these columns," Nobuaki goes on, making me feel like I'm on a historical tour, "were designed by the artist Daniel Buren. He is famous for his stripes. Actually, people call him the stripe guy."

I laugh and raise my eyebrows and say things like *Wow. Neat! Really?* But I have little to add. Everything is new to me. It's like finding a secret garden. All this time it has been within walking distance of my other spots, and yet I didn't know it was here. Rows of trees pruned into rectangles stretch to the arches on the other side. Rich blues, reds and yellows burst from flowerbeds surrounding a multi-streamed fountain.

"It's incredible," I say.

"If you think this is beautiful," Nobuaki says. "Imagine if we could have seen it when the Duchess Henrietta Anne lived here. It was said to be the most beautiful garden in Paris."

I try to imagine it, but it's difficult with all the tourists everywhere, snapping photos and strolling and relaxing on the benches. *What was it like when royalty strolled here?* I wonder. *What did they wear? What did they think about? Where did they go to the bathroom? Who was Duchess Henrietta Anne?*

The only way I can feel grounded in a place is to understand the mundane details of life. Otherwise I have a hard time grasping the history. I wind up in a shady compartment of facts and major events that blur together.

Nobuaki however, seems to have a crisp notion of dates and people. "After the Revolution, *Palais-Royal* was given to the public," he says. "It became known for its gambling and brothels."

I want to stop him there and ask him to elaborate on "the Revolution," that sweeping term that implies fires, chaos and head chopping. I want to know what it was *like* during that time. Not just who was killed and when. I want to know what the city *smelled* like, what it sounded like, and how an average chimney sweeper or a seven-year-old girl might have experienced the city when it was exploding. The French know the dates perfectly, thanks to rote memory drills during their early education, but I want more than just dates. I want a multi-sensory account.

Nobuaki might be able to offer insight, but he's busy showing me something else now, pointing to a tiny bronze cannon mounted on a concrete cylinder. It's in the middle of a long patch of pristine grass, on which it is forbidden to walk, according to a severe "*Pelouse Interdite*" sign.

"This cannon was erected in 1786 on the prime meridian of Paris," he says. "Every day at noon the sun's rays would pass through a lens and light the fuse. Actually, I think it still fires, but the original was stolen. This is a reproduction."

"How do you know so much?" I ask him.

"I love French history," he says.

We pass a couple of the restaurants that line the garden, along with speciality shops that sell stamps, pipes and perfume. At the very end, we stop to gaze in the window of one that features tiny music boxes. I don't need to check menus or price tags to know that these places are reserved for a *very* select clientele.

I'm puzzled, though. There are no buskers in sight, which either means that music is entirely forbidden here or the square simply has yet to be tapped. This could be it. *Palais-Royal* could be the intimate and enchanting busking paradise I've been looking for.

I'll be back for you, I think, as we exit through the far archways. *Tomorrow!*

LE GRAND COLBERT is located just beyond the garden. I feel myself shrink as we approach its glass entrance. A man dressed like Nobuaki opens the door for us and smiles with a respectful nod as we enter.

"*Bonsoir messieurs dames,*" he says. His eyes twinkle as if he's genuinely pleased to see us.

Nobuaki tells the man his name.

"*Suivez-moi, s'il vous plaît,*" the maître d' says, and leads us to our reserved table.

My weathered Blundstones tread silently across the intricate mosaic floor. Regal palm trees reach toward high, corniced ceilings, and dozens of spherical lights spring off columns that run along the centre of the room. Patterned mirrors line the walls and reflect the light, giving the place a surreal golden glow. When we reach our table, the man slips behind me and pushes my chair in as I sit.

"*Deux verres de champagne,*" Nobuaki says, as if asking for something as ordinary as water.

Our flutes arrive promptly, along with a small bowl of thin

crackers in the shape of flowers and two menus in leather casings. I push my shoulders back and straighten my spine. I may not be dressed appropriately, but I can at least try to adopt proper posture.

"*Santé*," Nobuaki says, reaching out for a toast.

"Santé," I echo, as I bring my slender glass to meet his.

Champagne, I discover, is hardly a liquid at all. It seems to be made entirely of bubbles, that slide, fizzing and tickling, down my throat and ricochet in my stomach. Even after a couple of sips I can feel its effects: a slight rushing inside my veins and a pleasant lightness to my thoughts.

AFTER A FEW MINUTES, a young woman arrives to take our order. Her dark hair is tied back in a tight ponytail and there is a hint of suspicion in her gaze, a barely detectable furrow to her meticulously plucked brow. I'll admit, we're an odd pair: an older, conservatively dressed Japanese man with a young violinist in tatters. I stare back at her, unflinching.

Nobuaki orders a steak and I ask for the macaroni, which is far from French but the only vegetarian option I can find on the menu. Nobuaki studies the wines and confidently selects something from the list.

"So why did you decide to become vegetarian?" he asks.

It's a classic question, one I've been answering for the last fifteen years, but tonight I decide to keep my answer simple. "Oh, I just love animals too much to eat them," I say.

Nobuaki nods. "It must be hard for you here. So much of French cuisine is centred around meat. Did you see what the man next to us is eating?"

I discretely turn to the table on my right. An elderly man sitting alone is feasting on a thick sausage. The inside looks like a flat, coiled up tapeworm.

"What is it?" I ask.

"Andouillette."

"Which is?"

"Pig intestine," he says. He laughs at my contorted face. "You've heard of steak tartare?"

I shake my head.

"Raw ground beef with a raw egg on top. A French speciality. They eat pig feet too. Pig everything. *Tout est bon dans le cochon.* The rich used to get the good parts and the peasants would find things to do with the rest. The tail, the snout, the ears, the intestines. Everything. The meals that the peasants once ate out of necessity are now coveted as delicacies. The same is true for many cultures."

I try to see what others are eating but they are too far away. The place is huge and nearly empty.

The waitress approaches with our wine and confidently drives the screw into the cork. It slides out in one fluid motion accompanied by a muted "pop." She pours a ruby sip into Nobuaki's glass, then steps back and waits. He gently swirls the liquid, tips it into his mouth, pauses, swallows, and gives a stern nod. The waitress fills our glasses, places the bottle on the table, then slips away to the kitchen.

As usual with someone I've just met, there's no shortage of discussion topics. Nobuaki is a classical music lover. It's a pleasure to speak in depth about composers and musicians. He's knowledgeable in music history, and even has multiple recordings of his favourite pieces.

I notice that Nobuaki's glass is empty, so I follow his lead with a few generous sips, which prompts him to refill our glasses. The wine does little to calm my stomach, and by the second glass I'm feeling flushed. Fortunately, the near future requires no fine motor skills, and I should be able to manage both eating and talking.

Nobuaki's face is also reddening, and with every sip he is becoming increasingly verbose. He is delving back into French history now, but my attention span is rapidly dissolving and before long I lose track of what century he's in.

"The end is near," he suddenly says, staring somewhere over

my head. His eyes have darkened and his skin has gone from pale to glowing orange.

"Pardon?"

I'm not sure if he's referring to the near empty wine bottle or if I've missed something in the conversation. Perhaps we've moved on to climate change.

"For me," he adds, then downs the last of his wine and slams the glass onto the table. He grabs the bottle and clumsily empties it into both our glasses. I scramble for something to say, while Nobuaki stares silently straight ahead, his face sunken and solemn.

I am drunk in a fancy restaurant in Paris. How could this be?

"*Et voilà,*" the waitress chimes as she sets our meals before us. "*Voulez-vous autre chose?*"

"*Encore une bouteille,*" Nobuaki says, and before I can protest she's gone again. How does she move so fast?

This time Nobuaki doesn't swirl the test sip tenderly but tosses it into his mouth and nods in the same motion. The waitress tops up our glasses and is gone again.

The sight of more wine fills me with panic. I don't know how much more I can handle, but I know that if Nobuaki drinks the bottle himself the scene is sure to be messy, so when he reaches for his glass I do the same.

"My friend," he says, his voice barely audible. "My best friend. Died a few years ago from a brain tumour."

"I'm sorry," I say. "That must be really tough."

"He was lucky," Nobuaki says bitterly, and takes another violent swig.

I stare at him, speechless.

"My time is near," he says, and his eyes begin to well. He grabs his fork, jabs it into the slab of steak on his plate and slices off a bite with his knife.

"But what do you *mean*?" I urge, trying to decipher if he's suicidal or terminally ill. Eating seems inappropriate, considering this turn of events, but if I don't absorb the alcohol with something I'll soon be on the floor. I force a large bite of noodles into my mouth and chew without tasting.

"I've been in France for three years," Nobuaki says. "On a student visa. I've been studying French and looking for work, but my money is running out and so is my visa. I can't renew it again. If I don't find something soon, I'll be out on the streets. I can't go on." He chews ravenously through his tears.

"Listen. Nobuaki. I'm... taking you very serious. . . ly," I say. My speech is starting to falter. My face is burning and my thoughts are swirling together in a blend of urgent fragments.

"I *am* serious. I don't want to live anymore." Another tear rolls down his cheek. He leans his head back and dumps the rest of the wine into his mouth. I am dangerously close to my limit, but I can't bear the thought of Nobuaki drinking the rest himself, not in a place like this. I take a gulp too, and hope that our combined tolerances will allow us to finish the second bottle without incident.

If Nobuaki is as poor as he claims, he likely can't afford tonight's meal. I have only the money I earned this afternoon, which isn't much, and this isn't the sort of place where you can leave a stack of dirty coins on the table. People here pay with clean cards.

"So you're unhappy," I say, as my thick tongue struggles to comply.

"Very unhappy," he says. He shakes his head and refills our glasses, spilling some onto the pristine white tablecloth.

"Isn't there anything in life that you love?" I ask, trying to steer his mind away from death.

He hesitates, then says, "No."

"French history? You were speaking passionately a few minutes ago. And beautiful architecture!" I say, a little too loudly. "And music!" I am shouting now, but I don't care. "You must love music or you wouldn't have invited me here!"

The old man beside us turns and glares. The intestines are gone. He's moved on to chocolate cake and an espresso.

Nobuaki's eyes slowly roll over to meet mine. *Do I have the same red, glassy stare that he does?* I force some more noodles, and with my mouth still half full I add, "And art!"

The siphon between thought and speech has lost all authority. I suddenly feel as if I have been put in charge of this man's life, that I'm now solely responsible for his well-being. I focus all of my remaining brainpower on this objective. Far too loudly, I list reason after reason for him to want to live. He remains silent, but nods his head every once in a while, which makes me think I'm doing a good job.

Soon, the second bottle is also gone, though neither of us have touched our meals for a while. My body is numb, the room is swishing, and nausea is creeping closer. I know we should go very soon, before something happens. A powerful sleepiness has invaded my skull. I need to lie down. Anywhere. The tiled floor looks inviting. Irresistible even.

The waitress appears with the bill. I'm amazed to see that Nobuaki already has his Visa ready and slips it into the black leather case.

"I would...like to...contribute," I say, tripping on the words.

"No!" he says firmly. "I invited you."

I'm too drunk and exhausted to argue, but I'm worried that tonight's dinner will be enough to send Nobuaki into bankruptcy. Maybe this was his plan all along. His *Last Supper*.

Then we are outside in the cool night air, staggering silently through the deserted *Palais-Royal* garden. The flowers are black and grey now and the tree symmetry is eerie, as if we're trapped in a fucked-up maze where everything is the same and goes on forever. If I knew Nobuaki better I would clutch his arm and we could support each other. If I were alone I would probably lie down on one of these park benches. I want to ask Nobuaki if he's changed his mind or if he's still planning on — I don't know how to even phrase such a question. Also I fear the answer. I say nothing and concentrate on keeping upright.

"I'm really glad you came tonight," says Nobuaki when we

finally reach the Metro entrance. His soft voice wavers. "Thank you. For everything."

Impulsively, I lunge forward and hug him. His body is cold and hollow, like a metal pole.

"Would you," he pauses. "Would you like to go to the *Père Lachaise* cemetery with me? I know it well. It's a beautiful place to visit. I could show you around."

With effort, I lift my heavy eyes up to meet his. A cemetery is not an ideal place for someone suicidal, but he's at least projecting into the future, so I say OK and hope that will be enough to maintain his motivation to live for the time being. I tear a page from my notebook and scrawl my number on it. Then, clutching the banister, I waver down the Metro steps.

I DON'T KNOW HOW I MAKE IT HOME, but I seem to have gotten myself here, because now I'm lying in bed. My ears are ringing and my head is swaying violently. I should be unconscious, but I'm worried that Nobuaki was serious, that I shouldn't have left him alone tonight. He might really be capable of —

My phone rings and I fumble for it in the dark. It's Nobuaki. Of course.

"I wanted to make sure you got home all right," he says. "Thanks again for a wonderful evening." His voice is clear, with no hint of alcohol or major depression and no reference to the evening's drama. "Also, how's Tuesday for *Père Lachaise*?"

"Sounds good," I slur, not certain I'll remember, but too tired to turn on the light and search for a pen.

"Great, I'll call you on Monday to confirm."

"Yes, yes, yes," I say, relieved.

I hang up and plunge into a deep, dreamless sleep.

FROM THE MOMENT I KNEW WHAT ONE WAS, I wanted to play the violin. But I had to wait. Lessons were too expensive. When I was nearly thirteen my grandma offered to pay and my mom found me a teacher and a violin to rent. For me, learning violin wasn't work, and I didn't have the burden of obligation that kids who are forced to play sometimes have. The violin was sacred. At first, I would took it out of its case often just to look at it, traced my finger along its curves, and plucked the strings quietly in my room. It smelled of wood and varnish — of the past. I liked imagining all the hands that had played it before me. When I lifted it under my chin and placed my cheek on the cool plastic chin rest, even before I knew how to play a note, I felt a part of a long line of heirs, generations linked by a love for the instrument. It was one of the only times in my life that I've felt perfectly aligned with an idea. I had no doubts. This was right. I was meant to play this thing.

At first, the sounds I made were painful. The violin is not an instrument that fits naturally with the body. You have to contort to make it work. Your neck is crooked to the left and begins to ache within minutes. Your right arm moves perpendicular to your left arm, which is concentrated on a different task altogether. It requires a brain rewiring. Even playing a simple scale was a discouraging challenge. The notes were whiney and sad. The bow bounced along the strings and my left hand struggled to keep up with the bow changes.

But this painful phase, which can sometimes last for years when children start young, passed quickly. I was old enough to grasp the concepts of the technique and young enough to intuitively interpret the posture, to pick-up the supple wrist and the relaxed left hand that those who begin the violin as adults almost never master. I learned quickly, whipped through the beginner pieces, and within a year was working on more serious music: concertos and sonatas. My violin teacher was the ideal blend of patient, kind and demanding. She pushed me forward, to be better than I thought I could be.

By the end of high school, I was preparing for university auditions. I spent months working on Bach's E Major Partita and Mozart's Concerto in D Major, that included a cadenza — the section where the orchestra stops and the violin shows off for a bit, which means it's fast and flashy. I worked hard, even though I didn't know what I wanted to *do* with the violin. All I knew was that I wanted to keep playing, because that's when I was happiest. The violin provided the right kind of structure. It came with a set of rules, a set of notes, and directions for how to play them, and within that framework there was the opportunity to add a personal touch, but nothing too pronounced. Just enough. When I was playing, even if it was in front of people, the outside world blurred. Only the music mattered.

Once I began studying the violin in university, however, something flipped. The usual nervousness I experienced during performances grew and grew, and soon became unbearable. In real life I could fake confidence in conversations or presentations in front of the class. I could easily take on an air, pretend to be someone else, and make jokes. But there was no hiding behind the violin. And being in a big new school with many talented players who had been playing their entire lives, my confidence took a major hit. When it was just me and my instrument in the practice room everything was fine, but as soon as I was in front of an audience, even a small one, the music unravelled. The fight or flight response, the body's natural reaction to acute stress, involves symptoms that make playing next to impossible. Chemicals are released in the brain to give a boost of energy. It's a survival mechanism to help us either kick our enemy's ass or get the fuck out. Heart acceleration, pupil dilation, sweaty hands: these things might help climb a tree, but on stage they caused my left hand to slide around on the fingerboard. And the most fatal of all: the shakes.

The first time it happened, I was in first year and playing in front of a nursing home. It was a required component for a music therapy class I was taking. The music was supposed to soothe the elderly residents, as well as offer entertainment and stimulation, but just before I began to play I was gripped by sudden terror. It wasn't the pressure. There was next to none. Half of my audience was unconscious, yet my heart was slamming against my ribs as if I was about to be executed, and as I played my hands trembled so violently that the bow bounced all over the strings. The sounds my violin were making were not unlike those of a complete beginner: squeaks and whines and stutters. By the middle of the song I was able to pull it together and finish the piece, and the next two songs were fine, but the damage had been done. Though no one but the seniors at the nursing home had been witness to the scene, I knew that if it could happen there, it could happen *anywhere*. I began to fear the possibility that my hands would tremble whenever I played. The idea haunted me. It was all I could think about, and the more I obsessed about it the more my hands shook, until they started to shake permanently, like a Parkinson's patient. I couldn't write properly or set a hot tea onto a table without it spilling. I lost confidence in my playing and in myself. Even if all I had to do was stand in front of an audience and play one single note, even if it was just an open string, I no longer felt I was capable.

One day during a lesson, my hands trembled so violently that my professor stopped me.

"Nisha, I want you to go see a neurologist," he said. "This is not right."

I did go to the doctor, but only to get Beta Blockers, a miracle drug many musicians use to hinder the fight or flight response. A classical guitarist told me about them. She claimed she couldn't perform without them.

"Careful with these," the doctor warned. "You have low blood pressure already."

The pills were meant for major performances, but I started taking them every day, just to make it through the rehearsals and lessons. With them, my hands didn't shake as much, but they caused headaches, nausea and made me dizzy. I could no longer concentrate on the music. I was too busy focusing on whether my hands were shaking, and trying to control the dizziness. The violin had become the cause of so much anxiety that I began to fear it. To loathe it, even. Most of all, I loathed myself.

I knew I couldn't continue to take beta blockers all the time. My body just couldn't handle it, and the mind game I was playing with myself had reached an epic level. All I could think about were my hands, and so they continued to tremble unless I took a beta blocker, which would immediately render me dizzy and nauseous. Then the medication would wear off and my hands would shake again.

Once I finished my second year of music, before things got any worse, I fled across campus to the Psychology Department. I'd taken a few classes already. Human behaviour was fascinating. Now, instead of being neurotic and depressed, I could *study* the phenomenon. I could write about it. In my last year of university I took a seminar in anxiety disorders, and wrote a long end-of-term paper on performance anxiety. Being on the other side of the disorder, reporting on it rather than suffering from it, was much preferable.

For the three years that I studied psychology, my violin went into hiding. Or rather, I forced it into hiding, because I could not bear the aspect of myself that the instrument had brought to light. It had triggered a form of madness I simply could not face. I had witnessed myself unravelling against the destructive potential of my own mind. And I'd seen enough.

WHEN I RAISE MY VIOLIN to my chin on the street, it is not a performance in the traditional sense. There is no real audience. I play only pieces I know intimately and have learned from memory from Suzuki method books, and some of the Bach Partitas I worked on in university. I am at home here. On the street, I can play freely, without worrying about my hand shaking. The *this-is-right* feeling has returned. I'm *supposed* to play this thing.

People judge me, sure. They love me. They hate me. They ignore me. They put love letters in my case. They call the cops on me. They give me money. The reactions vary, but most people look at me as if what I am doing is an improvement to the surroundings. That it matters. That playing violin on the street is better than not playing violin on the street.

My violin is my best friend and my saviour. It funds my sub-sistence and continues to introduce me to people and to this city. Here in Paris I have fallen in love with it again. It is bright and sings with extra joy after being in my closet for so many years. *I'm alive!* It says. *And I'm keeping you alive too. Don't ever leave me again!*

I won't! I tell it. *No matter what. I won't.*

I APPROACH *PALAIS-ROYAL*. The nervousness I usually get flutter-ing in my stomach when I try out a new spot is actually more like turbulent waves here. As I stand under the archway leading to the open area with the rows of striped columns, I can sense the potential. I want to play here so badly that I almost don't dare. If it doesn't work out, the disappointment will be crip-pling. Surely other musicians would have snapped this place up long before now if busking was actually permitted.

The only sounds here are of shuffling feet and tourist chat-ter. After fifteen minutes of hesitation, I decide that the worst outcome possible is that I will be asked to leave. It happens fre-quently enough. I can deal with it, and at least I will have played in someplace truly magical. I open my case, trying to decide on what I will start with. If I only get to play one piece, it should be something worthwhile. Something slow, to maximize the reso-nating potential. I don't have a huge repertoire. Bach's opening movement of the D Minor Partita. Yes.

As soon as I begin, it's as if the archway is polishing the notes, then setting them free to rise up and circle slowly, mixing to-gether in a sweet minor blend before fading away. My violin sounds like it's worth millions. The tone is warm and sweet and sensuous. My confidence rises and so does my gaze. People are stopping. Already I've made at least 10 euros and I'm not even at the repeat. There is an older man leaning on the columns beside a couple holding hands and smiling. A little girl in a red dress stops right in front of me, awestruck. A security guard approaches, shaking his head. *Shit.* I pull my bow off the string. "I can't play here?" I ask, kicking myself out before he can.

"I'm security for the *Palais-Royal* gardens," the man says, gesturing toward the Buren columns. He has black curly hair and a Spanish accent. "This archway technically isn't part of it. But someone from the *Comédie Française* might complain."

"And if they don't?" I ask, emboldened by the months I have already spent in this city and the variations that a "no" can encompass here.

"Well, you can try," he says. "I'm a classical guitarist. I've always wanted to play here too."

As I watch him strut out into the gardens in his blue uniform I begin a new piece, the third movement of Handel's Sonata in D, so joyful and triumphant in spirit that I used to play it for wedding recessionals. *It's mine,* I think. *This enchanting spot is mine!*

FOR THE NEXT THREE DAYS I return in the early afternoon, half expecting some other musician to be gorging on the acoustics, but the square is empty and silent. Inside the archway and across from where I play there is a grey door. It appears to be the actors' entrance for the *Comédie Française.* Many of them stop for a moment to listen before going in. Just now, one of them came over and put a ten euro bill in my case. The tourist traffic is steady, as are the coins. Finally, I have found my busking paradise.

Palais-Royal, I quickly notice, has its own set of homeless people. One afternoon, an older man with an accordion slung on his shoulder comes out from around the corner and stands in front of me, swaying to my gigue. A pipe hangs from his near-toothless mouth and leaks a sweet stream of tobacco smoke. I've seen him around these last few days, sometimes sipping rosé in the garden and once sleeping on a bench beside his instrument. Today he listens to me with his eyes closed and his chapped lips spread in a dreamy smile.

When the piece stops he shuffles over to shake my hand. He

doesn't speak French, but he points to his instrument and winks. Then he points to himself and says, "Marcel."

"Nisha," I say, taking his wet hand in mine.

"Romania," he says.

"Canada," I say.

And with a grin, he turns and shuffles back to the gardens.

Soon after, I meet a young blond man called Olaf, a Pole, and his friend David, a bearded Franco-Belgian. They approach me between pieces and take turns kissing the back of my hand. I speak French with David and English with Olaf. They have no language in common, and yet street living has bonded them into best friends.

"We sleep here," Olaf tells me, pointing to the grate of hot air a few paces from where I'm playing. "David snores," he jokes. When I translate this for David, he roars and punches Olaf's arm and they both laugh.

"I have five kids," David tells me, smiling with pride. "They live in Brussels with their mother. I just talked to my daughter yesterday. She's 16 and wants to come visit me in Paris." There is a pause.

I look at him, waiting.

"She doesn't know," he says. His voice breaks off, and he stares at the ground.

Olaf looks at me for a translation.

"He's talking about his kids," I explain.

Olaf nods. "Yes, he really misses them."

David wipes tears from his eyes. He is much older than Olaf. I wonder if somewhere inside he thinks of Olaf as his child, one he can at least take care of in his own way — unlike his children back in Belgium. He seems very protective of him, anyway. Olaf doesn't look any older than I am.

"We should get going," David says. He tugs at Olaf's arm and I watch them head off back to the gardens to scavenge and panhandle. In some ways I am not so different from them. I spend my days on the streets, too. I depend on the generosity of others for my well-being. I roam. I'm both a foreigner and a resident. I don't quite live inside society but tread along its fringe. I have few possessions and my schedule is what I make it. Maybe that explains our affinity.

On my way home, I see David and Olaf sipping vodka in a corner of the garden. I watch David pass Olaf the bottle. He grins and lifts his head back to take a large, terrifying swig. *They are not free,* I think on my walk to the Metro. *Not like me.* They don't have a safe place to go at night, and they are bound by alcohol. It ravages their bodies and keeps them prisoners. It steals from them their sense of self and time. The way they hold their bodies, it's as if the weight of gravity is too much, as if they are constantly fighting to stay upright.

ON MY FOURTH DAY playing at *Palais-Royal,* I'm in the middle of a piece when a voluptuous woman with long dark hair approaches me. My heart leaps with fear. When people interrupt, it's almost always to tell me to stop. But this woman smiles.

"I want you to be my teacher," she says.

I blink at her in surprise.

"I own the pipe store over there." She gestures through the archway. "Come see me after!" she says, and rushes away toward her shop.

An hour later, I scoop my coins into the storage compartment in my case. There are heaps and heaps, and many of them are 1 and 2 euro pieces. The case weighs a ton. My strap digs into my shoulder, and I know before counting this is my biggest day yet.

I carry my heavy case through the crowds, over to the pipe shop. The display windows are filled with hundreds of pipes, so many it is impossible to see inside.

As I open the door, it clangs some overhead bells.

"*Un moment,*" the woman hollers from the back.

I wait. There is barely room to turn around in here. There are so many *things*. Plants. Shisha tubes. Picture frames. And pipes. Hundreds and hundreds of pipes. There doesn't seem to be any discernible order to it all, though I don't doubt the woman knows where every item is located. I hear what sounds like books and stacks of paper fall over in the back, followed by some words that sound like Hebrew, and then the woman appears, looking flustered for a second, before she recomposes her smile and looks at me.

"*Ah! Vous voilà!*" she says. "*Venez.*"

She motions for me to join her in the back. I follow, trying not to knock things over with my case.

There is even less room in here, and I have to take my violin off my shoulders to squeeze in. The woman is sifting through a pile of CDs, knocking several to the ground until she finds the one she is looking for: Itzhak Perlman's *Perlman Plays Klezmer*. The woman slides the disk into a player and flips to a slow lamenting gypsy piece. The volume is near-max and the speakers are huge. Everything in the room rattles with the sorrowful melody of the song, and the woman closes her eyes, smiling.

When the piece is over she says, "Can you teach me that?"

"Sure," I say. "Do you know how to play the violin?"

"No," she admits. "But I have one," and sure enough, on a shelf behind her head is a green violin case.

I explain that she will need to do some preparatory work — scales and exercises to acquaint with the instrument. She nods.

"Can we start Monday?" she asks. "I want two lessons a week!"

"OK," I say. "But where should we do it?"

"*Ici!*" she says, as if the answer were obvious.

"Here?" I look around at the tiny space, not sure there is enough room for even one of us to bow. But there doesn't seem to be an alternative, so I agree to give it a try. And so I have my first kinda sorta job.

PALAIS-ROYAL IS A MICROCOSM of worldly paradoxes: contemporary art on a historical site, homeless people living where royalty once roamed, misery amongst manufactured beauty, classical theatre beside street music, and all of it teeming with characters, including the pipe woman. I am a character too, I realize. "*La princess du Palais-Royal*," David and Olaf call me. I'm part of the paradox now. Part of a tiny cultural ecosystem. If I belong anywhere in this city, it's here in the magical no-man's-land between *Place Collette* and the *Palais-Royal* gardens, teaching a woman to play klezmer music in a curio cabinet full of pipes.

I MEET NOBUAKI at the tall, gated entrance of the *Père Lachaise* cemetery. He leads me along the main cobblestone path into a village of mausoleums. They look like tiny marble homes. Some of them are the size of my apartment. The cemetery is like a big silent grey city, with elaborate sculptures and occasional specks of colour where people have left flowers. Many of the tombs are decorated with statues of angels, or crosses or crying women. Some are surrounded by tall iron gates. Others are plain marble slabs engraved with dates and names. Big trees line the main pathway.

Nobuaki has been to *Père Lachaise* so many times he knows where everybody is without a map. "Let's visit Chopin first," he says.

We leave the main path and head along a narrow passage. Before we even reach the site, I see the dozens of flowers surrounding it. On the top of the tomb, there is a sculpture of a woman weeping.

"That's Euterpe," Nobuaki says. "The muse of music."

I nod to the sad muse, and to one of France's favourite composers. There should be music here, I think. This place is much too silent for someone whose spirit was saturated in melody.

Next, Nobuaki takes me to Oscar Wilde's grave. His is more modern than Chopin's, with a large lipstick-kissed angel and many candles and flowers, yet it still doesn't do the man justice. "Don't you think there should be someone here reciting witty Wilde quotes?" I ask Nobuaki.

"That's a good idea," he says. "They could hire a theatre student. It would be a perfect summer job."

"True friends stab you in the front," I offer.

"We are all in the gutter. But some of us are looking at the stars," Nobuaki says.

"Either this wallpaper goes, or I do."

"His last words," Nobuaki sighs.

We continue our pilgrimage. The artists' tombs we visit might be much less elaborate than the looming mausoleums with statues, carvings and iron gates that hem them in, but it's the artists who have the flowers. Artists draw people, even in death.

On our way to see Edit Piaf, Nobuaki says, "When I die, I want to have a bench and a telephone at my grave. When people put the receiver to their ear, a recorded joke will play. It will make them laugh. People take death too seriously." While death is obviously on Nobuaki's mind — tough to avoid in a cemetery — he doesn't refer to it as an imminent event, and he isn't desperate, the way he was the other night. Though he has said many times that he would like to be buried at *Père Lachaise* one day, there is no mention of suicide or of the dinner at *Le Colbert*. I don't bring it up either. Right now, the air is light and playful. I want it to stay that way. "What will you put on your grave?" he asks me.

I have to think for a second. "Hmmm, maybe a comfortable wooden chair," I say, "one you can lounge in, and a little lamp. Then people could read out loud to me."

"Good idea," Nobuaki says, and laughs in the swiftly cooling air.

There are more than a few brown leaves on the ground. I don't know what Paris is like in the fall, and I don't know what it will mean for busking and my livelihood here. When you're from a cold climate, it's impossible to feel a cool autumn wind and not jump straight to winter in your mind. One street artist has told me the winter months will be too damp and cold to play. He said they will be unbearable.

Suddenly Nobuaki stops walking. I look around for the next dead celebrity.

"This is my favourite place in all of *Père Lachaise*," he says.

We're standing on a main path. It leads down a hill and turns a corner in the distance. I see nothing remarkable.

"This path," he explains, "reminds me of life. Big corners that veer out of sight. You don't know where they lead. You just have to follow them."

"Indeed," I say and we gaze at the metaphoric path for a few reflective minutes. Being foreigners, both of our futures are uncertain. We most likely won't live in Paris forever, but our fates are entirely unknown. Finally, we continue down the path and around the corner to the front gates.

After several hours of grave gazing, we're both blurry-eyed and lightheaded.

"Let me treat you to a coffee and a croissant," Nobuaki says, as we exit the cemetery.

"How about *I* treat *you?*" I say. I know we'll have a friendly fight about it when the time comes to pay.

We stop at the first café we see and take a seat on one of the outdoor tables. After the calm of *Père Lachaise*, the city seems to have accelerated, as if it's whirling in blender and we're in the centre watching it rush around us. I much prefer this experience to the last time I was with Nobuaki and it was my own head that was spinning.

We sit with our empty cups for a while, not speaking, hypnotized by the frequency of our surroundings: so dense, so alive. *Paris is a generous city,* I think. *It shares its energy, as if it has a hot white core that will never cool.*

When we finally get up to leave, Nobuaki says simply, "I love this city."

"I do too," I say, happy he is finding things to love again.

Scherzo

Faint jazz notes drift with a wet breeze over the Seine. I'm halfway across the Solferino pedestrian bridge after a morning in the *Musée d'Orsay* when they hit me. Van Gogh's raging skies and Degas's fuzzy ballerinas are still lingering behind my retinas, but now I'm being pulled from my museum-induced daze by the jazz. *An ensemble,* I think.

As I get close, I see it's just a lone figure in the sheltered passageway between the Seine and the Tuileries garden. He is in his 50s, with weathered skin and a thatch of grey hair, dressed in two wool sweaters, a bulky black scarf and a pair of frayed corduroy pants. He's crooning a relaxed rendition of *Sunny Side of the Street,* while accompanying himself on drums and accordion, and alternating between trumpet and trombone for the instrumental solos. His voice is warm with a light rasp. There are CDs for sale on a nearby table, and a top hat set in front of his bass drum for coins.

Sure, his act is impressive, but I'm enamoured with the location. The passageway leads to the Louvre gardens and is fully protected by an overpass. A highway runs above it, but there is no hint of droning traffic. Instead, it offers a flattering resonance and, to boot, the cobblestone pathway and adjacent lapping Seine make it delightfully aesthetic. Better yet, no one could ever complain about noise, as it is far from any residents or boutiques. *And* it boasts a steady stream of pedestrians. It is a busker's paradise.

I return to the bridge with my violin early the next day. As I hoped, the one-man band is not here. I quickly set up and launch in, starting with the slow, lamenting movement of a Handel Sonata, something to match the cool, cloud-covered morning. At first there are only joggers and a few aimless pigeons, but as I play on they are gradually replaced by tourists. There are plenty of young couples walking arm in arm, holding their cameras out in front of them as they kiss with the Seine as their backdrop. There are lots of families — not French families, which tend to be emotionally contained and well-dressed, but tourists. American mostly, with kids plagued with over-stimulation. As they come through, the kids are whining and throwing tantrums and their last meal is still smeared on their faces and clothes. My playing distracts them on their way by. They fall into interested silence and the parents reward me with coins and the odd dollar bill.

Now a gypsy appears. There was another one a half hour ago. It seems to be a standard interval. They are mostly women. Usually they wear long skirts and kerchiefs, but these are dressed like tourists, in jeans and T-shirts, and many of them carry backpacks or unfolded maps. They stoop before tourists passing by and pretend to find gold rings, which they offer to their victim of choice. Most refuse, but with some coaxing they can sometimes be convinced to accept it. The tourist will go on his or her way, only to be followed by the ring finder, who now wants money. If the tourist refuses, the ring finder become desperate, rocks back and forth, pointing to her mouth as if she's suddenly become a starving refugee. The person with the ring either throws it back or sighs and pulls out a wallet. It's a strange and uncomfortable scene that plays out over and over in front of me. Behind my violin, with the passivity of watching a nature show, I observe the tourists as they become prey. Some will get away. Others won't be so lucky.

By late afternoon, the traffic has declined sharply, so I decide to pack up. My shoulders are aching and the strings have turned my fingertips black. I hadn't expected to play so long and didn't bring any food. The music has been sustaining me, but now that I've stopped playing I'm aware of my stomach digesting itself, and when I stand after putting my violin away, my head spins. The strap of my violin digs into my shoulder from the weight of all the coins. This place is as good as I had hoped it would be.

THE NEXT DAY I return to the bridge, armed with two bananas and a thermos of tea. I'm going to stay all day.

After only half hour, though, the one-man band emerges from around the corner, with an instrument in each hand and a bass drum slung on his back. My mouth goes dry. *Will he be fierce? Will we have an unpleasant altercation?* I play warily now, using only half my bow.

He calmly sets his instruments down and stares at me. I pull my bow off the string and smile sweetly.

"*Je ne t'ai jamais vu,*" he says, squinting at me. His ashen cheeks are slightly concave and he's wearing the same double sweater combination as he did yesterday. He is not much taller than I am, but his body is fragile and worn, as if he's been dragging his drum for decades.

I lower my violin and push my shoulders back to feign confidence. He obviously isn't concerned about me. He has every intention of playing here, now. It's *his* spot.

I could argue, I think. *It's a public space, and technically it's forbidden to play anywhere in Paris except in front of the Pompidou.*

As if reading my thoughts, he tells me he's been playing here every day for years.

"I played here yesterday," I say.

A few months ago I wouldn't have been so bold, but there is a survival element to busking and I can't afford to let this place go so easily. Also, I'm learning the French art of compromise. *No* almost always means *let's discuss.*

"Except Mondays," he says.

He tells me he goes to a recording studio every Monday, so I could play then if I want. I sigh and hesitate to indicate that this isn't enough.

"I start at 1:30," he says. "You can play before I arrive. Every day if you want."

That'll give me an hour and half if I start at noon, I think.

I consider his offer. The traffic will be slower then, but still enough to make a decent wage. The man is a busking veteran, and with all his equipment he is far less mobile. This passageway is his livelihood.

"OK," I say.

Satisfied, he tells me to watch his stuff, then turns and walks back in the direction of his car, which is parked in a tiny lot at the side of the river. A few minutes later, he returns with a card table, a suitcase, and a tall white stool. He opens the suitcase onto the table and begins to spread out his CD collection.

"*Est ce que tu chantes?*" he asks.

"*Non,*" I admit. The truth is, I can barely carry a tune, have a vocal range not much larger than an octave, and I have no lung power. I am no singer.

He gestures to the CDs and says he has some songs he needs sung in English. "*Des chansons spéciales,*" he says, his voice lowered as if someone might be eavesdropping.

I glance at the table. He has a variety of albums that span several decades. Some feature him as a young man with dark flourishing hair, in a suit and bow tie, posing smugly in a red car in one and beside the Eiffel tower in the other. His eyes flicker as he reaches inside the suitcase and pulls out a disk. I stare at the cover. A bare ass, female, makes up the bottom third of the image, and a red rose protrudes from between the spherical cheeks. In the background, cotton-ball clouds are suspended in a blue sky. The name of the disk is *Overdose 69*.

These, I realize with alarm, are the songs he wants performed.

"They're sex songs," he explains, "for the Internet. Americans will download them if they are in English." He looks at me expectantly.

I pry my eyes from the cover, and say, "*Désolée, je ne chante pas.*"

His face and shoulders drop and he slowly turns to replace the disk in its secret location. He looks so disappointed, so thoroughly dejected, that I say I might know someone. An anglophone. A musician. "Maybe she'll do it," I say.

His face snaps back toward me, and his hopeful glow returns.

He hands me the CD and pulls a tattered business card from his breast pocket. His name is *Bernard*.

THE SINGER I HAVE IN MIND is Brigitte. She's a musician from my hometown. I don't know her well, but ever since I heard she moved to Paris for a Frenchman, I knew I wanted to be friends with her. She lives just outside the city, in *Boulogne*, a 50-minute Metro ride away. Bernard's invitation is a perfect excuse to invite myself over.

I text her: "I have a musical proposition 4 u."

Brigitte texts back: "I'm intrigued. I'm free 2morrow if u r."

THOUGH WE'VE NEVER MET, I give Brigitte a hug when she greets me at the station. We have so much in common, I feel close to her already. Her love story seems to have worked out better than mine, though. She and her French boyfriend have a nice little apartment, with a real bedroom, a kitchen and a living room with a piano.

Brigitte makes some chai tea and brings it into the living room. "So what's the project?" she asks.

"Uh, well," I say, not sure how to introduce the situation. "Basically this guy is looking for an anglophone to sing these songs in English."

I slip Bernard's CD into Brigitte's stereo. The female vocalist is professionally trained, and boasts a full-bodied jazz voice with a suggestive smoky growl. I don't understand all the lyrics, but I catch enough to conclude that they are perverted and some border on toilet humour. There isn't the poetic sensuality I was expecting. It's all about popping cherries and licking cum-sicles.

Once our laughter dies down, Brigitte says, "OK there's no way I could sing songs like that! But I'm too curious. I have to meet the man behind this music."

THE NEXT DAY Brigitte and I meet at the Louvre Metro, the stop nearest Bernard's oasis. We walk through the Louvre gardens,

down the steps toward the underground passage, and toward
the Seine. And there is Bernard, in the middle of arranging his
equipment. As we come close, he pulls a small metal flask from
his pocket and brings it to his lips. He turns, sees us, and grins.

"*Bernard,*" I say. "*Je te présente Brigitte.*"

"*Enchantée,*" says Brigitte politely.

Bernard tells her that she speaks with a nasal voice and will
have problems giving birth. Brigitte's eyes widen and she looks
to me. I offer an apologetic smile.

"*Non, mais, c'est vrai!*" he exclaims. He bends his knees and
gives a dynamic demonstration, grunting wildly and bouncing
up and down.

We stare, bewildered, while passersby turn their heads in-
quisitively.

Once he recomposes himself, Bernard asks if we've thought
about his proposition. I gently explain that neither of us are
comfortable singing his sex songs.

He pauses, but only for a moment to recalculate. "But I have
other projects! Other songs! Are you a musician?" he asks, leaning in toward Brigitte.

She nods.

"And you speak English?"

She nods again and leans backwards.

"*Chante!*" he demands.

Brigitte shakes her head.

"*Allez!*" he insists. "*Chante quelque chose.*"

He stands with his ear to her mouth in waiting. She looks to
me. I shrug and offer her an encouraging smile. Finally, almost
inaudibly, she sings a short excerpt: "*I wanna be loved by you, by
you and nobody else but you.*"

Bernard takes a step back, eyes narrowed in consideration.
"Let's try it," he announces. "Both of you, in the studio."

I look to Brigitte and shrug again, not sure what to do. *Both
of us?* I think. *Singing in a studio?* Brigitte shrugs back. Neither of
us are able to make a decision. I can barely sing, but maybe if we

were singing *together* it could be OK. *Brigitte can mask my short-comings, and it won't be as scary if we're together.* Plus, it's Bernard. There is something compelling about him. It's as if he's been trying his whole life to break into something, to "make it" in the world of music, and we are his key, his last hope, or so it seems by the way his pleading eyes sear into us. I feel myself breaking down. *It could be fun,* I think, *an interesting experience, something to laugh about later.* I raise my eyebrows daringly at Brigitte.

"*D'accord,*" she says, laughing.

"*Lundi!*" says Bernard, with a triumphant smile.

"I JUST CAN'T BELIEVE THIS GUY," Brigitte says as we ride the regional train to Bernard's friend's studio in the south-eastern suburbs of Paris. "He's either crazy or a true artist."

"Maybe both," I say. "He's been playing music his whole life. It's all he wants to do. It's all he knows how to do. And he's been playing on the street for thirty years."

It's midmorning, and we have the train car to ourselves for the whole forty minute trip, save for one older man nestled in the first seat and staring out the window.

"I wonder what he's going to get us to sing," Brigitte says.

Suddenly the butterflies in my stomach give an extra jolt. *I should never have agreed to this! I can't sing!* And here I am heading to a recording studio. I had figured I could fake it, but now that the train is whisking us closer I'm not so sure. My range is literally not much larger than an octave and my lung power truly is pathetic.

We cross the Seine and enter a suburban wasteland of warehouses and modern apartment buildings. *Not much longer now,* I think. *What have I done?* When we arrive at the station and step out onto the platform, Bernard is there, waiting for us. "*Suivez-moi,*" he says, starting up the barren street. His phone rings. "Shhh," he tells us. "It's my wife."

Brigitte and I look at each other, confused, and follow silently a few metres behind. After a few blocks, we are there. I was expecting a do it yourself basement set up with foam and egg cartons taped to the wall. Now, to my horror, it appears to be the real deal. The first room has several looming microphones, a keyboard and a drum set. Through a glass window in the wall, a man with curly grey hair and wearing a yellow checkered shirt is aglow before a massive computer screen.

"*On est là, Claude!*" Bernard hollers.

The man smiles and slides out of his leather chair. He opens the door to his glassed-in universe, kisses us on the cheeks, and invites us to sit down around the big table in the centre of the room.

Bernard tells Claude we are the girls he was telling him about. "*C'est des anglophones!*" he says, as if we're a rare specimen.

"Nice to meet you," Claude says, with a heavy accent, then laughs as if he's told a joke.

"*Bon, on commence!*" Bernard says, gleaming.

He reaches into his bag and pulls out the lyrics for a song and sets them on the table. It's "Taurus the Bull." I recognize the song. It's from the sexy CD.

"We said we didn't want to sing on this CD," I protest.

Bernard laughs. "*C'est pas grave*," he says. "It's not a provocative song. *Ça va aller.*"

Brigitte and I examine the lyrics. They feature farm animals copulating, while an aroused farmer looks on. In one verse, children watch through the living room window as bovines get it on in the field.

"OK, Claude," Bernard says. "Cue the music so the girls can learn the tune."

The velvet voiced woman from the French CD comes on the speakers. I listen in defeat to her wide vibrato and evocative nuances. I'll never be able to sing like that. I glance at Brigitte. She is smirking and shaking her head — either at the absurdity of the situation or the impossibility of our imminent task. At least she seems relaxed.

OK, I think. *We're doing this.* I try to manage a smile.

Claude plays the song twice so we can get the feel of it, then

Bernard claps, and cries, "*On y va!*" He escorts us to the other room and asks who will sing first.

Huh? I look up at him. *We have to sing separately?*

My plan of hiding behind Brigitte's voice is already foiled. My heart picks up speed and all I can think is *I don't want to be first.* My hand raises and I point to Brigitte. She gasps and slinks back slightly as Bernard approaches with a hefty set of headphones. He puts them on her head and places her before a large microphone. Then he leaves the room.

Through the glass window I see him take a seat beside Claude. His smile is electric. He probably thinks that his dream is finally about to be realized.

Brigitte's eyes are now gaping with what looks like fear. I try again to muster a smile, but can't quite get the corners of my mouth to rise. My heart is already beating fast and I feel a hot wave of regret wash over me.

Claude cues the music. The volume is so loud that I can hear it clearly from Brigitte's headphones. The introduction comes to a close with a crowing rooster, signalling the beginning of the first verse:

At the dawn of day. . .
Mother nature awakes
All the singing birds,
Wishing me a good day.
The soft wind caresses
The skin of my face,
And in the fields, nature reclaims her space...

The horny bull!
The horny bull!
The horny bull, takes the cow aside!
The horny bull!
The horny bull!
The horny bull likes a bouncy ride!

I HOLD MY BREATH so I don't disturb Brigitte's concentration by laughing, but I needn't have bothered. She doesn't even make it to the end of the chorus before she is overcome with giggles. I immediately lose control and fall to my knees, clutching my stomach.

Claude cuts the music. Through the glass I see he doesn't find the situation amusing. Bernard is frowning and has turned a shade greyer.

"Your turn," Brigitte wheezes.

"Maybe you should try it again," I suggest.

But Bernard is motioning for me to approach the mic. Brigitte smiles and places the headphones over my ears.

"Good luck," she says, grinning.

I take a deep breath. It's as if I'm standing on a high circus platform about to do a triple flip in mid-air before grabbing the anticipatory hand of a spinning co-trapeze artist. This simply isn't possible. *Why did I think I could do this?*

I concentrate on the lyric sheet, which is trembling in my hands. The introductory music begins. I hear the rooster crow.

I am astonished when, right on cue, my vocal chords comply. Sounds leave my mouth. I can feel my throat rattling, but I don't recognize the voice. A pronounced southern American accent has taken over. I'm singing in character, consumed by an inner hillbilly who has never before surfaced. The singing itself is objectively dreadful. My voice trembles, and I make several entry, rhythmic and melodic errors. Part of the verse dips below my range, reducing my voice to a mere croak. I only manage to finish the first chorus before the giggles return and I stumble away from the mic.

Bernard bursts into the room, frowning. He tells us to come into the control room to have a listen. It's obvious we're off to a poor start.

We file in and take a seat at the table, while Claude cues the recording. Mine is played first. I knew it was bad, but I wasn't prepared for this. It sounds like an elementary school talent show. My voice wavers in and out of tune, the rhythm is way off, and the country accent is out of control. I wince and feel my cheeks sear with shame.

Brigitte's take is better than mine. She has more control over her vocal chords and at least gets the entries right.

"We should have warmed up," Bernard says. "Follow me."

He shows us to a keyboard in the other room and begins playing ascending chromatic chords. Our task is to sing "The Horny Bull!" as loud as we can.

Together, we belt out the mantra, straining our larynxes until our voices crack and we're out of breath. My throat aches as if I've been screaming.

"All right," Bernard says after a few ascending and descending chords. "Let's take it from the top."

I stand nervously to the side while Brigitte slips the headphones on and bravely steps up to the mic. The rooster crows and she begins to sing. It's better this time — far from CD quality, but it's in tune and she adds a waver of emotion to select words, as if she's "feeling" it more. But she still doesn't make it beyond the first verse before laughter takes over and Claude cuts the music.

My second attempt is no better than my first. I try my best to maintain control, but the southern drawl overpowers everything and contorts my pronunciation — and my voice quality reaches a new low. I can see Bernard and Claude shaking their heads through the window. I don't dare glance at Brigitte, but I can hear her stifled laughter beside me.

Bernard summons us into the control room again. Claude says it's really a shame, because they like my country drawl, but Brigitte has a steadier tone. Overall we have failed terribly. Bernard launches into a lecture on music practice and the need for dedication and hard work. Claude chimes in that we'll have to devote ourselves a great deal more if we ever want to succeed. We can't expect to become singing stars without dedicating ourselves to it.

I wonder if Bernard remembers under the bridge when I told him that I didn't sing, that I *couldn't* sing. I don't have the energy to remind him. Brigitte and I sit silently, ashamed and bewildered, nodding and holding back laughter.

It spews from us as soon as we're back outside on the street.

"The horny bull!" Brigitte chants, on the way to the train.

"At the dawn of daaaaaaaay!" I sing in my new-found drawl.

"I can't *believe* we did that!" she says.

"What a terrible idea," I admit.

But I'm glad we did. I got what I had hoped for: the beginning of a real friendship with Brigitte. I'm sorry that we disappointed Bernard, but he's dedicated to these sex songs, so I'm sure he'll find someone better suited. I wish I didn't have to face Bernard so soon after my shameful display, though. We're co-workers now. I can't afford to stay away from the mystical passageway where the gypsies frolic and coins fall into my case aside the gently surging Seine. In fact, I think I'll go back tomorrow.

ONCE A WEEK I go to an Internet café on the second floor of a photocopy shop near the Pompidou. It is a stagnant, sweltering place with a dozen large humming computers and two swivelling fans clogged with grimy fuzz. It is dominated by a dense armpit odour, and the keys stick, but it's three Euros an hour — the cheapest internet around.

Amid a handful of emails from friends, with exasperated subject lines like "Are you still alive?" and "Where the hell are you?" is an email from Jérémie. He's returning to France next month to finish his thesis and will need his apartment back for a little while, just for the winter. He's sorry for the inconvenience.

A familiar pang of panic returns to the pit of my stomach. Even high-earning French professionals are denied simple housing here. I don't stand a chance. I'll have to call José and beg him for one of his tiny cells.

I leave the internet café and head straight for Nobuaki's. He's lived in New York, Berlin, and for the last three years Paris. Maybe he'll have some ideas or connections, or at the very least a sympathetic ear. I walk to his building, around the corner from *Place des Vosges*. He buzzes me up.

Just sitting at Nobuaki's kitchen table is reassuring. Everything is white and clean. The curtains in the windows are gently gathered together by silky ties. A white lace cloth is placed symmetrically in the centre of the small table, and the duvet on the bed around the corner looks like a blanket of fresh snow. It's difficult to imagine dust and disorder invading this serene setting. Classical CDs line the far wall, organized alphabetically by composer. Books, most of them about photography, occupy the bottom shelf. A Nikon camera and at least a dozen lenses sit on a small desk in a nook opposite the bed. The ceiling boasts ancient wooden beams, a reminder of the building's age. Hilary Hahn is playing Bach quietly from the stereo, and a faint sweetness wafts from a pink hyacinth in the kitchen window as I explain my plight.

"I'll look in the Japanese paper," Nobuaki says. "You'll have less competition." He places a white kettle of water on the stove for coffee, goes to the shelf by the bed and returns to the table with a thin newspaper written entirely in Japanese.

I marvel at the tiny elegant characters, while Nobuaki scans the housing ads — and frowns. "See anything interesting?" I ask.

"Hmmm," he says, shaking his head. "There is only one here that you could afford. It's 500 a month and it's in Les Vallées. It says it's a twenty minute train ride from Paris."

I stare at him, then nod slowly. I can't be choosy. I'll probably have to live outside the city. In the suburbs.

Nobuaki catches my eye. My uncertainty must be blatant. "Well, we should at least go see it," he says.

He dials the number on his cell phone, begins in Japanese but immediately switches to French. He makes an appointment for tomorrow at two.

"The landlord's not Japanese?" I ask when he hangs up.

"No, she's French. She doesn't even speak Japanese. Very strange. I'll come with you if you want," he says.

I nod and fold my arms across my chest. The situation has taken on a new level of reality. *Who would rent to a street musician? Who would want to live in the suburbs?* People without money, I guess. Prices drop significantly per square metre when you leave the boundaries of Paris proper. But so does the energy level. Paris is a windup toy that never stops buzzing. The energy is electric, with so many people packed in such a small space and so many ideas and desires shooting around. You can't help but absorb the energy into your cells, and to vibrate at a higher frequency. Actually, the suburbs are somewhat of a mystery to me. I've haven't spent any time there — apart from the recording studio with Bernard, and the first apartment I visited. I know the area is massive, though, with a population five times that of Paris itself. It includes some of the richest neighbourhoods in France and also some of the most desperate — huge social housing structures and areas that are so unsafe, I'm told, that even the police don't go there. I know that some people choose to go to the suburbs because it's quieter and they can raise kids with more space. They do their shopping at big supermarkets and have their breakfast in the garden on weekends. I know that other people live there because it's where they were born and it's the only place they can afford. The choices depends on the area, it seems, but me in the suburbs? I really don't see it.

Les Vallées. The name sounds nice. *The valleys.* It suggests nature, a place with rolling hills and a sweetly running brook — a country getaway for city folks on weekends and summer vacation. Like my hometown of Huntsville, known for its lakes and forests and its proximity to Toronto. "Oh, you're from cottage country," people said back in university when I mentioned where I grew up. Muskoka. My summer jobs were tending to the gardens and grass of the summer people from the city, washing dishes at one of the fancy resorts, and selling T shirts. We didn't trail behind big motorboats on water-skis. We had a pond instead of a lake. And acres and acres of dense forest. Only one neighbour for kilometres. Our necks were covered in blackfly bites in the spring and mosquito bites in the summer. I climbed trees so high the branches swayed in the wind. I ran barefoot through the woods until the soles of my feet got like leather. Our well ran dry in the summer and we had to pour pond water into the toilets to flush and have showers at friends' houses. Or just be grimy for a while. Moose and bears strolled through our backyard. We never locked the house and never got broken into. I learned the solitude of being alone in the middle of the woods, and how the forest changes at night. It can quickly seem hostile and frightening when the sun disappears and the night creatures stir. I think of the taste of wintergreen and wild leeks and maple water. I think of a beaver tail slapping a warning against a still pond, or a bloodsucker draining the life out of a frog. I think of a blue heron stopping for a rest, its tall legs jutting out from the dark water, and of tree frogs humming their hearts out all night long. Which one of these Les Vallées offers, I'll find out tomorrow.

I spot Nobuaki in the crowd by his black leather coat and a white silk scarf tied neatly around his neck. As we buy our tickets at the machine and board the westbound train, there is a knot in my stomach, as if I'm heading to an audition — a very *important* audition. Nobuaki seems equally nervous, and we barely speak during the train ride to the little suburban cluster of Les Vallées, ten kilometres northwest of Paris. It barely appears on the map.

Once we exit the station, we enter a calm neighbourhood with tall houses, lush gardens and big old trees. Brick walls line the street and metal gates protect each property. The sidewalks are empty. We pass no one on our way to the address that Nobuaki has written in his notebook.

Finally we stop in front of a big clay-roofed house surrounded by trees, with vines sneaking up the walls. Flowers are growing in window boxes, along the porch and in a layered garden to the right.

Nobuaki presses a buzzer set into the pillar of the gate. A few seconds later a latch lifts and the gate inches open. A woman appears on the side porch. When we get close enough, I see she's frowning.

She's probably only about sixty years old, but her round body, dyed beige hair and a generous layer of foundation and blue eye shadow make her appear older. Her navy blue nylon skirt and matching jacket bring to mind secretaries in the 70's — rigid with only a hint of femininity. She says she hopes the apartment isn't for both of us.

"*Non, non,*" reassures Nobuaki. "*C'est pour la jeune fille.*"

The woman turns to me. "*You're not Japanese,*" she says accusingly.

"*Canadienne,*" I say with an apologetic cower.

Her eyes narrow. After a few uncomfortable seconds, she sighs and says she only rents to Japanese people, but now that I'm here she might as well show me the place. She leads us across the garden to a mini house on the other side.

I look to Nobuaki. *Very strange*, his expression says.

The building is the size of a garage. Incredibly, it's a miniature version of the woman's house, with a clay roof and a big wooden door. Inside is a tiny bedroom, a bathroom, a kitchen and a big wooden desk by the window. I'm thinking fast. Les Vallées may be far from any social action, but it's quiet and I could still practice late at night. And it's a house, completely autonomous. One of kind.

"*Madame,*" I say, trying to sound earnest but not desperate. "I would really like to live here."

"*Venez,*" she sighs, turning toward her house. "*On va discuter.*"

Nobuaki and I follow her into a large kitchen tiled in beige. A mini dachshund in a cage on the floor yaps excitedly when we come in. One of his legs is bandaged, but he heaves himself violently against the bars to bark and then yelps with pain. It's hot in here and what smells like a quiche is baking in the oven. Decorative pitchers sit on a shelf, beside a row of cookbooks.

Antique plates hang on the wall. The woman leans down and coos at the dog for a moment, then straightens and motions for us to sit at the kitchen table.

Anxiety flutters in my chest like flames. I keep my eyes on the ceramic bowl of fruit in the centre and study the skin textures of the pears, mangoes, kiwis and bananas. How could I possibly convince this woman to rent to me?

"*Alors, racontez-moi,*" she says.

Nobuaki stares into his lap, anticipating my answer. With a deep breath, I meet the woman's gaze, and tell her the truth.

"I'm a street musician," I say. "I don't know how long I will be in Paris, but I need a place to live starting next month. Rent will not be a problem."

"Can you sign a one-year lease?" she asks.

I shake my head, and tell her that I only need a place for a few months.

She sighs and her eyebrows crumple. "This is *très embêtant,*" she says — very troublesome.

There are a few moments of silence, during which I consider begging and crying, but I manage to hold back. Finally the woman takes a breath and tells me with brimming eyes that her mother always helped foreigners. "She just died," she explains, wiping the tears with her index finger to avoid a mascara smudge. She straightens her shoulders with sudden conviction and announces that she will rent to me in honour of her mother. It's what she would have done. The woman smiles at me and a lightness falls across the room like a suddenly thinning cloud.

"*Merci beaucoup, beaucoup, beaucoup!*" I sputter, and if she wasn't French I might have hugged her.

Nobuaki shakes his head in amazement as we walk down the driveway. "You are so fortunate," he says several times.

It's true, finding a place in one shot in Paris is a miracle, especially under my circumstances. I know I have Nobuaki to thank for that. How else would I have found an affordable house listed only in a Japanese newspaper? The randomness of my life can

seem outrageous if I think about it in a rational way. But somehow, if I just live it, day-to-day, things fall into place. It's a bit
like crossing the street with your eyes closed. This month I live
in Paris. Next month, Les Vallées.

MENUETES

I trudge toward the Metro with my life on my shoulders. My big blue bag makes me look, and feel, like a backpacker, just passing through — a young twenty something heading to a youth hostel. After months of blending in here, I'm stared at in the street and eyed warily as I enter the packed Metro car. I struggle to support the weight of my bags against the sways and stops. No one offers me their seat.

My landlady is waiting on the porch in a long brown coat when I arrive. She isn't smiling. "*Vous voilà*," she says, and with an eerie calmness explains that she gave the apartment to someone else, someone who could commit to a year. Someone Japanese.

I drop my bag to the ground and stare at her in disbelief. She tells me not to worry, that I'm going to live at her mother's place, just down the street. It's even bigger, but the rent will be the same. "*Suivez-moi*," she says, heading down the driveway.

I force my bag back onto my shoulders and follow her under the tracks to a narrow residential street. She gives me sideways glances as we walk, but she doesn't speak. I have nothing to say either. I'm still recovering from the abrupt change in plans.

At a yellow brick building, the woman stops and punches in a code. The door unlocks with a buzz. I follow her in with my backpack and my violin.

Crammed together in a tiny elevator cage, we ride three floors up.

"I think you're going to like the place," she tells me.

I look over at her and manage a smile. *I'm not homeless. Whatever this place is like, it's not the street.*

The apartment door scuffs open and a pungent staleness streams out. It is assaulting, like a hospital ward that hasn't been aired in years. It smells ancient, like antique wood and ratty rugs.

"No shoes in the apartment," the landlady says, as she slips off her loafers. She scurries in her nylons across the carpeted dining room floor to open the window. *"Ah, voilà!"* Her voice has a rushed cheer to it, like a desperate real estate agent.

I set my bag down next to a dark varnished dining room table with sculpted legs that curve out at the top and taper to foot-like structures on the bottom. On the wall is a gold-framed mirror. In the corner, a grandfather clock's hands are frozen at a quarter past three. It's like a museum of reconstructed rooms. By Paris standards, the place is a mansion, with a large kitchen, a dining room, a living room and a full sized bathroom. There is a bedroom at the end of the hall, but we don't go in.

"My mother was very strict with the housework," she says. "That's why I prefer Japanese people. They are quiet and clean. I hope Canadians are too."

She hands me the door key and a piece of paper with the code for downstairs. Then, as if it's an afterthought, she informs me that I have a roommate. A Japanese man. He'll be arriving later this afternoon. She heads to the door, saying she's going to let me settle in and leaves me alone in her mother's apartment.

I stand in the middle of the dining room and shut my eyes as I try to accustom myself to this new environment. I hear the metal door of the elevator clang shut and the gears grind as it shutters to the ground. Then there is silence.

I have the unpleasant jumpy feeling of being in someone else's place without their permission, and the uncomfortable edge of anticipating their imminent return. The old woman's presence is heavy, as if she's just stepped out for a baguette. *Would she mind me living here,* I wonder? *She* did *like foreigners.*

Nonetheless, I decide to let my future roommate take the bedroom. And it's not out of generosity. I'd rather sleep in the living room without a door than invade a dead woman's sheets. I remove the cushions from the couch in the dining room and drag them into the living room for a bed. Then I survey my situation. My new lair has palm trees, spider plants and succulents that flaunt their vivacity beside the dusty artefacts. There is a decorative fireplace. Along the mantle sit a few smaller potted plants, a wooden clock and a haunting statue of the three wise monkeys respectively clutching their ears, eyes, and mouth. *No evil here,* they say. Above them is another mirror, directly opposite the one in the dining room. When I peer into it, I get a glimpse of the back of my head ad infinitum. The walls have a white and gold papered texture, and the floor is covered by a worn, light blue carpet that smells like old cheese. I couldn't feel less at home.

The kitchen is large, with a real oven, a stovetop and all the kitchen utensils and baking dishes needed to make any size of cake or casserole. In the fridge I find a jar of jam, a mouldy lemon, and a container of unidentifiable rotting leftovers that I'm not yet prepared to deal with. There's a teacup in the sink, but I don't have the heart to touch it.

In the bathroom, the old woman's frayed toothbrush sits in a holder. Creams and perfumes line the shelf in the cabinet behind the mirror. I inspect one of the bottles — a pink one, with a lemon-shaped atomizer. The scent is sharp and ambrosial, reminiscent of a funeral — too many flowers blending together.

I don't dare look in the shower. Discovering hair strands would only increase the woman's presence here, and I already feel like an intruder.

I peer into the bedroom. It is long and narrow, with a single bed by the window and a couple of books on the bedside table. I wonder if she died right here in this room, on this mattress, between these sheets. I step back and circle around the apartment again, not sure what to do. Everything seems off limits, like an alarm might sound if I touch anything.

Finally I go into the kitchen, fill a bag with rotten items from the fridge and bring it to the bin at the bottom of the building. The starkly barren street has an apocalyptic feel. *Who lives in this ghost town, and why?* The thought of spending the winter here makes me tingly with panic. Already the days are short and dreary. It is raining more often than not and a heavy blanket of moisture is steadily descending onto Paris. The leaves are turning brown and flaking away. Gardens have lost the lustre of summer, and flower boxes are becoming barren. Summer dresses have morphed to black coats, making some streets feel like a funeral march. I don't know how I'll survive here, far from the rush of Paris that provided a constant rush of energy. I might just invest in a fluffy duvet and not resurface until spring.

I cross the street to the supermarket across from the train station. It is only slightly bigger than a convenience store and offers a selection nearly as limited. As soon as I open the door, the cashier, a friendly Arabic man, welcomes me to the neighbourhood. I turn away from the produce, which is expensive and withered. I don't feel like cooking anyway. I settle for a baguette, Nutella, cheese, coffee, jam, and several boxes of tea for my upcoming hibernation.

Later, I'm pouring pour tea from the old woman's big green porcelain teapot, when an agonizing buzz at the door makes me spill onto my foot. *My roommate.* My heart speeds as I rush over wet-footed and open the door to a guy my age.

"*Bonjour,*" he says. "*Je suis Kosuke.*" He has hair down to his shoulders and is dressed in black. More funeral clothes.

I lead him to the bedroom. On the way, I explain about the recently deceased woman. I'm worried he won't want to sleep in her bed either, but he doesn't seem bothered. He drops all his bags off in the room and says a polite "*Merci.*"

When I return in search of sheets and blankets a half hour later, his video equipment is strewn across the floor and his clothes are nestled in the dresser. I want to ask what he did with the old woman's beige underwear and nightgowns, but instead I just close the door behind me.

Back in my room, I put my music stand in one corner, my bag of clothes in another, and set my pile of coins in front of the hearth. With no other belongings, it's difficult to take up any more space, or to be anything other than a visitor.

When I finally bed down that night on my narrow spring-filled mattress, the blankets are scratchy and the smell of wool and carpet is overpowering. Outside there are no sounds — no cars or people. I can hear Kosuke organizing things in his room. Like the hamsters I used to have as a kid, the movement is a presence, a gentle reminder that I'm not entirely alone in this old and tired place. I eventually fall asleep to the comforting rustles.

DUE TO THE ALMOST CONSTANT RAIN that follows, I end up spending even less time on the street than I did in the fall, and a great deal of time in the apartment, reading and writing and sharing pots of tea with Kosuke in the evenings. The place quickly becomes homelike, the way a camp bunk can take on a sort of familiar comfort. I've gotten used to selecting my clothes for the day from a pile on the floor and sleeping with only a narrow sheet pinned to the entranceway of my bedroom — a mere suggestion of privacy, since it covers only a third of the opening. *It's just temporary,* I tell myself. *I can pretend to be an extrovert for a while.*

Kosuke's eating habits are as poor as mine, only instead of Nutella toast he indulges in chocolate cereal. Kosuke is an artist. He makes short films and is taking Indian dance classes here in Paris. Technically he's enrolled in a language school, which provides him with a student visa, but he rarely goes to class. He's kind and gentle and curious. He grew up in Tokyo, far from my rural Canadian upbringing. Here, though, we lead similar lives centred around art, with few official obligations and no idea where we'll be in a year. We are two drifters caught in a time capsule situated in a ghost-town suburb of Paris. All around us the greenery has shrivelled and fallen away. Cue winter.

SIPPING TEA AT THE ANTIQUE dining room table with Kosuke last night, I started naming all the places from which I've been kicked out while playing in Paris. First, I told him about the time the police showed up at *Place des Vosges* after someone made a noise complaint. The three officers looked at my passport and wrote down the number, but they didn't ask any questions. They could have, though. And my illegal status would have been glaring. There was the time I was playing in front of a small garden in the Marais and a man dressed in a brown suit came over to tell me that he lived in the area and hated the violin. If I didn't stop at once, he would call the cops. His aggression and hatred were so unexpected they bore right into me. I instantly burst into tears.

"Don't cry!" the man ordered.

But I continued to weep as I packed up, and a young boy who had been listening with his mother ran over to give me five euros.

Finally, I tell Kosuke about the *Champs-Élysées*, where it is strictly prohibited to play, and the cops will show up within minutes to hassle any musician who dares.

"I want to film you getting kicked out by the police," Kosuke declared, "for a documentary on intolerance. Can we go tomorrow?"

SO, DESPITE THE HEAVY GREY CLOUDS Kosuke and I are seated side by side on the Metro heading to the *Champs-Élysée*. Me with my violin. Him with his video camera. I'm already starting to get nervous about the upcoming police encounter. Not only are such incidences unpleasant, Kosuke and I are both foreigners with not-so-stable visa situations. *Why did I agree to this?*

The escalator lifts us to the boulevard and we enter the bustling march of the *Champs-Élysée*. The pace is quicker here than anywhere else in Paris, and people walk with self-importance. Even the sneakered tourists seem to hold their heads higher as they pass by upscale shops or sit in overpriced establishments nursing their *café au laits*. In a setting so grandiose, you can't help but strut, giving off the thick aura of wealth, both real and desired. The buildings are as white as bleached bones and the sidewalks are at least five times the width of any anywhere else in Paris. There is money here, so either you have some or you act as if you do. Even in grey weather, the density is staggering — so many soles slapping against the pavement. In crowds this big, it's hard not to slip into the surging stream. For a moment this happens. My eyes glaze over and I walk forward in a mindless state. But then I remember why we are here. Soon I will have to break away from this rush and become something else. A spectacle. A defiant musician begging to be accosted by the police.

I just hope they don't ask questions. My visitor's visa ran out months ago, and there is a rigorous campaign aiming to rid the country of the *sans papiers*. I've seen visual minorities approached by police at random asking for their papers. Nobuaki has told me how he was interrogated for hours before they even allowed him to enter the country. They repeatedly showed him Chinese characters and demanded he read them. *I do not read Chinese characters. I am Japanese,* he told them again and again. Nobuaki still swears he's being watched sometimes on the street. Things like this don't happen to me, because I blend in, as long as I don't wear Birkenstocks or open my mouth. *If I begin to play here and the cops start to ask questions or see that Kosuke and I are together or, worse, that we had planned the kick-out for an art project, well, we could be deported by tomorrow.* They would only have to contact Kosuke's language school to discover that he hasn't been attending classes.

Still, the idea of risking our well-being for art is romantic and exciting enough to keep me walking, heart pattering, to a lamppost between a magazine stand and a Peugeot dealership. Kosuke gets out his camera and sets up a few metres behind on my left. I unpack, tune my strings, and begin, sheepishly at first, with a simple Bach minuet.

The *Champs-Élysées* works on a different principle than *Places des Vosges* or *Palais-Royal*. Here, hundreds of people pass by every minute. It's easy for them to lose themselves in the frantic forward march of the boulevard and ignore me altogether. This is what most people do, but out of a thousand there is one who will stop, smile, and reach for a coin.

I manage to make a few Euros before I see five officers closing in on my right. My heart starts to slam. I feign ignorance and keep the music going.

"*Mademoiselle,*" says the alpha officer, his voice cool and demanding. "*Il est interdit de jouer ici.*"

I stop and lower my violin with obvious disappointment, while passers-by turn to gawk. Even though I was expecting it, under the officers' critical glare I can't help but feel like a criminal. Then one of them spots the camera.

"*Hey!*" he yells and the pack rushes over to surround Kosuke. "*Qu'est-ce que vous faites?*" I hear one of them bark.

"*Film violoniste,*" says Kosuke, thickening his accent as if he were an innocent tourist.

I hate to leave him alone with the officers crowding around his camera, but it would be suspicious otherwise, so I walk up the boulevard and wait nervously for about ten minutes. On my way back to the crime scene I find him walking toward me, a few shades paler. He turns and we walk together up the boulevard.

"They erased my footage!" he says, outraged.

The incident only highlights the theme of the film. *Intolerance.* The city is plagued with it. Intolerance for accents is one. I'm so used to being greeted with a grimace when I speak to people outside of the busking setting that I feel I should apologize in advance ("Sorry for the accent, but do you sell soy milk here?") In some ways, this intolerance is helping me to work harder on my pronunciation and intonation. Anything to reduce the glares and grimaces. Intolerance for tourists, is another — slow walkers or map readers. Many Parisians avoid tourist-heavy areas for this reason. Intolerance for music. That one I know intimately. Getting kicked out from playing spots happens so frequently I've grown to expect it. Intolerance for colour. Cops randomly ask black people for ID on the street. "Is it a crime to be black?" I heard one young man ask once as he dug his wallet from his pocket. I met a black woman who changed her name to Céline because her own name was too African sounding to put on a résumé. Intolerance for heat and crowds. You know you're pissing off a Parisian when they utter an audible sigh. Usually another will follow, heavier and impossible to ignore. If the situation persists, a remark will be uttered. In the Metro once, a woman glared as she sighed. "You could take your backpack off you know!" she said. I looked into her hateful eye slits and smiled. "Yes," I said. "I know."

Intolerance is pervasive, but after today Kosuke and I have resolved not to mess with it for now. It's unsettling on a daily basis, but being surrounded by five angry cops reminded us that it can also quickly turn serious, and we're in no position to play such a game.

It's raining now — a cold horrid November rain. Playing in it would be worse than futile. Kosuke and I head back to our tiny suburb, a place so small it barely appears on any map. A place no foreigner would tread unless by fluke. Kosuke and me. The two flukes of Les Vallées.

THE TEMPERATURE HAS DROPPED steadily and the dampness is now a wall that assails me when I open the door. It is all encompassing, and edges through layers of clothing until it penetrates my marrow. My shoulders ache permanently from tensing. I thought I'd be able to handle this — I've lived through two decades of harsh winters and figured I would have no trouble with a measly 5°C. But this cold is foreign, fierce and unforgiving. I'd prefer a crisp -20 with a metre of snow to this wretched moisture.

I start wearing increasingly more layers, long johns under my pants and multiple shirts and sweaters. My fingers started to get so cold that I cut the fingers off my gloves and wear them while I play. They reduce my dexterity, so I have to stick to slower pieces. Even with the gloves, most days after 45 minutes my fingers are useless and I have to take refuge in a café.

I make less money in the cold. Much less. People aren't nearly as social. Most walk by quickly, their shoulders hunched against the wind, their faces buried in scarves.

"*Courageuse*," whisper some as they rush by. They're too uncomfortable to stop and listen or search their wallets for a coin.

"*Vous allez attraper froid!*" says one woman passing through the archway at *Palais-Royal*. She frowns at me as if I'm taking drugs.

I smile and keep playing, but she stops in front of me and waits. When I lower my violin she launches into a lecture about the dangers of "catching cold," as if it's a disease lurking in the dampness. It's not the first I've heard of this. French people are always going on about catching cold, though I'm not sure I know what they mean.

"Don't worry," I tell the woman. "I'm from Canada."

She nods, satisfied, and moves on.

But this is only an excuse to help the woman feel better. Winters in Canada are not like this at all. They might be long and involve snowstorms and ice, but the cold itself isn't so hostile, and it stays outside. The houses are designed to keep it out, with things like double windows, electric heaters that people turn up too high, thick insulation and, for the privileged, heated tile floors. The cold is confined to the outdoors. *As it should be,* I think.

I grew up in a winter culture, but that doesn't seem to exist here in Paris. Tuques, for example, are nowhere to be seen among the locals. Scarves are abundant, but even in the summer I saw people wearing those. They're more for fashion than warmth. There are no bulky androgenizing coats, warm boots with felt liners, wool socks, flannel or fleece. Instead of bundling up under covers and making soup and chili and tea and hot chocolate, as people in Canada do, Parisians seem to prefer to ignore the season altogether. They complain about it, sure. They don't appear to like the moisture any more than I do, but I don't see anyone doing anything about it. Why aren't they building moisture-free zones? Why aren't they investing in fleece body suits? Hot toddies and mulled wine should be available on every street corner. Working hours should be reduced to allow for more sleeping, and full spectrum lights should be at least partially subsidized by the government to prevent the seasonal melancholia I can feel festering inside me even now. Without snow, there is just greyness and sadness. It hangs heavy in the streets. It falls in sheets from the sky. It nestles under the eyes of the people in the Metro. And it's in the air that creeps into everything, making it all wet and weepy.

AFTER A CHILLY BUSK at *Palais-Royal* one afternoon, I pick up a few cans of Heineken at the grocery store by the tracks. When I lived alone, I never drank at home, but now that I have a roommate I feel like acknowledging Friday night. Also, I need a break from all that tea.

Kosuke is sitting at the dining room table on his computer when I arrive home. Without saying anything I put one of the cans beside him.

"Oh! Thank you!" he says and promptly cracks it open.

I open one too and we clink our cans together. The cool bubbles tickle my throat in an old friend way and remind me of post exam celebrations. Even though I played only two hours today and made very little money, the taste of beer makes me feel as if I have accomplished something.

Before he's consumed even half, Kosuke's face is lit up like a lantern and his eyes look like they've been painted over with shiny nail gloss. His speech begins to fall apart, leaving his sentences fractured and stalling. By the time he finishes the can, he's properly plastered and his speech has lost almost all its articles. With narrowed eyes he starts telling a ghost story from his childhood.

"I am five," he says, with a solemn face. "I see man standing at end of hallway looking at me. He is stranger. I come close and see man is transparent. I see intestines and stomach and heart."

I search Kosuke's face for hints that he might be joking, but he looks just drunk.

"He tell me not be afraid," Kosuke says slowly. "Then he disappear."

"Hummph," I grunt, then nod, not sure what to say. Ghosts are not something I think about often, like God, and I find stories like this troubling. What do you say when someone claims to have seen Jesus or ghosts? Remain politely respectful? I see what might be a twinkle in Kosuke's eyes, but there is a good chance it is alcohol induced.

"Kosuke, is that a true story?"

He nods, but the corners of his mouth twitch slightly.

"Kosuke," I start, and he erupts with wild drunken laughter. The story of the ghost brings us to the topic of death, and he begins to talk about his father. When Kosuke was younger, I learn, his father died from what he describes as stress. Kosuke tells me he once warned him never to become a slave to society. I wonder if Kosuke's dad was inflicted with one of the culture specific disorders I studied in university. Japan had a few. One was Karoshi. *Death by overwork. It might explain Kosuke's free spirit and curiosity,* I think. It might also explain his eclectic choice of activities: Indian dance classes, film making and electroacoustic music courses. And it could also be why he travels so much: in some ways, Kosuke has suffered greatly from his father's death. In other ways, it has enabled him to go against the pressures of society, to be constantly exploring. He inhales life with deep, enthusiastic gasps, and tries new things with the fearlessness of a child. One day last week he came home with brand new roller blades. He put them on, applied wrist guards and went immediately to the street. I watched him from the apartment window as he edged forward on stiff legs, falling, getting back up, falling, getting back up. He was gone for over an hour, and when he came back he was glowing with inspiration and fresh air.

"When I get good," he told me as he undid his blades, "I'm going to film while roller blading."

I thought of how I'd quit roller blading after a single fall, and how the incident was still recent and humiliating in my mind. Kosuke didn't even seem to register all the falling he was doing — he was focused on the strides.

I brought us two beers each, but Kosuke's eyes are already starting to close. He wavers to his feet and says, "I go to bed."

I smile as my humble and fearless roommate sways down the hallway to his room and falls asleep with the light on. How different we are. While I want to blend in, to burrow and to belong, he wants to taste and move on. In a way, it is fear itself that brought me here to France: fear of following the narrowing corridors of academia, of limiting myself to a specific social phenomenon confined to an institution. I didn't fear financial instability the way many of my peers did; I feared entrapment. I wanted a new place that I could settle into at my own rhythm. I wanted a language that I could be intimate with, free from the rigid classical music world, and a city that I could embrace. Or that would embrace me. And meaning, of course — a reason for doing anything at all. People sometimes say that I'm brave to busk in a foreign country, but I don't see it that way. This is the most comfortable place for me to be, on the edge of society, with no major goals that I can mess up. I can't fail at this, because busking is an ongoing condition, not a means to an end. There is no ultimate point of arrival, no defined goals or expectations. I could use a dose of Kosuke's inhibition and ability to take risks, though. If anything I've become a little *too* comfortable in this busking lifestyle, and here in the cocoon of Les Vallées. After all, *Buscar* is a Spanish word that means to search.

I SET OUT FOR ANOTHER DAY of shivery partitas and sonatas. The dry heat of the Metro gives way to a wall of moisture, which wallops me as I walk up the final flight of stairs to the grey, cloud-covered streets. I hunch my shoulders against the hostile wind and head to *Place des Vosges*. I bought a thermos yesterday and have come armed with some heavily honeyed chamomile tea, which I hope will increase my busking stamina. My wage has taken a serious hit from the weather, and though I saved quite a bit over the summer, with my higher rent it may not be enough to last the winter. I have to keep playing.

From a distance I see a man seated on a stool beside Maâmar. He's wearing a black windbreaker and his wiry grey hair splays out over his shoulders. At his feet is a brown violin case. When he sees me coming, he stands and grins. I have never met him, but I know who he is. I recognize the wild grey curls and the sharp green eyes, and of course the violin is a give-away. It's Tim, the violinist Maâmar was sketching a few months ago. So many times I would arrive to play and Maâmar or George would exclaim, "You just missed Tim!" I had begun to wonder if Tim was a running joke between the painters.

"*Nisha,*" he says, standing to greet me with the *bises.* He smells like a folk festival, a comforting blend of sweet grass and clown makeup.

"*Tim, enfin!*" I exclaim.

"I've heard a lot about you," Tim says in accentless English.

"Oh, you speak English!"

"My mother's American," he says with nonchalance. "I went to school in the States. Julliard."

A group of Italian tourists arrive and crowd around the paintings. Since George isn't here today, Maâmar leaves us to take care of them.

Tim slings his violin over his shoulder and says, "Want to get a coffee?"

We wave to Maâmar, who is deep in selling mode, and head to a nearby café. The outside terrace has a wall of thick plastic around it and a couple of long glowing heaters inside. The patrons are huddled at the tables closest to the heater, the way newly hatched chicks crowd in front of heat lamps.

After a jumpy bow-tied waiter has taken our order, I ask Tim about Julliard. Maâmar had told me that Tim played well, but I'd never imagined at a world-class level. Julliard is *the* place for child prodigies. So many of the violin greats graduated from there: Midori, Sarah Chang, Perlman, Nigel Kennedy. . . .

Tim unzips his jacket and loosens his dark green scarf. His irises are deep emerald pools, and he has the same serene smile

I've seen on church ministers and New Age healers, an every-thing-will-work-out-in-the-end pleasantness that sets those around them at ease.

"Yeah, I studied with Galamian," he says.

"Wow," is all I can say. Galamian is the editor of my complete solo violin works by Bach. He's a household name in the violin world — the Tolstoy of the fiddle.

"I was supposed to be a prodigy," Tim laughs.

"And what happened?"

"There was a death in the family. I inherited a bunch of money. I never liked the competitiveness of the violin world, so I quit and lived like a king for ten years. It was wonderful."

Two espressos are set before us with an enthusiastic "*Voilà!*" I stir in a pack of sugar, curl my hands around the tiny cup and listen as Tim describes his travels to India, Fiji and other parts of Asia — a spiritual quest. He studied the art of meditation with mentors in each place he went.

"I didn't touch the violin for years," he says, "but I eventually ran out of money and had to come back to France. I took lessons from Dominique Hoppenot. Have you heard of her?"

I shake my head.

"She founded a violin method," he says, "a metaphysical ap-proach that aligned with my teachings in Asia. She was a won-derful woman, very generous. She had small hands like yours," he says as I bring my coffee to my lips. "She died, though. A few years ago. Cancer." He pauses for a moment and stares down at the table with a semi-smile of fondness. "She wrote a book on the method," he adds.

"What was the method?" I ask, amazed that classical music could be associated with metaphysical. Of course, music is a cru-cial part of many spiritual practices, a way of deepening trances, a way of connecting to higher levels of consciousness, but my university training was mostly focused on pedagogy and tech-nique, far from the spiritual realm.

"It's a blend of music and meditation," Tim says. "Music is a vehicle for meditation. Even on the street, when I play, I am not aware of what's happening around me. I'm not thinking about mistakes. They don't exist. I am one with the music. I *am* the music. It's the greatest feeling in the world!"

He grins, revealing a row of tobacco-tinged teeth. To demonstrate the positioning, he twists his left arm forward, directly in front of him, with his head facing straight ahead. He brings his right hand, curled in a bow hold, in front of his face and in line with his left hand. His expression relaxes and his eyes take on a distant quality.

"It allows for stereo sound and there is direct contact between the body and the instrument," he explains.

"You don't use a shoulder rest?"

I can't imagine playing without the padded Kun that secures the violin on my shoulder and maintains a distance of a couple of centimetres between my body and the instrument.

"No, no shoulder rest. You have to feel the vibrations of your violin. That's very important. It's awkward at first, but you can use sponges until you get used to it. When you achieve this state, Nisha, it's…well…pure bliss."

But busking has so many distractions. It requires so much outward energy, and eye contact with those passing by and constant smiles.

"So, you actually manage to meditate on the street?" I ask.

"Oh yes! Playing on the street is the perfect challenge, especially in this cold!" He waves his hand at the plastic wall. "But I don't *choose* to play on the street. I mean, I don't love it. I have to support myself. And I only play to make enough to live. My uncle lets me live in his studio for free, so I just need enough to eat and smoke hash. That's about it. I compose music at home, and I've got other projects, films mostly, but I'll need lots of money for those." He laughs, then says, "I'd like to hear you play sometime."

I cringe at the thought of playing for someone so accomplished. *My old neuroses will probably come flooding back,* I think, *and I'll be ravaged again by incapacitating anxiety.* It's not an idle fear. Even on the street, if someone stops to listen with the collected, knowing gaze of a musician, my playing tends to suffer. My hands waver, my fingers become stiff, and my memory lapses. I fear judgement, not being good enough, and mistakes.

As I sit here across from Tim, though, I wonder how things might have been different if in university I hadn't been obsessing about my shaking hands but strove to attain this blissful state that Tim has described, where music and musician are synonymous. My muscles might have relaxed, my fingers might have remained nimble and reactive and the bow might have sailed smoothly over the strings. I might have even kept going.

It's a nice thought, but just thinking about playing violin in university causes my lungs to contract. I breathe in deeply and my exhale is a long, drawn-out sigh. It's too late for a career in classical music — I was far from Julliard material anyway, but I wonder if I could study and adopt this method, as a way of reconciling with the violin, of being able to play in front of a real audience again. Could I replace my fear of making mistakes with a search for inner peace, using music as a vehicle? It sounds too good to be true. But if this were possible, the violin would take on a different reality. So would busking.

Before I can ask Tim about learning the method, he stands abruptly and announces, "I must go. I'm meeting the woman I love." He jots his number onto a napkin, and I watch him disappear around the corner, his violin slung over his shoulder.

I make my way slowly back to *Place des Vosges*. Of course, the spot is open. In the winter I rarely have to worry about competition. Almost no one plays outside. But Tim does. And although the weather hasn't changed since I arrived here an hour ago, I shiver less thinking about him playing here, under the same arches, suspended in a music-fuelled meditation. As I go through my repertoire of lamenting winter pieces, the cold is less something to endure and more something to overcome. It is almost pleasant.

A TEXT MESSAGE drags me from my late morning dreams. *"Rendez-vous cet après-midi. Amène ton violon. 14h. 11 rue Victor Letalle."*

It's Marie. She approached me on the street last week, said she knew a guy who hired musicians to play in his bar. I liked her immediately — a young, bubbly woman who works at a bookstore and spends her money on concerts and art shows. Her cell phone was buzzing constantly, with calls and texts from friends all over the city: performing, concert going, and partying. Marie's the same age as me, but her short hair, the dark circles under her eyes, and her commanding confidence make her appear older. I told her I didn't do things like this, that I don't *perform*, but she seems to have set it up anyway. I don't know if my nerves can handle such a thing, but now that a *rendez-vous* has been arranged, I decide to at least go and meet the owner.

After an unbearable hour playing through a sheet of dampness, I head to my appointment. It's in the 20th Arrondissement, a neighbourhood I don't know at all, and it takes me a while to find the place. Eventually, on a street barely larger than an alleyway, I see the tiny establishment, *Au Copains,* hidden among apartment buildings and a couple of schwarma places. A small man with short black curly hair is sitting in one of the chairs by the window. He watches me approach and stands with a smile as I enter.

"Je suis Mohammed," he says, taking my hand in a tight, friendly grip.

He motions for me to sit, then disappears behind the bar and returns with a cup of mint tea so sweet it makes my cheeks throb. The paintings lining the walls feature streaks of earthy browns, greens and yellows with gold highlights. Small saucer shaped chandeliers hang from the ceiling and a long string of tiny white lights run along the top of the wall. The tables have been painted with red swirls. Posters for upcoming events plaster the window.

Mohammed tells me he is a big supporter of the arts. And, he says with a modest smile, he's a painter and a drummer himself. "Now let's hear you play!" he says, leaning back in his chair.

I push away the nerves that are beginning to seep into my limbs and take out my violin. I play the Gavotte from the G Major Bach suite. It's the piece I'm most comfortable with and least likely to screw up. As I reach the first repeat, I glance over, see that Mohammed is frowning, and stop playing.

"Do you know anything faster?" he says. "Something with more rhythm?"

I only know a handful of fiddle songs, but I play the one I know best, the Swallowtail Jig. Mohammed leans forward in his chair grinning and nodding his head to the beat as he drums on the table.

"*C'est ça!*" he shouts. "Play that kind of music! *Parfait!* I pay my musicians 25 Euros and they pass around a hat. You can make good money this way," he says. "But you have to fill the bar. That's all I ask."

I glance around. The place isn't big, but my friend pool is still quite limited. I'm not sure I can fill this place, and I'm not sure I'm up for a performance either. I'm not even a fiddler. I only know a couple of tunes.

Mohammed dashes behind the bar and returns with two glasses and a bottle of punch — his own special blend.

"*Santé!*" he says, bringing the golden liquid to his lips.

The punch is heavy with rum. I return to the cold afternoon drizzle, dizzy and disoriented. Not only have I just agreed to perform at a bar, I realize as I tread toward the Metro, but I am going to have to stretch five minutes of music into an evening of entertainment. *What have I done?* I think, as the train whisks me back to my unconscious suburb. *What have I done?*

IN THE METRO ON THE WAY to play at *Palais-Royal,* I notice a rich woman in a fur coat toss her scarf over her shoulder. It lands gently on the shoulder of a poor immigrant Chinese woman sitting beside her. Neither notice and the two women ride three stops sharing the same silk scarf. *My dad would get a kick out this,* I think. *He might even write a poem about it.*

Sometimes I wonder how my dad is. A couple of months after my parent's marriage ended, I was back for Christmas break, and he invited me and my brother and sister out for lunch at a local diner. It was a noisy place, with families chattering and getting top-ups of oily coffee. He began telling us about his new love, a wonderful woman he'd met at a poetry group. An American. Over grilled cheese and fries, he told us about the foot rubs he gives her and the romantic walks they take in snowstorms. He made their bond seem divine. He wasn't seeking our approval. It was more like he was trying to convince us of something — that he was loveable, maybe. Or that he was fine. No, better than fine — he was better than ever. He was moving on.

"Why so soon?" I asked. It seemed unfair that he should be enjoying himself so much while my mom was still grieving.

I figured he would say something lyrical about true love not being bound by time, but he said only, "Adults can't be alone."

"Can't, or don't want to?" I snapped.

He didn't answer. In time, he became a silent figure. Even when I was a kid, there was a heaviness to his presence that made me clam up, often too self-aware to speak. Nothing seemed natural or appropriate to say. By the time I moved away for university, we had become strangers. And now we're now like old acquaintances who think of each other from time to time. He doesn't know that I spend my days playing under ancient archways and on bridges over the Seine. He doesn't know that I live on the canal and speak French. He doesn't have my phone number and he doesn't do email.

His comment annoyed me at the time. Now I know that being alone can be glorious. My solitude in Paris has allowed me to engage deeply with my surroundings, far more than if I'd stayed with Pierre. I wouldn't have stayed out the other night until 2:00 a.m. talking to a photojournalist from Miami. I wouldn't have gone to the ballet last week. I also wouldn't have crashed Harold's upstairs neighbour's party and met a dozen artists from the States. Since my home life is solitary, I have to turn outwards for connection. It allows a unique openness to the world, a desire to connect with humans of all kinds, from sweet grannies on the Metro to roughed-up homeless dudes with dogs. Being alone in Paris has allowed me to connect with the city in a far deeper and more meaningful way. Adults *can* be alone. They're just scared to death of it.

I think of my dad now as a man that I know. This is how I ward off resentment. As long as he remains a sad poet with good intentions, our duet, however faint, however dissonant, can continue. Maybe I'll write him a postcard describing the scarf scene. The two women have gone now. The scarf only joined them for three stations. Then the rich lady got off and two stations later the Chinese woman left. Now the Metro is nearing my stop, *Palais Royal - Musée du Louvre.*

"*Pardon,*" I say, clutching my violin close to me as I make my way toward the door. "*Pardon, pardon, pardon.*"

It's a few days before the gig and I think I have the music part figured out. A friend back in Ontario has mailed me a book of Canadian fiddle music. The tunes are super simple and fast enough that I won't have to worry about my bow hand shaking on any long drawn out notes. I'll take half a beta blocker just in case, but I'm not concerned about the music anymore. I need to fill that bar.

I send out text messages to the patchwork of people I've met while busking. I try to imagine them all in one place, but the image is disorienting, like at the end of a play, when all the actors come out and hold hands for a bow. In my mind all my friends exist in different settings. Bringing them all together in the same space is unfathomable, but then again, the bar isn't central, and it might be difficult to convince anyone to sacrifice their Thursday night for an evening of sight-read fiddle tunes.

The day before the gig, I run through the fiddle book. The

tunes are catchy but repetitive, and they're very short. I'm not sure how I'll keep things lively enough for an evening of entertainment. Traditionally, songs like this would be learned by ear, memorized generation after generation, and would never be played solo. There'd be other fiddles, guitars and wooden spoons in a rowdy bar or kitchen, with liquor in a perpetual pour. At least I can count on the alcohol. Mohammed has that covered. And maybe he has some extra spoons lying around.

The day before the gig I send out a reminder email and hope for the best.

I ARRIVE AT *AUX COPAINS* 30 minutes early and find it already half full and in an animated state. Marie is seated at a table in the back, with six other people. Judging by the laughter and flushed cheeks, they've already been dipping into Mohammed's punch. There is a row of middle-aged men perched at the bar, eating peanuts and chuckling with Mohammed, who gives me a high arm wave from behind the bar. I'm pleased to discover that there is already enough noise to successfully drown out my violin. That's the way it should be, after all, a background drone of upbeat jigs and reels, not a performance but an atmosphere — festive and participative, with stomping feet and banging tables. It's not a sit-back-and-relax kind of thing but rather a get-smashed-and-cheer event.

Mohammed leads me to the corner beside the bar where I am to set up. As I'm unfolding my stand Brigitte arrives with her boyfriend and three of his university friends. They wave and take a seat by the door. A few minutes later, a group of middle-aged men straggle in and take the table nearest me. Mohammed comes out from behind the bar to greet them with hearty handshakes, which gives away their status as *les piliers du bar* — the regulars. By the time I've got my violin tuned and the music on the stand, Nobuaki is sitting at the back and Céline has arrived and is looking for a place to sit.

Mohammed is ecstatic with the turnout and offers a round of

punch on the house. If it was a classical concert, playing violin with alcohol in my veins would be unthinkable, but these fiddle tunes need grit, they need to be roughed up, so I take a sip of Mohammed's potent brew, and with it tingling in my throat and warming my stomach I lift the bow to the strings. Most of the people tonight are caught up in the festive atmosphere, are introducing themselves, chatting and ordering drinks. Loud waves of laughter surge occasionally from Marie's table — they're the drunkest of the bunch. So I bring the bow down hard, making a cloud of rosin as I begin the first fiddle tune, slamming my foot with every beat. The bar joins in, clapping and nodding their heads with an occasional whoop. Their enthusiasm pushes me to play louder, faster, with even more energy, not even considering wrong notes or intonation. It's the *esprit* that counts. With all the clapping and cheering, Mohammed's bar is almost beginning to resemble a genuine East Coast pub, though a real fiddler would scoff at my classically trained attempt. I should be standing up and *shredding* bow hairs, with my whole leg pounding the beat.

Passers-by on the street are drawn in by the joyous vibe. There is something pleasing about the predictability of these tunes. There are no surprises and even the minor melodies are so vigorous they end up sounding cheerful. I glance up a few times and see that Kosuke has arrived and is talking with Céline and Brigitte. Sophie, a writer who interviewed me for an article about busking, is also here. So is Lionel, a folk singer I met while playing near the Pompidou. Drinks are steadily consumed, which keeps Mohammed busy. He is rushing to and from the counter, taking orders and offering his punch to newcomers. Between pieces, he thrusts his own beer glass into the air and toasts to the music, which causes the tiny bar to explode with roaring and stomping. I grin out at the audience. Some are strangers, but most are familiar faces, all people I've met through music. Tonight, clapping and drinking and cheering is the result of randomness and attraction, a gift from Paris herself.

SUDDENLY I'M AWARE OF IT, the jagged winter rain has softened to nurturing showers, which are beginning to breathe life into flower boxes. The sun is showing itself more, slipping out from between the sheets of clouds for hours at a time — enough to inspire dark buds along tree branches. The feeling of it pouring across my face is so novel I end up stopping on the street and slipping into a mini daze. Playing is getting easier with the rising temperatures, and passersby are beginning to relax again. Winter is losing its footing. Coats have been giving way to spring jackets, and today short-sleeved shirts appear, exposing the first elbows of the year.

As I play for these new spring specimens, the sweet sting of nostalgia hits me. I realize that soon I'll be going back to Jérémie's place and Kosuke will be leaving for a trip to the UK. We may never see each other again.

That night he comes home after his Indian dance class zinging. "Let's go roller blading!" he says.

"Huh? Now?" I look out the window. It's already getting dark.

"It'll be fun," he says. "I've been practising. I'm much better at it now."

I haven't been out since my fall along the canal, but my roller blades are sitting right by the door and Kosuke is already heading to his room to get his, so I reluctantly dig out my wrist guards from the laundry pile in the corner of my room.

We start off without direction. The night is cool, but we're soon flushed from our strides. I follow Kosuke down a side street, and after a few minutes we come upon a roundabout with an abandoned building in the middle. We circle around it, over and over, increasing our speed and confidence with each rotation. The rhythmic scraping of the blades against the pavement puts us in a trance. We push faster, harder, with no regard for our physical selves, and I soon lose sense of my body altogether. I don't know how long we've been going around before Kosuke suddenly breaks the vertigo and veers up a small street on the right, then to the left. There are no cars, so we claim the middle, allowing our strides to become long and exaggerated.

"Keep going," Kosuke suddenly yells. "I'll go this way. We'll meet on the next street!"

He turns left and starts uphill. I keep straight, then at the next intersection go left. After a few minutes I discover that it doesn't go all the way up but curves to the right again. I follow it around the corner, hoping it will veer back around, but it only twists more to the right. I race back to where Kosuke and I split ways, but I can't see him anywhere.

The euphoria shifts to panic. It's completely dark now, and I can barely see. Cold sky spittle is starting to dampen my face and clothes. I skate forward with increasingly frantic strides, gazing up each intersecting street. Kosuke could have taken any of these, but as far as I can tell each one is deserted. I go up and down them, squinting in the thick greyness for Kosuke-sized shadows. After about half an hour of scouring, I realize with a flash of fear that I have no idea how to get back home. Really, no idea. The streets are foreign and silent, save for the rain slapping against the pavement. And Kosuke is gone.

Shivering, I stop to attempt some rational thought. If I stay put, I'll only get wet and will never find my way home. If I keep moving I *might* find Kosuke, I *might* find my way back, and I *might* lessen my likelihood of hypothermia. So I take off, slower now, into the black rain.

My hoodie and jeans are soon drenched and my shivering intensifies. I call Kosuke's name a few times, but my voice is lost in the dampness. I reach a larger street, and since I have no idea which way to turn, I choose randomly — left. I keep a steady pace and stopping at each intersection to squint up and down. The first three streets are empty, but on the fourth I see a small blob in the middle, nearly invisible in the shadows.

"Kosuke?" I yell, as I race toward the figure, which as I approach I see is turned sideways, lying on the road. It is Kosuke, propped on his elbows, blinking in the falling rain.

"Kosuke! Are you OK?"

"Yes," he says. "I fell. I am just so miserable."

I help him off the ground and we continue, arm in arm, down the street. It's teeming with cold rain now, and we're no closer to home, but now that we've reunited my panic has been reduced to a manageable thrum. We return to the larger street, and, clutching onto each other's wet sleeves, struggle to maintain control during our descent. As we near the bottom, we come upon a man hunched behind an umbrella and starting up the hill.

"*Excusez-moi!* I say as we clumsily slow to a stop, swaying back and forth trying not to fall. The man peers out from under his umbrella and his eyes widen when I ask directions for Les Vallées. He tells us we're far, very far. We'll have to take a train. There's a station at the end of the street.

Kosuke and I spend thirty minutes huddled and shivering in a little glass shelter on the train platform. There are no gates at these suburban stations, so when the train finally arrives, we glide ticketless onto the empty car and ride three stops to Les Vallées.

"That was fun," Kosuke says, as we ride up the cage elevator to our apartment, drenched and nearing collapse. I study his pale face. His mouth is slightly upturned. His dark eyes radiate with kindness, as they always do, even when he's drunk or lying on the pavement in the rain. I still can't tell when Kosuke is joking. Maybe a part of him always is, just a little.

We've been each other's sidekicks for the winter. Two hibernating creatures holed up in our suburban den, sharing teabags, Nutella and chocolate chunk granola. Now with the winter receding we must venture out on our own, out into the wilds of the urban environment. Me to Paris. Kosuke to Scotland. Both of us reclaiming our solitary styles. I hope to take some of Kosuke with me, though. His lightness. His fearlessness. His gentle kindness. And I'll keep roller blading, no matter how many times I fall. Not falling was never the point. I know that now.

BOUREE

In Les Vallées my circadian rhythm slowed to that of the town. All the rain and grey made me sleepy. I traded coffee for tea and slept a lot, nestled in the scratchy covers of a dead woman. Her ghost lingered — in her things that her daughter wasn't ready to deal with and in the fibres of the carpet that she had tread upon for years until it had become thin and faded.

Now that I'm back in Jérémie's apartment, my heart rate has picked up again. Colours have brightened. New spring leaves appear almost florescent as they flip outwards. The streets are thick with odours of bakeries, perfume shops and rotisseries. This place is alive. It throbs. It honks. It sings. It screams. The sidewalks have swelled, and as I walk toward *Place des Vosges,* I make unflinching eye contact with those I pass, smiling at strangers and even chirping a few "*bonjours*" to those who smile back. I have a drunken lack of inhibition. I am in love again, with this city, and with everyone in it.

The painters greet me with kisses. George is wearing a beret and a scarf and is smoking a pipe. Maâmar is still wearing his tuque. He's the only Parisian I know who owns one. His gloves have the fingers cut out, like mine, and he is working on a new painting of the square, a night scene with a crescent moon and a spooky purple aura.

The archway is free, so I set my case down and take out my violin. The music flows with renewed joy and ease. Once I am warmed up with a few easy pieces, I launch into new ones I practised over the winter. It's warm enough outside now that I can introduce them to the street. I start with the A Major Handel Sonata. The first two movements are filled with trills, short chirpy bowings and syncopated rhythms, and the slow movement is so short it's like a passing thought before we're back into fast, playful triplets. My violin is bright and cheerful today, almost as if I've changed instruments. I beam at passersby, and they respond with smiles and nods and coins, and one older guy tosses in a 20 Euro bill.

After *Place des Vosges* I saunter over to play at *Palais-Royal*, where a guy puts a fistful of purple tulips in my case, probably plucked from the royal garden. David, the Belgian, stops to listen for a while, before kissing my hand and moving on to panhandle on the other side of the garden. Actors from the *Comédie Française* nod at me on their way to rehearsal, and Rakel, the pipe store owner, stops on her way back from lunch to request an extra lesson this week. There is another gypsy song she's dying to learn. A father and daughter dance together under the archway as I play through a Bach gavotte. An ancient woman dressed all in white with skin like paper stops and says to me, "Never, ever stop playing."

On days like today, when the music is as smooth as cream, when the coins pile up, shiny and hot, when smiles are everywhere, I think I could busk forever.

WHEN I ARRIVE BACK at the apartment in the early evening, a book leaps out at me from Jeremie's crowded bookshelf as I walk in the door. The spine, sandwiched between two musicology text books, is an unassuming shade of dark grey with white lettering, but it is the title that catches my attention: *Le violon interior*, by Dominique Hoppenot. Shit! All this time, the manifesto of Tim's metaphysical violin method was close enough for me to reach without getting out of bed.

I slip the book from its perch and flip through the pages. There are a few sketches showing the positioning of the violin and bow, but most of it is text. I've never read a book in French, but I'll have to try. It's the only way to get to the information locked inside. It'll be a damn struggle, but the fundamentals of Tim's method are in here waiting.

Later that night, after a roller blade along the canal and a tomato salad, I sit on the mattress with my back against the wall and make my way slowly through the first chapter, reading several sentences twice to get the meaning. Spoken French is easier than written. It has a smaller vocabulary and includes elements of sign language, intonation and expression that team up to create meaning. Now, though, it's just me and the printed words. As I read through, the voice in my head is monotone, with stutters and stops, like a pre-schooler doing an oral reading test. I force myself not to look words up in the dictionary and press on through the dense undergrowth of elegant phrases, hoping that by the end of the chapter meaning will unfurl into something tangible.

The first chapter is called *Le mal du violon,* and discusses the hardships associated with the violin — everything from physical pain to psychological damage. The violin, Hoppenot writes, can become an enemy and a source of pain. The pleasure of playing is often taken away through the continuous emphasis on technique and the neglect of emotional components, such as joy and expression.

I have been lucky, I realize, because the violin did not actually become painful in the way that Hoppenot is describing until I studied it in university. Before that, my teacher taught a balance of technique and emotion, gently correcting my technical imperfections without compromising my motivation. My lessons often involved visualization and imagination, which emphasized the emotional aspects of music.

"Think of a little brat in the schoolyard. Play this line like that," she'd say from her teaching chair, a steaming mug of herbal tea cupped between her palms. When she rose to correct my hand position, her fingers were hot and comforting.

"You have to have a split personality in this section," she said once, when I was working on a Beethoven sonata. "Think of a woman who tells her grown children how much she regrets not spending time with them when they were little and in the same sentence asks them how they like her new curtains." Later, when I was working on a Mozart concerto, she put on Verdi's *La Traviata* to show me the heart breaking lyrical passages in the final act, where Violetta is dying of tuberculosis and pining for her lover. In these ways, she taught me that expression was a critical element, and not solely dependent on technique.

It was in university that I experienced the debilitating pain that Hoppenot refers to. That's when the focus fell squarely on what was *wrong*. Though my school was mild compared to others — I can only imagine the vibe at Julliard — technique reigned. For the first few months, I had to relearn basic elements, tilt my wrist higher, bend my index finger less, and instead of learning pieces, I was assigned exercises to correct the "problems." The music disintegrated into a pile of notes, and each one was a battle, as I tried to juggle intonation, clean shifts, left elbow slant, right wrist bend, supple right hand, straight bow, wider vibrato and lower right elbow. Expression was suffocating amongst the technical requirements, and the attention on the physical aspects made me hyper aware of my body and hopelessly self-conscious. As the music fell apart, I began to fear my violin. If I wasn't practising, I was ravaged by guilt and a constant hum of anxiety. As soon as I opened my violin case, a different frequency of anxiety would flood through me — fears of not being good enough, of failing, of being judged. I unwittingly turned my professor into a father figure, whose love and attention I craved, and the violin was the only tool I had to get it. As my anxiety mounted, so did the shakes, and at night I would toy with quitting the violin. It would be a form of death to abandon it, after all I had invested, but eventually I couldn't see an alternative. I wasn't the only one suffering. I saw my peers storm out of master classes, weep after private lessons and stagger red-eyed out of the practice rooms.

I jam a pillow behind my back and continue reading as a gentle night breeze seeps in the window beside me. The violin, Hoppenot writes, is a notoriously difficult instrument to master. *And I am far from mastering it,* I think. My professor once told me that when he was a student he virtually lived in the practice room. He would play all night long and be woken, shivering and bleary eyed, when the custodian walked in with cleaning buckets the next morning. Maybe he told me that story to demonstrate what level of dedication was required to "succeed."

It was obvious I wouldn't. Any improvements I made in the practice room I lost during lessons, when my body trembled and my heart went haywire.

"This is the violin world," I thought at the time, "where music is serious, everyone follows one path, and everyone is judged according to specific criteria." Technical ability above all else. Sensitivity was part of it, but farther down. And creativity and joy barely made the list.

At the end of the first chapter, Hoppenot suggests that if musicians and pedagogues could understand that teaching methods can evolve, the violin would stop being simply a difficult, tyrannical instrument that we struggle to master, and become an authentic voice allowing those who truly seek it access to themselves and to resonate their inner string.

FUELLED BY THE FIRST CHAPTER of Hoppenot's book, I call Tim and ask for a lesson.

"Of course!" he says. "I'd be happy to give you one."

Since we both live in small studio apartments, we arrange to meet in the *Palais-Royal* garden. I arrive five minutes early on another coat-less afternoon with a kind breeze and soft warm light radiating from behind a thin layer of clouds. Tim arrives five minutes late, walking briskly with an emphatic grin, his violin case swung over his shoulder. He's wearing a frayed brown corduroy vest jacket and his wiry grey curls lap around his face.

"Wonderful to see you," he says, as he sets his violin case on the bench. He gives me the *bises*, and his sweet grass scent lingers in the air. "If you're ready, let's get started."

As I open my case, I don't feel the usual debilitating nervousness. This is not an average violin lesson. It's about authentic voice, the joy of playing, and self-expression. This time, I'm seeking access to myself. I'm looking for my inner string.

Tim takes my violin and gently positions it under my chin,

almost completely perpendicular to my body. Without a shoulder rest, it sits painfully against my collarbone. I clamp my chin hard to maintain my grip, but still have to support it with my left hand. It feels weird. It feels wrong.

"You'll have to get a new chin rest," says Tim. "One that sits in the middle of the violin instead of on the left. Now, instead of your thumb to the side, it bends back and goes under the neck of the violin like this." He adjusts my hand so that the pad of my thumb, the place where violin teachers draw happy faces to make sure it remains perpendicular to the neck, is completely hidden from view. This adjustment of the left hand makes my left arm twist farther under the instrument at a painfully contorted angle. Again, it feels forced and I can't help wincing.

"Good!" says Tim. "Great!"

Passers-by are staring at us. I blink helplessly. My left arm aches already. Tim tightens my bow and puts it in my right hand, then he raises my arm above the strings.

"Perfect," he says with a satisfied nod. "Of course it won't feel natural at first. That's normal. If you remember when you started the violin, it also did not feel natural."

I do remember. My teacher tucked the violin under my chin and brought my left arm down so that I was supporting the instrument with only my chin and shoulder.

"If I went to the store and back, would you still be in this position?" she asked.

"Yes," I said, but truthfully it felt terrible. It strained my neck, and I was terrified I would drop the instrument, which was a rental at the time.

"Try a two octave G major scale," says Tim.

I start slowly, doing my best to produce a clear tone, but the notes are muddled, as my left hand struggles to maintain the awkward position. Tim stands ready and pushes my thumb back into place several times when, out of habit, it slips beside the neck. The scale is uncertain and out of tune. My left arm burns.

"This is all I want you to practise for now," he says. "Getting into this position so your muscles become accustomed to it. Then you can work on a few scales. Put a sponge in place of the shoulder rest as first, if you find it too difficult without it."

I nod again. I haven't yet said a word. It's humbling to be in the role of student again, and this new position is foreign and difficult. It will take a lot of work to get my limbs to agree to such angles, and that blissful meditative state, I realize now, is a long way away.

After I play the scale again with only slight improvement, Tim gets his violin out to demonstrate. He begins the third movement of the Bach G Minor Partita, gliding effortlessly through its fury of 16th notes. His fingers move expertly up and down the fingerboard, shifting seamlessly and landing in tune despite the severe twist of his left arm. As he plays, he stares in the direction of his fingers but his eyes are vacant and unblinking.

"You're a busker, so you know what it means to be in the Now," Tim says, when he reaches the first repeat and lowers his violin. "You've definitely tuned into it."

I nod. I know what he means — that tenuous state where time stands still and conscious thought ceases, a blend of hyper awareness and sleep. I dip in and out of it, but it never lasts for long. I've never been fully immersed, not the way Tim is when he plays.

HE CONTINUES TO RAVE about this blissful state and the importance of being aware of only the present moment. "When you can let go of the past and the future and concentrate on the Now," he says, "that is true freedom, Nisha. And that's the beauty of the method. It helps you get there." As he sets his violin in its case, he adds, "With the sound coming in both your ears equally and the instrument vibrating against your body, you can become one with the music and with the world."

With our violins resting in their open cases, we sit on a bench. Tim talks while I listen and nod. It is increasingly clear that this is more than a violin method and more than a state — it is a complete lifestyle. He meditates for several hours a day and eats only a bowl of rice in the morning. His existence, as he describes it, is simply varying degrees of what he refers to as the Now. The present. He deepens it through meditation, with and without the violin, and even on the street he is able to distance himself from his surroundings, or rather *become* his surroundings by erasing the boundary of where he ends and everything else begins.

"What you're doing is moving beyond thought," he says. "While you go about your day, try to separate yourself from your thoughts, maintain awareness, be in the Now."

The more he speaks, the less I think I understand what it means to be in the Now. *Does it mean without memories? Without concern for the future?* If so, it's not far from what I'm already living, an escape from my past and without plans for the future. But it goes deeper than that. It's a constant state of acceptance and awareness. *Can one live in an effervescent city like Paris and maintain this calm, blissful state? Doesn't one have to be sedentary, alone on the edge of some reclusive cliff?* I don't ask Tim these questions. Not yet. It's all too new. Tim takes out his notebook and scrawls out a reading list for me, books by Eckhart Tolle, Ramana Maharshi, and Osho. Then he stands, zips his case shut and says, "I have to go now."

He kisses my cheeks. "Good luck," he says. "Let me know when you're ready for another lesson." And then he's gone, into the crowd of baby carriages and slow-moving tourists. I remain sitting for a long time, my thoughts like soccer balls, ricocheting off my skull walls.

"*VOUS NE POUVEZ pas jouer ici!*"

I pull my bow off the string and stare at the man jogging on the spot in front of me. He's wearing baggy yellow sweatpants, a sky-blue jacket and a purple headband that pushes his hair into sweaty grey spikes. His eyes have the gloss of an overworked philosopher, someone capable of theorizing life's deepest mys-

teries but unable to match his own socks. He glares at me as he
jounces up and down, but I maintain a cool gaze. Without a
police badge, he has no authority to stop me from playing. He's
probably just a local lunatic.

"I live here at *Place des Vosges*," he says. "And the residents
have voted against music. No more musicians. If you continue
to play," he warns, "I'll call the police."

My Adam's apple contracts and my tongue becomes heavy
and useless. *It can't be true.* Musicians have been playing here
forever. It couldn't be over, just like that. I search the man's eyes
for understanding, or at the very least a hint of empathy.

"*La vie n'est pas juste*," he says with a grin, and jogs to the
end of the archway, where he waits for me to pack up before
disappearing around the corner. I stand there for a few minutes,
paralyzed by the pain of rejection and what this means for my
livelihood. No more *Place de Vosges?* Finally, I trudge away, along
the *Rue de Rivoli* with what feels like a hot chestnut wedged in
my throat. It's as if I've just been exiled from the family home.

THE NEXT DAY, I decide to return to *Place des Vosges* — for two
reasons. First, I am beginning to doubt the man's authority. Only
the extremely rich live here and he looked more like one of the
sleeping-bagged homeless guys than an aristocrat. Second, *Place
des Vosges* is too precious to abandon just because an eccentric
jogger told me to. If I've learned anything in France it's to fight
for what you think is right. Rules are rampant, but they are more
like guidelines and most often ignored.

I'm barely halfway through my first piece when a monster
BMW motorcycle with a wide plastic dome blasts up onto the
sidewalk. I leap backwards to let it pass, but it stops in front of
me. The driver is dressed in a dark pinstriped suit. He is strapped
in and leaning back as if lounging in an easy chair. His grey hair is
combed back and his face is stoic with a hint of a menacing sneer
— the only feature that reveals him as the jogger from yesterday.

"*Bon, j'appelle la police*," he says, adding that the police will take my violin. "You'll regret it."

He revs the engine and speeds back onto the street. I return my violin to its case and slump to the ground under the archway with my back against the cool stone. I blink away oncoming tears, as a group of oblivious tourists shuffles toward me, taking pictures of the archway and oohing in gallery windows.

I don't know how long I'm sitting before I hear, "*Bonjour!*" I look up and Tim is beaming down at me, violin slung at his side.

"Tim!" I stand to greet him. "I got kicked out by a guy on a motorcycle!"

"Oh yes, that fool," he smiles almost wistfully, as if remembering a schoolyard bully rendered harmless over time. "He's been bothering us for years."

"So he does live here?"

"Yeah." Tim points to the other side of the square. "Over there."

It's far enough away that the man couldn't possibly hear the sound of my violin from his palace.

"Are you going to play?" I ask.

"I was planning on it."

"What about the guy?"

Tim shrugs.

I sit back down against the wall as Tim, without even a warm up note, begins the Bach Chaconne. The archway suddenly fills with an arc of swelling melody and Tim's stare deepens as he dissolves into the notes. His left hand stretches wide to accommodate the opening double and triple stops, then slides gracefully up and down the fingerboard for a passage of calm before the series of runs. To my amazement, passers-by mostly ignore him. A few try to make eye contact, but Tim's gaze is elsewhere and they quickly move on. I am so enthralled with his playing that I don't even hear the distant growls, until suddenly the motorcycle rips onto the sidewalk, devouring the music with its roaring engine.

The man looks at Tim with narrowed eyes. "*Il est interdit de jouer ici,*" he says.

Tim smiles warmly, as if at an old friend and says, "*Certaine-*

ment, monsieur."

"Partez tout de suite!" The man commands. His scowl deepens. It looks as if he might spit on us.

"Bien sûr, monsieur. Pas de problème." Tim packs his violin away while the motorcycle man waits. *"Bonne journée."*

Tim's smile glints like a shield. The man revs once, then blasts away on his bubbled bike.

I glower, sweaty with rage. Not only is this guy obscenely rich, he must not even work. He's appointed himself the full-time music police to "protect" the citizens of *Place de Vosges*, who also must not work or else why would they care if musicians played during the day?

"You were so nice to him," I say.

I thought all French people, even enlightened spiritual ones, became fiery in the face of injustice. That was the impression I got from the protests I've seen — thousands of men, women, children, seniors, and adolescents, charging down the boulevard carrying banners, flags and noise makers, megaphones and masks and hand painted signs. They blow whistles and thrust their fists in the air bellowing with such fervour it sends shivers through me.

"Well, there's no need to be aggressive," Tim shrugs.

"So, you're stopping?"

"I'll come back another day," he says. "Let's go to the media library. Maybe we can find some violin duets."

I nod and follow him to *Rue de Rivoli*, and as we walk together my fury deteriorates from the softness of Tim's presence. He tells me he's taking the train to visit his mother tomorrow. "She's a millionaire in the south of France and I can barely feed myself." He laughs. "Then I'm going to Amsterdam for a week. The busking is better there. And," he grins. "I can get hash much more easily."

The sun is blasting with confidence. There will be no showers today. It would be a perfect day to busk, but my heart needs more time to recuperate after this devastating development.

After half an hour we reach *Les Halles*, a massive underground complex in the very centre of Paris, which houses a cinema, a shopping centre with hundreds of boutiques, a food court, a swimming pool, and several converging Metro and RER lines. I've seen pictures of this place in the early 1900s when it was the main Parisian market, the *Marché des Halles*, with piles and piles of fruits and vegetables, wooden wheelbarrows carrying pallets stacked high with sausages or lettuce, cheese wheels or wine, and thousands of merchants selling their wares, shouting their prices, drinking at the nearby cafés, then later visiting the ladies of the night along *Rue St. Denis*. The chaos must have been staggering — all those bodies scuttling about with wide baskets filled with provisions for the week, all that yelling, the bloody carcasses and the sour stench of sweat and rotten vegetables. Now, as we slide down an infinite escalator to the sterile shopping centre all I smell is perfume and plastic.

Tim shows me to the Media library, which is a musical paradise, with entire walls of scores, hundreds of CDs and DVDs, multiple bookshelves and magazine racks. I goggle at the sheet music, flip through a book of Eckhardt-Gramatte solo violin caprices, a compilation of Beethoven sonatas, and some Vivaldi concertos.

"Maybe they have the Leclair sonatas for two violins," says Tim.

We search for a while, though I'm not sure why. Even if they did have the music we're looking for, neither of us is eligible to get a library card since we don't have official addresses. Administratively, we don't exist. After a while we pry ourselves away empty handed.

"We could try the Bach violin concerto," Tim says. It's a piece anyone who has learned to play classical violin has studied at some point. He stops on a small landing between two staircases as we exit *Les Halles*. It is half sheltered and half exposed, with the sublime Saint-Eustache gothic church towering behind.

"Here?" I'm sceptical. It's still part of the commercial complex. Surely there are cameras with security men just watching in waiting.

"Why not? If we get asked to leave, we'll leave. If not, *tant mieux.*"

We get our violins out and I push my open case forward. We pound the concerto's strong, regal intro with confidence and manage to stay together through much of the sinuous counter point and staggered rhythms, but halfway through our memories falter and the music trails off.

We laugh and lower out violins. I'm energized by the power of playing with another musician, especially another violinist. The way it pushes the music forward, the way you have to listen differently to yourself and to the other player, constantly adjusting.

"That was fun," Tim says, putting his violin away. "And this is an OK spot."

It's true, this staircase has potential. It is heavily frequented, even during the day, with a gentle lingering resonance, and the newly renovated *St. Eustache* provides a scenic backdrop. We even managed to make 3 Euros, which we split between us.

We'll both be back, I'm sure of it. Especially with the BMW-bubbled guard patrolling our beloved *Place des Vosges*.

THE SUN IS GENEROUS and warm as I play at *Palais-Royal* for a couple of hours in the afternoon. It's the right kind of hot, not the kind that encourages swearing and collapsing but the kind that is comfortable, that encourages ice cream eating and pretty dresses. The coins flow and the music is easy and sweet. I stare at all the babies and they always, *always* stare back.

"*C'est la Princesse du Palais-Royal!*" David says to Olaf. They wave at me and skip past the archway. They're in a good mood. Maybe they're having a prosperous day too.

In the early evening I return to the staircase where Tim and I played yesterday, just in time to catch the homeward bound locals. The sun is lower, the light softer, and the footsteps on the shiny steps are subdued, like tiptoes. The traffic on the staircase is steady. Most people are on their way up, fresh out of the Metro system. It's a viscous blend of suited men with brief cases, professional women in high heels and skirts, and a stream of disoriented tourists, fresh from the airport and clogging the flow as they drag their suitcases up each stair. The locals who are not already listening to their MP3 players look up in surprise when they see me. They've probably never seen a musician here.

The longer I play, the more I understand why. It isn't the busking gem Tim and I had hoped for. It's a small, hidden nook along a busy trajectory — the travellers have yet to regain their individual status bestowed by the outside world. They are still part of the rolling masses, and by the time they spew onto the steps, notice me, decided what they think about me and whether they want to give me a coin, it's too late. They're patting their pockets or shoving their hands in their purses as they head up the second staircase. Then they glance back apologetically and continue forward. Everyone has somewhere to be here. There is a frantic feel, like the last 100 metres of a marathon, when racers, numb to pain and outside noise, start to sprint. For many people here, this is the end of an hour-long commute, the final stretch until they reach open sky. A good busking spot needs more than just traffic. It needs a preparation zone, where people hear the music from a distance, decide if they like it and locate a coin before they even arrive. There needs to be sufficient space for people to stop and listen or at the very least not risk getting rear-ended if they stoop to drop a coin. The staircase simply doesn't pass the test.

I've already decided to stop at the end the piece, when a guy in a purple collared shirt slows and drops a euro in my near-empty case. He smiles and leans on the railing beside me to listen. His jeans and helmet of dark brown hair that billows around his head gives him a PhD student air, but his stiff collared shirt suggests professionalism. He's good looking, too. *Very* good looking. Every time I glance up he looks away, but when the piece ends our eyes meet.

"*Tu joues bien,*" he says.

I ask if he plays an instrument. He laughs, which I take as a no. He motions to the staircase and asks if he could read while I play.

"*Avec plaisir*," I say.

He pulls a book out from the back pocket of his jeans and sits at the bottom of the second staircase, while I play through a few pieces. I'm making no money, but I'm playing for him now, and that is compensation enough. Something strange is going on. I can't keep my eyes off him. The music requires very little brainpower. I could play these pieces asleep. My mind, my *attention*, is on him. Every time he looks over at me a cool stream of smoke smoothes down my spine and circles in my stomach.

Inner alarm bells sound. *Don't let him go!* I segue from one piece to the next, trying to build up my near-empty reservoir of courage. He could have a girlfriend, a wife or even kids. He could be gay. He might only be interested in my music. My heart thrums louder and off time with the gavotte I'm mindlessly moving my fingers to. The thought of him rising and disappearing up the steps inspires a flash of panic, so I stop at the next cadence, not even bothering to finish the piece, and fire him a smile. All he has to do is come over, I decide, then I'll ask him for a drink.

I kneel beside my case, remove the few coins I made, and lay my violin in its place. From my periphery I see him approaching and my heart ignites. I zip my case closed and stand to face him. His blue-green eyes are the same colour as mine. I wonder if he can see my pulse pounding in my neck. His unhurried demeanour tells me I don't have to ask him anything. The attraction is so tangible I can taste it.

We walk up the stairs together. He is a head taller than me and walks at an energetic clip. He tells me his name is Frédéric. "*Et toi?*"

"Nisha," I say it slowly so I won't have to repeat.

"What does it mean?" he asks.

"It means night in Sanskrit," I say. "And Frédéric?"

His laugh is incredible, like a high-pitched tropical birdcall, so loud and unusual it makes me laugh too.

"Well Frédéric is a pretty common name, you know. I think it means a peaceful ruler. *Un gentil chef.*"

We head along the pedestrian *Rue Montorgueil*. It's a chaotic mess of baguette, wine and cheese buyers, and line-ups that spill onto the street — locals picking up provisions for dinner that night. We have to zigzag around shoppers and yappy-dog walkers and slow-moving tourists.

"So are you a philosopher?" I ask, noticing the book title: *Humain, trop humain. Un livre pour esprits libres.* Who else carries around Nietzche in their back pocket?

The bird laugh quivers in my ear again. "No, no. I work in pharmaceuticals."

"A pharmacist?" Now I picture him in a lab coat, filling prescriptions.

"No, I work in logistics," he says. "I make sure medical supplies get to hospitals and pharmacies throughout Europe."

He stops in front of a café called *Le Tambour*, with a red exterior and an outside terrace. "I'm meeting a friend here for dinner," he says, "but we could have a beer in the meantime."

My heart swoops with disappointment. I wanted him all to myself. I wanted the night to stretch on and for the outside world to make a dome around us and melt to murmurs and blotches of colour. I wanted to lose myself in this strange new state that has taken hold of me with the strength and rapidity of an injection.

We take a seat at an outside table. Right away, a "*Bonjour!*" blasts from behind. I turn to see a colossal man, thick in the middle, with a long flowing beard. He has a white apron tied around his waist and a meaty hand rests on his hip in waiting.

We both order Leffes.

The man lumbers to the bar and returns with two thick round goblets of honey coloured beer. Frédéric and I clink them together and smile. His face is symmetrical, and not with chiselled warrior angles but soft, kind ones. His eyes are sharp with intelligence, calm, and aware — but without judgement. He is quick to offer wholehearted laughter, but when he starts talking about the Red Cross work he does with homeless people in his spare time, his face becomes solemn. He switches to English, which he speaks with heavy zeds and rolled Rs.

"They are not the problem," he says of the homeless population. "Society is. Most of them suffer from mental illness and they need treatment. Most of them came from large, poor families. Homelessness is completely preventable."

His features tighten like an archery bow preparing to fire.

I tell him about my homeless buddies at *Palais-Royal* and he beams. "I *know* them!" he says.

"You *do?*"

"Yes, that's where I volunteer, in the 1st and 2nd *Arrondissements.*"

We work ourselves into a frenzy, discussing government failures to deal with homelessness, empty election promises, and the general lack of research on *la grande exclusion*, those who have been ignored and forgotten by society. Frédéric has fire in him, a steady flame that provides warmth, makes my fingertips tingle and my chest expand. This fire, I realize as I listen to him talk about the homeless, could also be used in battle. His hands clench and sparks sail off his tongue as he declares the need to protect the homeless. The longer we talk, the more attached I feel myself getting, as if tiny anchors have linked us and if he stood suddenly I would be pulled up with him.

"*Désolé pour le retard!*"

I turn to see a bald middle-aged man approaching our table. He's round, flustered and out of breath.

"*Nisha, je te présente Bruno.*"

I'd forgotten all about Frédéric's friend. I stand to give him the *bises* and reluctantly suggest that I be on my way. As I hoped, they both insist I stick around for another beer. The wizard man is already standing behind us, and Frédéric orders us a round. Then both Frédéric and Bruno produce cigarette packs.

"I only bought these because I knew I was going to be seeing him," Bruno says, pointing a thumb at Frédéric, who shrugs and lights his cigarette with a plastic Bic lighter.

The beers become a bottle of wine, then food, then another bottle. When the night air gets chilly we move inside the restaurant, which is long and narrow and decorated with an Alice in Wonderland collection of Paris street signs, woodcarvings and clocks. The bar stools are made from old bus stop signs and along one wall is an illuminated Metro map. Florescent fish swim in a glowing aquarium along the bar. Shining stoplights give the place a psychedelic feel. It's packed with diners and drinkers, and there is so little space between the tables everyone seems to be eating together, as if at some friendly banquet. We have long talks with our neighbours. First we discuss tourism with a gay couple from New York. Later we tackle an immigration conversation with three inebriated Algerian men. The communication is fuelled by wine, laughter and hand gestures and the whole place quivers with unabashed expression.

After the Algerian men leave, Bruno and Frédéric begin discussing the current Israel-Hezbollah war. Their views clash instantly, since Bruno is Jewish and Frédéric just got back from visiting a friend in Lebanon. Their conversation swiftly escalates to a full-fledged argument. Bruno defends Israel's military actions in loud shrieks, while Frédéric pounds the table with his fist, slamming Israel for its recent airstrikes on Lebanon. The two men speak in French, fast and furiously. Their voices raise exponentially, with increasing frustration. As the tension swells, their drinking follows suit. Bruno's face becomes deep red and sweat drips dramatically down his face, while Frédéric's voice breaks and trembles. My mouth goes dry with worry and I sit completely still, staring at the table and wondering how their friendship could ever survive such an incident.

Finally, when the wine is depleted, they fall silent. Bruno sighs and wipes his face with a serviette.

"*Ça va?*" My voice is a squeak after their booming rhetoric.

Bruno turns to me, confused. "*Bah oui,*" he says.

Their argument seems to have been as natural as ordering their crèmes brûlées, simply another element to a satisfying meal. They appear to have even enjoyed it, and now they're relaxing in its aftermath. Then, as if no disagreement had transpired, Frédéric asks about Bruno's daughter, who also plays violin.

"She's great," Bruno says.

"His daughter is gorgeous," Frédéric tells me, and before the pang of jealousy can dig too deep, Bruno flips open his wallet to reveal a six year old girl with dark ringlets and a sweet shy mouth.

"I'm having a great time," Frédéric finally says, "but it's almost two in the morning, and I have to catch an early train tomorrow." He slowly rises to his feet.

We file out into the night. The Metros have long stopped running so we walk to the neighbouring street, which is busier, and Bruno flags down a taxi.

"*Merci. C'était un plaisir*," he says, before he slips into the back seat and disappears behind the tinted window.

There are a few moments of silence as Frédéric and I adjust from the loud, smoky establishment to abandoned streets, silent and damp, with a yellow glow coming from the street lamps.

"Are you tired?" asks Frédéric.

"Not at all," I say, though my head is fogged with wine and fatigue. "I always stay up late," I add, which is true, but usually not this late, and never after having had so much to drink.

"If you want," he says. "I could show you the view of the city from my rooftop."

"OK," I say, trying not to sound too enthusiastic. Nothing has happened yet and I don't want to assume anything. I'm analysing the situation with debilitating self-awareness, studying Frédéric for signs of affection or neutrality or boredom or infatuation. So far, it's hard to tell. Frédéric and I haven't been alone enough, yet, and he seems to give the I-really-like-you gaze to everyone.

"*Chouette*, follow me," he says.

We walk side by side snaking through the near-empty streets.

Despite the time, Frédéric stops at the historical plaques and translates them into English. "This plaque explains why this neighbourhood has so many Egyptian names," he says. "They were named during Napoleon's expedition in Egypt. It was fashionable to give Egyptian names to things. It was the beginning of the fascination with ancient Egypt." He points to the building above the plaque where three big head sculptures stare out into the shadows, their elf ears sticking out behind thick hair that spreads down to their shoulders. Above that I can make out some hieroglyph-like drawings of horses and chariots that in the darkness appear like cave paintings.

"Now we're on my street, *Rue D'Aboukir*," he says, as the street we're on dissolves into another one. "Actually Napoleon Bonaparte lived here once, back when he was just a poor guy and this was a crappy neighbourhood. Now it's chic. It's called the *Sentier*. It's famous for its clothing shops," he gestures to a boutique across the street. In the unlit window, I make out a rack of sparkly dresses and tapered jeans with sequins. "There are thousands of little brands waiting and hoping to be discovered," Fréderic adds. "Some well-known names started here. Naf Naf, for example. And Chevignon."

"Where are the clothes made?" I ask. My voice is thin in the damp night air.

"Some still make their stuff here," he says. "Mostly on the second floor. The clothing business used to be dominated by the Jewish community, but when the Chinese took an interest and started making clothes in China it was hard to compete, so lots of Jewish landlords converted entire floors into little apartments to rent to guys like me."

Frédéric stops at a narrow glass door and punches in his code. Five floors up, he turns the lock on his door. I follow him into an apartment of clinical cleanliness.

"My mother cleaned the place yesterday," he says.

I'm not sure what's worse, the idea that he is a clean freak or that his mother cleans his apartment.

"She is retired and a bit bored," he explains.

Books are everywhere. There are hundreds of them, lining all available wall space. One shelf is dedicated to thick art books with names I've never heard of. Another one is filled with graphic novels organized by series. One bookshelf is built right into the wall, with interior lights that cast an ambient glow on the gold page leaves of Balzac and Voltaire volumes. Through the closet door I see piles of soft cover books, three rows deep and threatening to topple.

"My apartment is small," he says apologetically.

"Not so much," I say.

It's at least three times bigger than my place, with a separate area for the kitchen, a full sized bathroom and the rest of the apartment is open-space. Frédéric's bed is in the far corner, smothered by a horizontal shelf packed solid with CDs and more books. By the window is a couch and two chairs. I claim the couch and hope he will join me, but Frédéric goes to the other side of the coffee table to sit in a small, blue, felted chair. I wonder if he plans on kissing me at all, or if I've misread the signs and he's just looking for a friend. My confidence is seriously starting to wither.

"Do you read *bandes desinées?*" he asks, motioning to his graphic novel collection.

"Just ones for kids," I say. "Astérix mostly."

"Aha. Astérix. Classic."

Frédéric launches into a detailed explanations of his favourite writers, artists and series, plucking volumes off the shelf and spreading them on the table. He speaks increasingly faster, and only in French. His eyes are red and glossed with fatigue, but his mouth keeps moving and his voice and soft consonants are as lulling as a car engine. A fierce fatigue descends. The steady drone of his voice cuts out as my eyelids fall shut. I pry them open again. He doesn't seem to have noticed. His voice continues to hum and my eyes close again. My head falls to the side, but I lack the strength to summon it back.

When I open my eyes again I see that Frédéric is already at the window.

"Shall we go on the roof?" he asks.

I struggle to stand on sleep-laden legs and follow him to the window, which gives onto a courtyard. I follow him out, and along the unstable scaffolding — that makes an outrageous clamour in the otherwise silent night air. On the other side of the courtyard is a shaky narrow ladder that leads to the roof. Frédéric scoots up and disappears over the side. I take my time, cautiously climbing the slippery rungs until I can step onto the precariously tilted roof.

Suddenly Frédéric's warm hand surrounds mine. At first I think he's helping to steady me as I waver on the slant, but he maintains his gentle grasp as he leads me to the edge of the building. We climb onto warped boards that lie over an upward extension of scaffolding and gaze out over the damp city. The lights that normally illuminate the monuments have long been extinguished.

"*Sacré Coeur* is over there," he says, pointing to the dark mound on our left. We're not holding hands anymore and I wonder if he had taken my hand in a friend way, a lover way or if he even grabbed it consciously at all. He now seems completely absorbed in the cityscape.

"That's the Montparnasse Tower," he says, motioning to the left with his head. "They built it to prove they could make a sky-scraper. Most French find it ugly. The Eiffel tower is over there." He points. "It was also considered ugly when it was built."

I lean forward for a better view and promptly lose my balance. Frédéric grabs my elbow and we sway back and forth for a moment on the shaky boards.

I lift my head to thank him and our mouths meet. His is warm and tastes faintly of *crème brûlée* and smoke. I clutch both his elbows to keep from falling over and our kiss deepens. He exhales through his nose and I breathe in his sweet smoky air. When our lips finally part we stand side by side in silence, gazing out over the buildings. Before long, the streetlights switch off in one big blink and the city lingers in blue-tinged darkness. Hand in hand, we are witness to the still moments between streetlights and sunrise.

A CRAZY THING HAS HAPPENED. Something outrageous. It's already apparent as Frédéric and I walk downstairs, bleary with fatigue, and push through the frosted glass door into the cool morning light and he kisses me good-bye before sprinting to catch a taxi to the train station: the city has changed. The sun is pure and potent, as if someone has just pulled sunglasses from my face. The buildings gleam like bleached bones, and as I walk down *Rue Montorgueil* the colours — fresh yellow flowers in black pails, a pyramid of oranges, rows of strawberry tarts, a window full of macaroons — are almost too much. Odours of croissants and fish and fresh fruit permeate the air. Even sounds are amplified: street cleaners spraying the cobblestone, passing scooters, clanging church bells. It's as if a dial has suddenly been cranked. The vibrancy of the city is not only fully accessible now, it's staggering. *This* is the Paris that people dream of visiting, the Paris that is shown in movies and described in books. I needed love to access the whole canvas, and now, here it is, a masterpiece unveiled. I stumble my way down the street, bewildered. In my hand is a bag of graphic novels. It's my glass slipper, the only thing that allows me to believe that I didn't dream Frédéric and our rooftop kiss.

The weekend that follows is a haze. I play at *Palais-Royal*, then try a spot in the Latin Quarter, where I'm chased away by a restaurant owner — a sour-faced woman who shoos her hand at me as if I'm a fly hovering over a steak. Normally my throat would have lumped up and I might have even slunk home discouraged, but I'm untouchable right now. Instead of taking the Metro in search of a new spot, I wander the Latin Quarter, where large men stand at the doors of restaurants to lure tourists with jokes and charming smiles. A round-bellied man whose job it is to break cheap china plates in front of a Greek restaurant winks at me before slamming another one against the cobblestone in front of the entrance. The smell of steamy gyros, French fries, falafels and crepes creates a greasy wave in the summer heat, and even *that* I find pleasing. It's part of the whole that is Paris. Even the urine soaked alleyways that I usually hurry past are charming to someone in my state. Same with the tiny dog turds from the little local terriers. And the crowded Metro. And the thick diesel fumes. This is madness.

On Sunday night Frédéric texts from the train. "Meet at the giant head in front of Saint-Eustache tonight at 7?"

"*Bien sûr!*" I write back. *Of course. Of course. Of course.*

I arrive a few minutes early with my violin, my notebook and a few extra clothes. The "head" is a sculpture the size of a car. It's round and smooth and tilted to the side, with a giant sandstone hand cupped close to the ear. I wait for Frédéric on its giant index finger. When he appears from behind the head, I jump down to greet him. We kiss like long lost lovers, then I take his hand and we start up the street to his house. My hand fits perfectly into his. His palm is warm against mine and his fingers curl around my knuckle. Linked to him like this, I feel mighty, as if we're a joined force, an entity of our own.

It's hard to talk about love and avoid clichés. The very nature of it is cliché. The drunken joy. The way your spine unfurls as you walk. The way your brain is highjacked by thoughts of the other person. *I wonder what they're doing now. And now?* The way you've lived your entire life without this person and suddenly they are imperative to your day. The self-abandonment as you hand your heart away, knowing it could be crushed. Perhaps the thrill of that potential crush is part of the rush, like riding your bike too fast down a hill on wet pavement. The crash would be so devastating, it makes the moments even more pure and sweet and magical. Maybe you know you're in love when you're no longer bothered by such clichés.

Frédéric and I race through the relationship stages like slalom skiers. Time miraculously stretches out before us and we devour the city with uncurbed voracity. We do everything together. I become one of those uninhibited lovers entwined on park benches, the ones I used to watch and silently curse because their affection accentuated my own loneliness. Frédéric and I talk and talk and talk with a near frantic urgency. My mouth is dry from saying so much. We have our whole lives to catch up on and our whole lives to live. Not to mention the present — according to Tim, the most important. French and English meld until I am no longer conscious of what language we're speaking. One night we listen to podcasts on atheist philosophy. Another night we watch Betty Boop cartoons until 2 a.m. I read him the only English novel he owns: *The Picture of Dorian Grey.* He reads me *Le Petit Chose* by Daudet. We stop at every historical plaque, and each new fact sharpens my image of Paris. A building I pass several times a week happens to be the oldest house in Paris, built in the 14th century. We stop outside of Bateau-Lavoir in Montmartre, an old piano factory that has been made into artist studios. It's where Picasso worked. I wouldn't have noticed it on my own. I was always too busy looking for playing spots. Now the history of the city is starting to unthaw.

Sleep seems like a waste of time, but once in a while, lying in bed, we'll fall unconscious mid-conversation. Our minds might be hyperactive, and our hearts on fire, but our bodies eventually decide to step in and close up shop. This love is a reckless love. We are losing ourselves in one another. We are losing a grip on who we were before we met. I am aware of it happening, but the truth is, I don't even care.

ONE SUNDAY AFTERNOON, Frédéric suggests we go to the *Place de la Bastille.* It's only a five-minute walk from *Place des Vosges,* but I had no idea that on Sundays it hosts the largest market in Paris. *Ah bon! How could I have missed this?* There are hundreds and hundreds of vendors.

We enter and start down a long row of produce — shiny eggplants, frizzy lettuce heads, bundles of fresh basil, mint, chives and oregano. I think back to my sad meals, the withered salads I used to make from the cheap produce down the street. The flabby carrots. The soggy cucumbers. Here, everything promises texture and flavour, crunch and juice and sweetness. I stop in front of a display of figs, some of which have been cut in half to show their deep burgundy interior.

"*Vous voulez essayer Madame?*" the vendor asks.

I nod, taken aback at being called *madame* for the first time. Until now, I've always been *mademoiselle*. I'm OK with it, though. I can handle *madame*. The man cuts me a quarter. It is unbelievably sweet, with the seeds lending a light, satisfying crunch. *It's like eating love,* I think. At its ripest moment.

"*Je vais en prendre,*" I say, taking a small handful.

We turn down the cheese aisle. Some of the cheeses here are arranged behind glass like valuable jewels. Some are giant wheels on pedestals, and the vendors yield machete-sized knives. Some are tiny, shrivelled, expensive balls of mould. Others are large hunks with the mould proudly present as green circles and black dots. We spend a while here, mulling and pointing and testing. I try one that tastes like it was harvested from milk festering between two cow teats. It is sour, with a beast-like tinge. Frédéric laughs as I try to mask my horror from the vendor. Spitting it out is not an option. Finally we reach a compromise: a creamy St. Nectare, an aged mimolette that looks like a slice of cantaloupe, and a ferocious roquefort because it's Frédéric's favourite. On our way home, we stop on *Rue Montorgueil* for a baguette, a fistful of daisies and a bottle of red wine that Frédéric plucks from the shelf without a flinch of hesitation.

On Saturdays when I play at *Palais-Royal*, Frédéric comes along with a book and reads in the garden. When I finish, we get a roasted vegetable panini from the nearby bakery and eat it near the fountain. Then I drop my violin back at home and, if the weather's good, we go back out to explore: covered passageways, hidden courtyards, wine bars and cafés, chocolate cake

and plum pie and Saint-Julien. On Sundays I play near the Solferino bridge before Bernard arrives. Frédéric brings a book then
too, but is usually too distracted to read — all the passers-by, all
the people who stop to talk, the gypsies, the tourists, the young
Parisian men wearing scarves even though it's summer. Frédéric watches the spectacle with amusement, and watches me play
with admiration. He has never had a music lesson in his life. For
him, it's as if I'm pulling doves out from my sleeves. At night we
sleep entwined — even in sleep we can't bear to be apart.

One day after work, Frédéric comes home with a green and
purple romanesco broccoli. It is huge and alien-like with spiral
tentacles. It looks like it belongs under the sea, if not on another
planet. "I don't know what to do with it," he says. "But it made
me think of you."

Instead of eating it, we go to the department store a twenty
minute walk away and pick up some plasticine and cotton balls
and blue sparkles. Then we spend hours turning Frédéric's coffee table into a fantasy land. We break the broccoli into small
pieces and scatter the cone-shaped flowerets along the wooden
surface. We pull the cotton into thin, delicate layers around our
psychedelic trees and toss the sparkles over everything. The rest
of the evening we spend moulding characters out of plasticine
for our new world. When we are finished, we have a mystical
land that we leave undisturbed until the flowerets get old, begin
to wither and rot.

I MEET TIM at *Palais-Royal* for another lesson. I've been working
on his method at home, playing scales and even maintaining
the position he's taught me as I practice (slowly) the presto of
Bach's Partita in G Minor. As long as I continue to play in the
street, though, I can't completely commit. When I'm busking, I
have to revert back to my old ways. I need my shoulder rest and
my thumb parallel to the neck to play properly. Tim assures me
that this new way of holding the instrument and the serene state
of mind that goes with it will take time to master. He stands in

front of me and corrects my posture immediately, whenever it slips. It requires so much concentration that by the end of the lesson I'm dizzy and exhausted. I lower my violin and sit on a bench, while Tim launches into the spiritual side of the method. "What you're trying to attain is a state of no-mind, of non-thought. Do you know what I mean?" he asks, taking a seat beside me.

"I . . . think so," I say.

I'm trying to keep up, but often Tim's language is too abstract for me to grasp completely. I learn most simply by watching him. His irises radiate with a special light source — deep and warm. I've seen it in others, too: religious people, people who meditate, and people who have done a lot of psychedelics. They possess a certain spark that instils in me both envy and fear. I'm beginning to worry that to attain it I will have to give up a chunk of myself. That I wouldn't be *me* anymore. Then again, Tim seems so *happy*. He looks at strangers as if they were his best friends. His resting face is a calm semi-smile. I've never seen him worried or upset or angry.

Today, though, he's busting with ultra-happiness, and as we're packing up, he explains, "My mother sent me a bunch of money last week. "I spent it all on recording equipment and a new computer."

"Of course you did." I laugh.

"Now I'm as broke as I ever have been," he says, "but I can finally work on my art projects. My next meal is of no concern." He shrugs.

"I believe you," I say.

Tim doesn't seem to have *any* concerns. Part of me wants this joy too. It's like he's tuned to a radio station on an open frequency most people haven't found.

Could I find it, I wonder, *with practice? And who would I be if I did? Don't joy and love exist at least partly through their contrast with sadness and loneliness? And isn't it wonderfully human to experience the whole gamut of emotion, the heart-wrenching along with the beauty? And even if I could eat a perfect pie for every meal, wouldn't I eventually want a little sand in there, a touch of something sour to keep things interesting? Or perhaps I'm just another stupid human addicted to suffering and pain, identifying with my past and fretting about the future.*

Tim's violin lessons are often more like philosophy classes. I don't leave with a tune in my head but with questions, most of them without answers.

EVER SINCE FRÉDÉRIC and I met, our relationship has unfurled like one very long date. For the last two months I've barely been back to my old apartment, just briefly for clothes and books. One evening, Frédéric comes home from work and announces, *"J'ai de bonnes nouvelles!"* Good news. He explains that his aunt is going to work in Africa and has offered him to live in her apartment. "It's on a pedestrian street beside the *Centre Pompidou,*" he says. "And I want you to live with me. If you want."

The decision is not difficult. We've barely spent a night apart since we met. But I will have to give up my apartment. I don't need its luck anymore, I tell myself. It's OK to let it go. With only a slight twinge, I propose it to Sophie, a friend of Brigitte's, who needs a place in Paris while she finishes her novel. She gladly pounces on it. *Et c'est fait.*

One evening, a few days before the move, I go back to my old place to get the last of my things. I spend a long time looking around the tiny space that used to be my refuge. It wasn't so long ago, but it's already as if someone else lived here. It's like visiting a set from a movie. *Did I really sleep there on that little mattress for a year? Did I really eat my breakfast there at that window? Brush my teeth in that sink? Practice and read and write in here?* I feel an edge of solitude and fear — emotions that I kept below the surface as I went out to meet the uncertainties of each day. When I came here I was like a child — barely able to speak French, with little to no idea what life was about here, how this society worked, or how to interact with people. I have been raised by this city. I've learned a language, a culture and a way of life. And most importantly, Paris taught me how to be alone — truly and wholly alone. And now that I know how to be alone, I no longer am.

SHOULDERS LADEN WITH BAGS of books and clothes, I leave my old place with a pang of wistfulness, as if I'm leaving that girl behind — as if I have to say good bye to her as I close the big blue door and traipse for the last time down the carpeted hallway, descend the resonating staircase, and step out into Paris — but as I walk along the quay and gaze at the deep blue lights reflecting from the cinema in the water I realize I'm not saying goodbye to anyone. I'm just saying hello to another version of myself, just stepping into her now.

On the plane, over a year ago, on my way to Pierre with my head full of dreams, I thought I would find a brand new me in Paris. I thought a new language and a new city would be enough. As if selecting a new self from a catalogue, I chose someone self-assured and fearless, someone mature and fun, and with a touch of class. I never found her, but I did find myself again, and all the things I've ever been: the five year old seeking fatherly love; the shy adolescent, afraid of judgement and rejection, and the serious student, striving for perfection. I'm still foolish and weird and sensitive — everything I ever wanted to be and everything I didn't want to be. I must also be things I haven't even discovered yet. The novelty, I realize, is not a new self but a different combination of the characteristics that make up who I have been and already am. Not being me was never an option.

Maybe now, knowing this, I can just *be*.

THE AFTERNOON IS DARK with threatening clouds, but I decide to play until the storm hits. Since our new apartment is only a ten minute walk from the *Saint-Louis* bridge, I go there first. If it rains, I can easily retreat.

Even from a distance I can see that the bridge is free. The

other buskers are cloud-wary and sensible, although so are the tourists. The humidity is so high it's hard to breathe and everything seems already wet. My clothes feel like they were taken out of the dryer too early. I know I won't make much money, but I'm here now, so I set up and begin with long, drawn out melancholic pieces to match the low, heavy clouds. Compared to the protected archways where I usually play, I am vulnerable to the elements, but I like the charged energy, the way the wind throws my hair and pulls at my bow. I'm playing more to the sky than anything else.

Suddenly I look up to see Nobuaki standing before me, like an apparition, dressed all in white, with his scarf streaming out behind him. His face is pale, nearly translucent, and his expression is blank. I gasp. *I haven't dropped in on him in a while.* His hair has grown almost down to his shoulders, and a pang of guilt shoots through my chest. *I haven't seen him in several months.* In his right hand is a black metal cane.

"Nobuaki! How are you?"

"Not good," he says, his voice low and wavering. "Can you come over when you're finished playing?"

"Of course," I say. "Nobuaki, what happened?"

"I. . . had an accident," he says, then turns and continues over the bridge with a pronounced limp. Dread floods my stomach as I think back to the day we met — his threats of suicide, the depression that I'd taken for a passing phase.

My concentration is lost, so it's not long before I pack up and start walking to Nobuaki's. The rain finally hits on the way, all at once, as if triggered by a switch, and falls with an angry force. By the time I reach Nobuaki's blue door, across from a flower shop and only a few paces from *Place des Vosges,* I'm dripping.

Inside, instead of the usual coffee brewing on the stove, a bottle of wine sits menacingly on the table. The liquid looks black from the door, where I take off my soaked shoes. Two polished glasses sit in waiting. The rain is slamming on the metal roof outside the window in loud pops. I tiptoe in my wet socks and sit at the table across from Nobuaki. Without speaking, he opens the wine and fills the glasses.

It seems wrong to be drinking in the afternoon, like having chips and candy for breakfast, but I don't know what else to do, so I clink glasses with him and take a sip. The wine's dark, woody flavour slides down my throat and I feel it hit my stomach, cold at first, then warm. It's good wine, but today it feels dangerous, and churns in my stomach like poison as I wait for Nobuaki to tell me what has happened. For several minutes he stares at the table while the rain slaps outside. I let my eyes sift over his apartment. It hasn't changed at all. His camera lenses are still lined in a row and his CDs neatly arranged beside his photography magazines. Everything looks the same, but I know it's not. Nobuaki's eyes are dark and sad.

"I tried to kill myself," he finally says.

I stay quiet and wait for him to go on. He continues to stare at the table for a few minutes, then takes a sip of wine. It looks toxic. I take a sip too.

Finally, in a low, wavering voice Nobuaki tells me about his months of depression, and how they were followed by an episode of acute paranoid psychosis. "I thought everything and everyone was against me," he says. "The baker, the pharmacist, even the ticking clocks were in on it."

He pauses for a sip. A long, self-destructive gulp.

"I stopped going outside. I didn't call anyone. I didn't see anyone. One day the doorbell rang. I didn't answer and a few minutes later a guy was breaking in through the window."

"What did you do?" I ask.

"I yelled at him and he ran away." Nobuaki smiles as he recalls the surprise of the amateur thief. "But it proved my suspicions that everyone was out to get me," he says. "Except for you," he adds. "You were never in my delusions."

I nod and wait for him to continue.

"It was July, nearing my birthday," he goes on, in a voice so quiet I almost can't hear it.

I bend forward. My breath is shallow as I clutch the stem of my empty glass.

"I was too exhausted to go on," Nobuaki says. "Not with the world plotting against me. So I took a bunch of pills and a whole lot of alcohol."

His voice breaks and he begins to weep. "I woke up two days later, paralysed," he says through his tears. "And my apartment was in shambles. I must have thrashed around in a state. I don't know what happened. I don't remember any of it. I crawled to the phone and called the only number I could remember, an old friend in Tokyo. She called the French authorities, who came and took me to the hospital. I was there for two weeks," he says, topping up our glasses.

I take a sip, now glad for the wine, which buys me a few moments to scramble for the right thing to say. All that comes is: "You're lucky to be alive."

"I know," he whispers.

Guilt is heavy in the air. *I should have called him more often. I should have made an effort to drop in when I was in the area.* Many times Frédéric and I passed close by, even had a coffee on a terrace only a few streets away, and yet I didn't even think of calling. I was too caught up in our love bubble. *I've been a lousy friend,* I think. *Especially after all that Nobuaki has done for me.*

He pours the last of the wine in our glasses. One large sip each, which we drink together.

When the bottle is empty, my head is spinning. I need a plan. A future engagement with Nobuaki, something for him to look forward to.

"I have a boyfriend now," I tell him. "I want you to meet him and see our new place. We're moving in next week. Would you come over? I could make zucchini pancakes."

"Zucchini pancakes? I have never heard of that." He forces a light laugh and the air thins slightly, enough that I feel OK leaving him.

"I'll call you soon," I promise as he closes his door.

The sound of the lock turning behind me echoes in the stairwell. I stare at it for a second. I only understood locks once I moved to a city. In Huntsville, we didn't even have a key. But locking from the *inside* I have never done.

Nobuaki referred to the incident as an "accident." That's also how my dad's ex-girlfriend described his suicide attempt three years ago. She called to tell me he was in the hospital. I was in third year university, struggling with a statistics assignment due the next day.

"Your dad's had an accident," the voice sobbed on the other line.

I knew who it was, even though we'd never spoken on the phone before: Karen. My heart slid in my chest as I pictured my dad falling off the roof at a job site or smashed up in a car accident.

"He tried to kill himself," Karen whispered. "He's in the ICU. I'm so sorry."

We stayed on the line a while, as she told me about their recent break-up and some previous suicide attempts in the last weeks. I surprised myself with how smooth my voice was as I tried to calm Karen and her raging guilt. The news of the accident was still cool at my fingertips. It hadn't yet reached my vital organs.

"Listen," Karen said. "I've changed my number. It's unlisted. I still care for your dad, but I can't have him in my life anymore. I hope you understand."

"I do," I said. But I also was annoyed, that it could be that simple — a change of a number and address. Move on. Chalk it up to a bad relationship.

"I love you," she told me before hanging up.

Yeah right, I thought. And that was the last I ever heard from her.

Like Nobuaki, my dad had chosen pills and alcohol.

After the phone call I sat for a long time in heavy, empty silence. There was no guilt. Just weight. By that time I knew that nothing I could do would make my dad happy. He was in his own prison, and I wasn't in a position to help him. We had barely spoken in over a year. Now when I think of my dad, I wonder. How he's feeling. If he still considers it. Suicide, I mean. I get the death wish thing. In early university, when the performance anxiety got bad and my self-loathing raged, death could feel like a potential out. A relief. And there are times when the meaning drains out from everything and a terrible apathy reins. And yet. I never would. Even during my deepest suffering, part of me always knows that it is a phase, that eventually my mind will settle down and my heart will fill again, and laughter, though it seems outrageous and impossible, will rise up from inside.

Maybe somehow I can remind Nobuaki about laughter and lightness. Maybe I can show him that with a new frequency, different music is possible. I think of Tim's perma-smile. Different music is definitely possible. It's just a matter of finding the right frequency.

Vivachi

OUR NEW APARTMENT IS PINCH-ME INCREDIBLE. IT'S SITUATED on a pedestrian street beside the *Centre Pompidou*, in the very heart of the city. The living room window overlooks a cobblestone square, with benches and leafy trees. With the windows open, there is no sound of traffic — just people: footsteps, laughter, cutlery from the café on the ground floor, three floors below. There is so much life happening on the street that I spend great lengths of time gazing down at it from our window. Homeless people meet on the benches to talk. Lovers make out in the moonlight. Gypsies skip through the crowds, engaged in their inventive — and repetitive — scams. Tourists take rests in the shade of the trees. From here I can see the spot where I tried to play when I first arrived in Paris and was immediately stopped by the police. They told me I would disturb the residents. Back then, the idea that I might one day *be* a resident would have made me laugh.

The apartment is quite big. The living room, dining room, kitchen and two bedrooms are actually separate spaces, which is luxury by Parisian standards. Compared to both of our old apartments, it's a mansion. I have very few possessions, so I move in easily. It takes Frédéric a few days. All those books. I work on assembling the shelves and he puts the books where they need to go. Since the apartment belongs to his aunt, it is a neutral zone we both can share. I keep expecting Frédéric to freak out. He has never lived with a girlfriend before, never even been serious about a girlfriend.

"But with you it's different," he says.

As for me, I have spent over a year claiming my space in Paris, and I am ready to share again. I want to. I've spent enough nights reading or writing in silence, or practising on my own for hours. I am relearning the joys of familiarity, of seeing the same face every day, and of letting someone know me — really know me. It wouldn't have worked with just anyone. Frédéric is different. I trust him. I set up his shelves and he fills them with words. Really, the only concern I have about living together is what we will eat, since we are both clueless in the kitchen. I have at least assembled a few salads in my lifetime, but Frédéric seems to have been merely spreading cheese on a baguettes for the last ten years.

After a few monkish meals, it becomes clear that one of us is going to have to step up. We can't live solely on bread and cheese, and my haphazard snacks of olives, crackers and carrot sticks isn't going to cut it. Since Frédéric works full time with a long commute, I am the obvious candidate.

I start slow and simple. After busking one day I buy some potatoes, carrots and onions. I throw them in a pot of boiling water, then add some chickpeas and salt. The result is boring and bland, but Frédéric, who has never before made a soup, raves as if I have performed a circus trick. The next evening, with leftover potatoes and onions, I attempt home fries. The onions burn to black crisps and the potatoes turn to mush, but we eat anyway, with large quantities of ketchup to mask the taste of charcoal.

"I love mashed potatoes," Frédéric says.

"Tomorrow, I'm buying a recipe book," I announce, determined to improve.

"Actually, I was thinking tomorrow might be a good night to meet my parents," Frédéric says. "They asked me to have dinner with them. Would you like to come?"

"Ah! Really? Do you want me to?" I know Frédéric hasn't told his family about me yet. Or any of his girlfriends, since they never lasted long.

"Yes," he says. "I think it's time."

FRÉDÉRIC HAS TOLD ME only a little about his parents. They live in a country home on weekends and Paris during the week. His father works as an accountant and his mother, who was also an accountant, is officially retired, but stays in the city most weeks to keep her husband company. At first I am happy to get to meet them, but now, as I walk to The Tambour, where Fred has made a reservation, I begin to fret. *Should I address them using tu or vous?* This is important. I'm better at *tu*, and it would make things less formal, but *vous* would be more respectful. *What will I say if they ask what I do for a living?* This is important, too. It will be among the first questions. And they've both had successful careers. I'm not sure if they'll appreciate my illegal street musician status.

When I arrive, heart pounding an unsteady beat, Frédéric and his parents are already seated in the back. It's the restaurant where we spent our first evening together, and just like last time the wizard booms out a *"Bonjour!"* as I walk in the door. I approach the table and everyone stands for a round of kisses and more *bonjours*. Then we sit down. I take a seat across from Frédéric, beside his dad.

"Tu as un accent," is one of the first things Frédéric's mother says. She is an attractive woman in her late 50s, with a youthful bob cut, wearing a green dress that matches her eyes. She asks me where I'm from.

"Canada," I say.

She tells me they went to Canada on vacation a couple of years ago.

"Québec?" I ask. Many French people I've met have spent at least one vacation in Quebec. They always glow about the hospitality, the scenery and the *drôle d'accent*.

She shakes her head. "Ontario. We had a terrible time." She describes the region, two and half hours north of Toronto, a place with nothing but lakes and trees, hundreds of kilometres of trees. I swallow and nod, as she describes the region in which I was born and raised. "We went on this hike in the forest," she says, "and got completely lost for hours. Then a huge animal burst through the trees."

"What kind of animal?" I ask.

"Something enormous!" is all she says. "It was horrifying!"

Frédéric's father, a round man with silver hair and a wise

twinkle in his eyes, nods his head.

I am not offended. In my experience, people who didn't grow up in nature seem to either find it cute, and risk putting themselves in danger as they approach a cuddly bear or a mother moose and her baby, or, like Frédéric's parents, find it so foreign they feel threatened. I don't tell them that I come from the region of their animal scare. They can find that out later.

The wizard approaches with the menu — a large chalkboard that he lugs from table to table. He props it on a chair before us and saunters away. Frédéric takes the opportunity to gently explain to his parents that I'm vegetarian. They look at each other with concern, then to me. For a moment no one speaks. Then Frédéric's mother turns to him and asks, eyes narrowed, if he has also become vegetarian.

"*Non, non,*" he reassures her and, as if to prove it, when the wizard returns to take our order, he asks for a steak tartare. His dad gets a steak, rare, and his mother orders a filet of fish. I sheepishly order my salad and his parents exchange another quick glance.

They'll get used to it, I think.

There is a brief but longer and more uncomfortable moment when the attention shifts to me. Questions are asked about my family, my education and what I'm doing in France. I answer as honestly as I can, and when they ask what I do for a living I tell them I'm a musician. *I'll explain later,* I think.

"One of our nephews is a musician," his mother says, which makes me laugh. Everyone has one of those in their families. The artsy weird one.

Frédéric's father is quiet and observant. It's his mother who keeps the conversation at a steady sprint. She has an extraordinary reservoir of energy, and her head moves rapidly back and forth like a sparrow. I adopt the quiet pensive position of Frédéric's father, while she and her son discuss the annual barbecue that Frédéric organizes at his parents' place in the countryside. It's coming up quickly, and his mother scolds him for not yet sending out the invitations. She needs to know how many people are coming, so she can plan the menu. They've already ordered a baby lamb for the event.

Then Frédéric's mother turns to me. "Don't worry," she says. "I'll find something vegetarian for you."

The evening wraps up with *crèmes brûlées*, espressos and goodnight *bises*. On our walk home, I'm glowing triumphantly, because there were no major disasters during the meal. I didn't fuck up at all.

"Just so you're aware," Frédéric pipes up when we're nearly home. "You really should have used *vous* with my parents."

"Really?" I say, shocked. "But they used *tu* with me."

"It's not always reciprocal," he says, and smiles. "It's also not a big deal."

Still, at least I didn't spill anything or make an unwitting sexual remark, as is so easy to do in French. I'll have opportunities to spill things and make mistakes later. This time, I just needed to make an OK impression. The vegetarianism might have thrown them off, but I'll have time to make up for it at the upcoming barbecue.

As I HEAD TO *Palais-Royal* for my usual busking session, I hear the high trills of a violin echoing in the distance. At first, I don't believe it could be true — until I get closer and find a flaxen-haired violinist boldly playing concertos in my spot. In MY spot! *Palais-Royal*, my precious gem, my livelihood, is under attack. I'm too stunned to move. I stand in the distance watching her. She's my age and has a stack of music on her stand. She is playing loudly and with a confidence I have never possessed. After a few minutes, I turn and rush away, outraged at the intrusion. For non-buskers, this is like arriving to work one morning to find someone at your desk speaking casually into your phone and typing things into your computer. Not only are they in your workspace, they will also be claiming your salary. And there is nothing you can do about it.

The next day I come early, ready for battle. The spot is empty and I begin to play immediately, but with not with the same joy and abandon that I usually embody here. The girl arrives an hour later, violin in hand, and approaches me with a friendly smile. To my surprise, she is sweet and subdued, but part of me resents her for taking what I irrationally believe to be mine. *It's only one person,* I tell myself. *Relax. We can share the spot.*

But this is only the beginning. In the weeks that follow, I arrive to find a menagerie of musicians: violin and cello, flute, two guitars, a saxophone, a cello, a clarinet and, one day, a buxom soprano. The musicians are young, and come from Mexico, Kazakhstan, Russia, Holland, and England. Like me, this is one of the only ways they can earn money in Paris. Somehow, word got around that *Palais-Royal* is a busking paradise. And it travelled quickly. Now when I show up, someone is usually playing and I have to wait hours for a turn. With *Place des Vosges* also in peril, the remaining options are few.

I find myself wandering around the city again, circling the streets, violin in hand, searching for another busking haven. I explore narrow streets on the Rive Gauche, bridges by the Seine, rumoured locations near the *Bon Marché* and a supposed archway in *Saint-Germain des Prés*.

The streets are no longer mine.

SOPHIE, THE WRITER WHO TOOK OVER MY SUBLET, sends me an email telling me about an ad she saw in a magazine. They're looking for female foreigners for an article on all things French. And they promise champagne.

"*J'ai pensé à toi.* Might be fun," she writes.

I picture a group of girls my age sitting around a table in a crowded, smoky bar, laughing and bonding over flutes of champagne, while a journalist observes and takes notes. I feel integrated enough now that I think I might be able to offer some insight. I respond to the ad. A few days later they write back. They'd love to have me.

The session is to take place at a restaurant called The World Place, located near the *Champs-Élysées*.

On the day of the interview, I busk earlier than usual so I can come home and change. I drop my violin and put on the best clothes I have. My gig clothes: black pants and a black shirt. I also tie a black scarf around my head to add a sense of style. Then I brush my teeth and head off to the *Champs-Élysées,* which is walkable from our apartment.

I haven't been to this area since Kosuke and I were stopped here by the police, and as I walk along the wide glittering boulevard, I again feel small and out of place. At least this time I won't risk deportation.

I am greeted at the tall glass door entrance by a handsome black man dressed like a groomsman, in a slick black suit and bowtie. "*Bonjour,*" he says, eying me warily.

"*Bonjour,* I'm with the magazine," I say.

His eyes soften slightly. "*Suivez-moi,*" he says.

I follow him into a palatial interior. Plush carpet melts under my feet. Sound-absorbing walls provide the calming, subdued ambience I've grown to associate with wealth. If I wasn't here with the magazine, they wouldn't even let me in the door. My fake-fancy black clothes wouldn't even come close to their dress code. There is no main light source, only strings of small shimmering lights off to the side, a few tiny bulbs embedded in the ceiling like stars, and candles flickering in glass holders along the front desk.

The impeccably tailored groomsman leads me over to the edge of a veranda that looks out onto a gymnasium-sized dining area. The patrons are speaking softly, seated in chairs as big as la-Z-boys, with thick white cushions propped behind them. In the far right corner is a raised area with crisp white couches, bright lights and looming umbrella reflectors. My stomach lurches at the sight of two large movie cameras.

Oh god, I think. *A television show!*

"*Par ici,*" the man says, and I follow him down a spiral staircase made of polished wood. *Oh god, oh god, oh god.*

My legs falter as we approach the gleaming couches. A film crew dressed in black is standing in waiting. A young man with short gelled hair checks my name on his clipboard and tells me to take a seat on one of the couches.

"I thought this was for a magazine," I squeak. My heart is starting to hammer against my ribs as I imagine being interviewed for a live talk show.

"It is," he says. "But we tape the sessions for our website."

A brief wave of relief allows me to climb the stairs and take a seat on a firm white cushion. A large black man lumbers over with a microphone the size of a ladybug and tells me to clip it to my collar.

"*Excusez-moi,*" I say, "but what magazine is this for?"

"FHM," he says and hands me a previous copy. "A magazine for men. It's for *Le Bar de Filles.*"

I flip through the pages to the last *Bar des Filles* article. It features a group of middle-aged women being asked questions like, *With age, do men last longer before ejaculating? Is a penis at 18 more beautiful than at 40? In the past, what sexual techniques have you shown to men?*

These aren't the light-hearted questions I was expecting. I thought we'd be talking about how the French dip croissants in their coffee, wear scarves in the summer, and take effervescent multivitamins. I figured maybe we'd get into relationship dynamics, but certainly not sexual positions. *This is just like Céline's party game,* I think. Except that my answers will be recorded and shared with the world.

A tall young woman with the rigid posture and haunting stare of a runway model struts up the stairs, hips swinging, and takes a seat beside me. She is wearing tight black pants and a loose cheetah print top. We introduce ourselves. Her name is Tanya. She's from Russia and has been living in France for three months.

"Your French is good," I say.

"Yes," she nods. "I'm intelligent."

There is an awkward silence, though she doesn't seem bothered by it. I scramble for something to say, then go for the classic, "What are you doing in France?"

"I'm looking for modelling work," she says. She brushes her wavy brown hair to the side. "*Et toi?*"

"*Je . . . joue du violon,*" I say. I leave out the part about playing on the streets. I'm marginal enough as it is right now.

Another participant arrives — a girl from Cameroon. She isn't as tall as Tanya, but she's equally as glamorous. She, too, is looking for modelling work, and is dressed for the part, in tall boots, tight pants, and a black cleavage-accentuating shirt.

After the third girl arrives, I realize that the magazine had clearly placed the ad on some sort of casting website, a website I would never have visited, and that *all* the participants will be model material — except for me. I'm dressed as if I'm going to a funeral, and the black scarf wrapped around my head is slowly coming loose.

The journalist, a confident, grey-haired man with smooth skin and a wide smile, approaches the stage, bouncing with energy at every stride. He introduces himself and sits down across from us with a Heineken and a large notepad.

"Do you have any questions while the others arrive?" he asks.

"Will you be asking these kinds of questions?" I ask, holding up the previous article.

"*Bien sûr,*" he says, gleaming. "We'll be talking about *everything.*"

The girls giggle and exchange giddy looks. They are already starting to bond with one another. I stare ahead in pre-traumatic shock and wonder if it's too late to bail.

Then the fourth girl, a Mexican in a tiny black dress, tiptoes up the stairs like a brittle princess and takes a seat under the hot lights. *Model,* I think.

A waiter dressed in traditional black and white approaches to take beverage orders. The others ask for drinks with names I've never heard of. Flustered, I order a glass of water.

We are instructed to fill out a release form, as well as note our breast size, as they will be sending us lingerie in the mail. I wear sports bras and yoga tops, and while I could make a guess at my North American size I have no idea how they measure in Europe.

When I confess to the journalist that I don't know my size, the other girls exchange glances. "My *European* size," I specify.

The journalist grins and examines my chest. "*85 B*," he says with conviction. I smile, though I can feel my face flush.

A few minutes later the fifth and final girl arrives. We all turn our heads as she marches up the stairs in tall red boots that go past her knees. Her skin is the colour of creamy coffee and she's wearing a grey mini skirt with suspenders over a tiny black top. Her make-up is as thick as paint. She is from Gabon, she says, and she claims her name is Romance.

Not fair, I think. *The rest of us just divulged our real identities. No one would name a baby "Romance."*

The waiter returns and places the girls' colourful cocktails before them, in specially shaped glasses. I receive my water in a tall orange juice glass with two floating ice cubes. The journalist takes a sip of beer and announces that it is time to begin. I look down and notice a toothpaste stain on my shirt. I have an urge to lick it off, but the cameras are already rolling

To start, the journalist explains his method. He'll pose a question, then go around the circle. Each girl will answer in turn, while he takes notes. Do we understand? We nod.

"Excellent. My first question: How are the French at flirting, compared to the men in your country?"

Romance is first to respond. She says that the French are too timid. They hesitate around women. "They lack confidence," she says, licking her glimmering ruby lips.

I try to keep my gaze on her flicking eyelashes, but my eyes keep returning to her clip-on microphone that is sinking steadily into her ample bosom.

"Nisha?"

My breathing quickens. I turn to face the journalist. As a matter of survival, I ignore the frightened self that is urging me to dash out of there, and slip instead into a confident, boisterous self, push my shoulders back and smile. As I speak, a photographer starts snapping pictures of me with a lens the size of a telescope. I don't wince at the blinding flash. I pretend this happens all the time.

I hear myself talk as if I'm listening to someone else — someone bold and experienced. "Canadians don't flirt the way they do here," I claim. "They wait a while before they approach a woman they like. I first found the French to be daring and forward."

The journalist takes notes with a broad smile, then asks the remaining girls their opinion.

The Mexican talks about how obnoxious the French have been. "One pulled up on a scooter and asked if I wanted to have sex!" she says and everyone laughs.

"Are the French *good* at flirting?" the journalist asks next.

When it's my turn, I let loose, cracking jokes and sharing anecdotes, while the others laugh and the journalist continues to scrawl in his notebook. After being approached on the street countless times by men, I ruthlessly make fun of their pickup lines, bashing their classic "*tu veux prendre un café?*", a line used so often, the one that Pierre used on me back in Canada. I tell them about other lines French men have used. I mention Michel, back when I first arrived in France, who asked me if I wanted to see his paintings. I reveal to my captive audience that I am a musician and that men often claim to be photographers looking for models or filmmakers seeking to "collaborate." Everyone is laughing hard, including the cameraman and I bask in the centre stage performance.

The next few questions are not difficult. They involve the way the French dress, if they are muscular, if they are sexy, and if they cook well. The questions are phrased in a general sense, and I answer them that way — not in reference to Frédéric but to French men as a whole, based on everything I have learned through conversations on the street, coffees with strangers and from what others have told me. The frightened part of me is rocking back and forth at the back of my skull, but I'm on a roll and can barely hear the whimpers.

The next question changes the tone. "Are the French good in bed?" asks the journalist.

The Cameroonian girl jumps in eagerly, to claim that the French don't take enough time for the preliminary stuff. "They move too fast," she says.

The other girls nod in agreement. The journalist turns to me. I am trapped in my clown suit. The others stare at me, waiting for my next witty remark. I can't clam up now. I grin and give a nod as if to say absolutely.

The journalist hesitates, waiting for elaboration.

"*Avant ou pendant?*" he asks.

I hesitate. I have no idea what the French are like in bed, as a general thing, but I've been kissed by enough random guys to know that they are quick to show affection. There's no way I'm going to talk about my experiences with Frédéric. He's unlike the other young men I've met here, and our intimacies have been sacred and sweet and have no place in this mess. My mind falters, like the static between radio stations. With both cameras swivelled at me and every pair of eyes, I grin and say, "*Les deux.*"

The girls laugh hysterically. The cameraman on my right fights to keep the camera steady through his laughter and the journalist takes a long swig of beer and says, "Wow!"

He jots more notes and I realize that what I've just said is going straight into the article and straight onto their website. My head is spinning now, as if I'd just stepped off an amusement park ride.

"What position do the French prefer?"

"On all fours!" yell the girls in unison.

The journalist nods as if in agreement.

My shoulders tense up and I feel my face flush. It's increasingly harder to maintain the clown act when I'm so obviously lacking in experience next to these beauty queens. The Russian has only been here for three months and already she has a wealth of knowledge and anecdotes about French men in bed. I try to imagine the level of experience required in order to distinguish what is personality and what is culture when it comes to sex.

"What's the craziest thing you've ever done with a French guy?" asks the journalist.

Oh god. Here we go.

The Russian shares her sex-in-a-backseat story, and Romance has had a sex-in-an-alley adventure. I feel the clown suit slipping off. My face burns when the journalist asks for my anecdote. I shrug. I can pretend to be someone else, but fabricating an experience is something else entirely.

"I've never done anything like that," I say.

The journalist blinks in disappointment. The charade is over.

The questions intensify like a fireworks show, become increasingly intimate, which causes the journalist to get more and more excited. His smile is gaping now, his eyes wide as he pries for the juicy bits. Nothing is taboo. Just when I think they can't get worse, the journalist blasts another at us.

"Do you consider yourself a sex fantasy?" he asks.

To my surprise, the Cameroonian confirms that she is her boyfriend's fantasy. Romance is too. The Mexican and the Russian nod.

The journalist looks to me. The clown suit is completely gone now. I sit naked before them.

"I'm not a sex fantasy," I say, and by now this comes as no surprise to anyone. I feel my throat tighten.

"Do the French have small penises?" asks the journalist, his eyes narrowing as if he knows the answer already.

"*Oui!*" the girls chime, and I see him shake his head sadly and note universal agreement in capital letters.

"And now for the final question," he says. My shoulders curl up to my ears and I hold my breath. "Would you marry a Frenchman?"

The Mexican is already married to one. The Russian nods with hesitation. The two girls from Africa say, "*Absolument.*"

"Nisha?"

What can I say? I sigh, shrug and answer, "*Pourquoi pas?*"

"How was it?" Frédéric asks when I come in the door. I join him on the couch, heavy with remorse. I didn't mention him in the interview, but I made comments tonight that could be interpreted as being about our sex life. His friends and family could come across the magazine in a doctor's office, a subway or on the train.

I tell him bit by bit what happened, cringing as I relive the horror. I describe the shocking questions I was forced to answer and my initial attempt at being funny by bashing the French. Frédéric listens with amusement and laughs when I tell him I thought the article was about flirting and fashion.

"I thought you knew what you were getting into," he laughs.

I describe the beauty queens, the things they wore, the comments they made and the sexual things they had done. He doesn't even seem concerned about what I might have said or about his friends reading the article. I ask him if he wishes I was a sex fantasy like the other girls. He pulls me into his arms and says, "*Je t'aime comme tu es.*"

He hasn't exactly answered the question, but surely a sense of humour beats out short skirts and ruby lips. I'd rather be a clown than a sex fantasy anyway.

FRÉDÉRIC'S MOTHER loves flowers. They are blooming everywhere on her property — bursting pink and white roses, giant purple balls exploding at the end of tall stems, clusters of tiny yellow flowers that look like butterflies, interspersed with long red petals that shoot outward like fireworks. Flowers I've never seen before. There is a small pond surrounded by a mini bamboo forest. Across from it, an enormous flowerbed stretches along the side of a hill, filled with lavender, round bushes speckled with radiant blue flowers. There are trees with delicate red and yellow leaves, tall tufted grasses, and yellow flowers with long tube-like petals that twist up long delicate stems. Bees zigzag from feast to feast, butterflies flip in the breeze and a cuckoo bird (until now I thought they resided only in clocks) calls out from a neighbour ing tree. Nestled between fields of sunflowers, Frédéric's parents' 15th century home stands beside a narrow river. Its exterior stone walls are a warm sand-coloured limestone. A staircase turret gives it a castle-like authority.

We have arrived early for Frédéric's annual barbecue, to help with the preparations — but not early enough: we've barely finished the tour of the property when his friends start to roll in — more than a dozen in total. I've met a couple of them in Paris, but this is the first time I've seen most of them, and the first they've even heard of Férédric's *petite amie.* There is a flurry of kisses and boisterous discussion with each new arrival.

Frédéric's mother soon summons all of us into the backyard for the apéritif. On a red and white checkered tablecloth sit bowls of chips, pretzels, pickles, cherry tomatoes and tiny cubes of cheese. Bottles of wine, beer, cassis, orange juice and Coke sit in waiting. No one serves themselves. Frédéric's parents pour the drinks. It appears to be a part of a welcoming ritual.

"Nisha, you have to try our homemade walnut wine," says Frédéric's mother. She hands me a glass of amber liquid that is sweet and nutty and very easy to drink. I finish my glass before the rest are served, so when everyone raises their glasses to inaugurate the barbecue I toast with an empty one. *Merde.* I'm also hungry enough to eat the contents of all the bowls, but the level of self-control displayed by the other guests is astounding. I watch Isabel, a high school chemistry teacher, take a single chip and chew thoughtfully as she discusses municipal politics with Cyril, a shy man who sells security systems and who so far has only indulged in a cherry tomato and a pretzel. I reach out and exercise ultimate restraint as I take just one pretzel and one chip and focus on retaining the names and professions of Frédéric's friends. They are mostly from his engineering school, and have established, high paying careers. I'm obviously from a different world, yet I don't feel as if I have to win them over. Frédéric is my VIP pass into their social circle. My lifestyle is alien to them, but they take it in stride and fire a steady stream of questions my way.

"What's the minimum wage in Canada?"

"What kind of social system do you have there?"

"How is the parliament set up?"

"Why don't you have a Québecois accent?"

When the apéritif wraps up, one of each snack item remains in the bowls.

NOW THE WORK BEGINS for the evening's feast. Many of Frédéric's friends nap in the back yard. Others play pétanque in the driveway. His mother heads to the kitchen, while his dad and a few other guests start to work on roasting the freshly slaughtered lamb. First they saw its head off, then someone rams a pole through its body and places it over a lit fire. While it's not considered barbaric, for Parisians lamb-skewering is still a special event. A *countryside* affair. Many of them take pictures of themselves beside the skinless and now headless creature. Finally, Frédéric's father takes his position beside the beast. His job will be to feed the fire and turn the carcass round and around as it roasts in the flames, basting it every once in a while with a mustard concoction that drips into the fire and causes it to spit and sizzle.

To escape the carcass, I head to the kitchen. There I find Frédéric's mother multitasking at an inhuman rate. She's got several cutting boards on the go, simmering saucepans, a full blender, and various dishes popping in and out of the oven. She tells me she scoured her cooking magazines for a vegetarian appetizer and finally decided on layers of tomato, fried eggplant and mozzarella cheese broiled in the oven. The main course, besides the lamb, is mashed potatoes, green beans, sautéed marinated mushrooms, cooked endives with béchamel, and a green salad from the garden. Dessert is a chocolate mousse and baked Mont d'Or, which, she explains, is a rich cheese served warm and eaten like a fondu. I happily spend several hours helping with the chopping, peeling, grating, and sautéing as Frédéric's mother chirps in her singsong voice about everything and nothing. She is a remarkable talker, mentions everything that comes into her mind, which is comforting, since I never have to worry about making conversation.

In the early evening, we all head up the hill to where Frédéric's father is proudly displaying the charred beast. Everyone cheers when the butcher arrives — an older man with a moustache, a beret, and a brown cardigan sweater. The wine bottles reappear and there is another apéritif, this time standing around the carcass as if it were a work of art just unveiled. I sip my walnut wine and try not to look at the massacre. Soon, there are so many conversations going on, it's difficult to know which one to join. I end up mostly listening in on several. After about half an hour, the blackened beast is taken from its perch and laid out on a table, where the butcher sets to work, filling plates with steaming flesh. Once the tall white candles are lit along the middle of the table, the meal officially begins.

Baguettes by the dozen are placed in three mounds along the table and bottles are in constant pour. Some neighbours from the nearby town have also been invited, which brings the attendance to over twenty. The table thunders with discussion. With the upcoming election, it's impossible to avoid politics, which adds extra heat to the conversations. Frédéric, who is seated a few chairs down from me, gets into a brief but impassioned argument with a right-winged friend about government allocations. Although Frédéric has never had to rely on government assistance, he is passionately defending the poor, pounding the table at the idea that those on welfare are simply lazy. Most of Frédéric's friends are on his side. They nod when he speaks and occasionally jump in with *oui* and *c'est vrai!* The right-winged friend soon backs down and the conversation fades into an amicable discussion about public transportation in Paris versus Marseilles. Just like that.

Frédéric's sister, a pretty woman with a strong, no-bullshit presence, is sitting across from me. Her three kids are also nearby, and I am able to pick up some valuable table etiquette through her corrections.

"Sit up straight," she chides her oldest daughter. Then, "Hand on the table," to the middle one.

My left hand has also been sitting idly on my lap and I discretely bring it out and perch it on the table as instructed. Frédéric's sister notices and fires me a wink and a warm smile. I smile too, and say, "I'm learning."

I don't just take cues from her. I gaze around and notice that all the adults are eating with their forks in their left hand and carefully trimming off bites with their knife in the right. This goes beyond my current capabilities. It's all I can do to lift my wine glass by the stem and refrain from holding my fork in my fist. Despite my deficient table manners, and the lack of lamb on my plate, I feel deeply imbedded in this scene — not an observer but a participant.

When the plates are cleared, small bowls of chocolate mousse are distributed. This, I watched Frédéric's mother make earlier. As with many French recipes, the ingredient list is minimal. The tricks are in timing, temperature and technique. She gently melted dark chocolate in a double boiler, while beating air into egg whites and gradually adding sugar. Then she very slowly combined yolks with the melted chocolate, before folding the whole thing together — lightly, so the air bubbles weren't disturbed. Then she popped it into the fridge. The result is airy, rich and smooth. I hear a few mmmmm's of pleasure resonate. Frédéric's sister wipes the dark stains from around her children's mouths. I take a serviette to my own just in case.

Next, the baked Mont D'or arrives, garnering a collective cheer. Everyone gathers around it and takes turns dipping Italian bread sticks and endive leaves into the hot liquefied cheese.

When the last of it has been scraped from its round pine boxes, coffee is served — dark espressos that make we wonder how anyone will get to sleep, as it's already close to 10 p.m. Many take their tiny cups outside to enjoy with cigarettes and the stars.

Finally, once all the dishes and crumbs have been cleared and the neighbours go home and the kids are in bed, the cognac comes out. The candles continue to flicker as the conversations lower to a gentle hum. I curl up beside Frédéric on one of the couches and eventually fall asleep on his shoulder to the lulling murmur of his family and friends.

"It is through the non-activity of the conscious mind, that we will be able to reconnect with the breath, to become accustomed to silence, to live moments of interior well-being."

This seems like something Tim would say, or something from a New Age yoga retreat, but this sentence, and others like it, I discover in Dominique Hoppenot's book, *Le violon intérieur*. It was first released in July, 1981, my birth month and year. I'm getting through it, slowly due to the French, but it complements Tim's lessons and reiterates his insistence that no-mind is bliss. I'm still working on the no-mind stuff. Hoppenot's message is that a state of inner stillness is necessary in the quest to reach individual musical potential with joy and grace instead of struggle and pain. She says that music "comes from the inside first." I think this is what she means by "resonating the inner string."

"Once you achieve this state," Tim says at the end of another lesson. "It's truly incredible."

Inner stillness. Bliss. Enlightenment. Some take a lifetime to find it. Tim himself travelled the world for ten years. It could flip on like a switch, as it did for Eckhart Tolle, who says he then sat on a park bench in the ecstasy for two years. Of course, most never come close to this level of happiness. But it's what everyone wants, isn't it? To be happy? People just have a different plans on how to get it.

Those who have it, though, send a simple message: happiness

is just freedom from your shitty mind.

A COUPLE OF DAYS after my lesson with Tim, I show up at *Place des Vosges* and find that the painters are not there. Then I remember that they're both on vacation. I have the whole archway to myself. I set up where the painters usually display their work and begin to tune. The open strings resonate under the archway, providing a soft base layer over which I begin the first movement of the Partita in D Minor.

There's an old man in the garden, walking slowly along the path in my direction, using his black cane for support. From the abrupt and rigid way his left leg bends, I can tell it's artificial. As he gets closer and the sound of my strings reaches his ears, his pace slows, just a touch. He looks up, a little to the left, a little to the right, and then he spots me in the shadows under the archway. It's dark in here, and cool. The sun can only get in as it sets, and by then its rays are sweet and subdued.

The old man crosses the street and enters the archway. He leans against the wall and meets my eye. Then something magical happens. It's the same magic that has always happened here on the street, but it's only after reading Hoppenot's book and having lessons with Tim, that I can articulate it. I'm not sharing music, I realize. I am sharing joy *through* music. This is why I don't get stage fright on the street. The music comes from inside. It begins with a little spark that travels from my chest, down my arms, through my fingers and into the strings. The strings pass it to the wooden body of my violin and it rises into the air through the tiny holes. It circles around the archway, ricochets off those 17 Century walls and swirls into the ears of the old man who is leaning there. He smiles. I smile back at him, and then at a middle-aged woman in high heels, clipping by in a hurry. She slows her pace, stops and opens her purse.

"*Merci mademoiselle*," she says as she puts a coin in my case. She smiles. I smile. He smiles. More people stop. They smile. The music changes. It becomes richer and warmer.

It's hot butterscotch now. And instead of a spark in my chest, a fire is burning there. Most of the people who stop don't own classical CDs or go to baroque concerts. This is not about what or how well I play. It never has been. Something else is happening here. Something that could not happen on a stage.

Playing on the street is not a musical feat — it is a balancing act. It's joy on a high wire. I dare to feel it, then I dare to share it. As people pass by, I toss them sparks and they return them, with smiles and nods and thank-you's and coins. And after an hour of this, my chest is now white hot. *This is bliss,* I think. *This is resonating my inner string.* I don't need a new violin method. It's right here on the street, literally at my fingertips, but I can't do it alone. It takes other people, hundreds of people tossing the joy back and forth, taking the risk of feeling it truly. Despite it all.

"*La petite Cosette*," people sometimes call me, after the character from Hugo's *Les Misérables*. This is partly in reference to the way I dress, which has always been raggish — pants with rips and patches, tunics and a news-boy-style cap or coloured gypsy scarves. Far from a sex fantasy.

Justement, Cosette in Hugo's novel is not a sex symbol at all. She is hope.

GIGA

I STEP OUT THE FRONT DOOR OF OUR APARTMENT AND AM GREET-
ed by sweet steam wafting from the little crepe stand beside our
building. The full-time employee is from Bangladesh and is one
of the best crepe rollers around, and by far the nicest.

"*Bonjour!*" he chimes, his smile stretching wide across his face.

"*Salut!*" I say with a wave.

Before me is the Pompidou. I see it every day, but it still im-
presses me with its bold primary colours and giant transparent
tubes. At night it looks like an alien ship, the way it's lit up and
blinking. By day it resembles a Skittles factory.

I pass the sprawling terrace of *Café Beaubourg*, on the ground
floor of our building, where the chairs all face forward and the
tourists gaze straight ahead at the Pompidou parvis. There's a
guy out there, performing shirtless with a crystal ball while his
speakers blast the Bach G Minor Fugue for violin. He's been
here for the last two weeks, mesmerizing crowds as the ball leaps
out of his hands, seemingly on its own accord, and rolls across
his body. His finale is a handstand while doing the splits with
the ball nestled on the back of his neck. The act requires serious
concentration. Sweat glistens on his torso and back.

I carry on toward *Palais-Royal*. I haven't played there in a
week, but it's Tuesday, so there will be less competition than on
a weekend. If it's occupied I'll continue on to the Louvre, to
a bridge over the Seine, or to Bernard's oasis. Wherever. As I
make my way past *Les Halles*, a group of teenage gypsies are pretending to be deaf and asking people to sign pledge forms. They
skip gracefully around me, grinning. They've seen me before and
know I'm wise to their schemes. They are surviving in their own
way, and while they might be a nuisance to some, they are ulti-
mately harmless. Some of them are even having fun. They aren't
mean-spirited. They just play by different rules.

As I approach the royal courtyard, I hear no music, only footsteps and some children laughing by the fountain. I can relax. Playing at *Palais-Royal* is like putting on an old favourite hoodie. I'm beyond comfortable here.

As I open my case, I decide to start with a new piece, the theme song from one of the many films Frédéric has introduced me to: *In the Mood for Love*. The violin melody is slow and haunting, the kind of beauty that is also edged with pain. It's a waltz, which is different from what I'm used to playing, but it's fun to mess with the 3/4 time signature, exaggerating the downbeats and trailing off on the other two.

A young woman with long blond hair stops and leans against the pillar to listen. I take liberties with the tempo, add trills and extra flourishes, slide up to the high notes on the D and A string and widen the vibrato. My bow and left hand synchronize and playing becomes effortless, like a kite that suddenly catches a breeze and lifts to the sky. Near the end, the notes swoop high on the E string for a final wail, then ease back down to end on the G string, low and forlorn. When I look up, the young woman's face is wet with tears.

"*Merci madamoiselle*," she says. She drops a coin in my case and continues through the archway and into the garden.

Suddenly I hear a shout. "*Hé! Bonjour Princesse!*"

I look to my left. It's the Pole and the Belge, my homeless buddies. They both have bottles of rosé and wide grins. I begin a Handel sonata that starts slow and loving, like a lullaby. They come up and stand less than a metre away and sway with eyes half closed and open-mouthed smiles that reveal missing teeth. Passers-by frown and veer around them. My wage is reduced to virtually nothing, but I don't mind. Playing for my homeless friends is one of the only things I have to offer them. After about twenty minutes, they take turns kissing my hand, then sway around the corner, probably for an afternoon snooze. I pick up the pace with some Seitz concertos, which are easy but sound impressive, with fast string-crossings and double stops. They are not well-known pieces, but the mood is peppy and bright.

On my way home, I stop at a fruit and vegetable stand for zucchinis. Nobuaki is coming for supper tonight and I promised him zucchini pancakes. I also get some tomatoes for a salad and fat ripe figs for dessert. At the fromagerie across the street I pick up some comté, some cantal and some chèvre, and from the bakery two fresh baguettes. I'm getting better at food shopping, but I still don't dare select a bottle of wine. I haven't learned the subtleties of regions and dates and grapes. I'm banking on a bottle from Frédéric's stock.

Nobuaki arrives early, so I invite him into the kitchen to talk while I work. I'm still an awkward and uncertain cook and must meticulously follow recipes if I'm to make anything edible. It takes time. I pour us both a glass of beer and we say the traditional French *santé* as our glasses touch. Nothing could be more appropriate tonight than to drink to Nobuaki's health. I'm happy to see that he has gained colour and weight since I saw him last and that he seems in better spirits.

"Did you bring your photo albums?" I ask.

"Yes," he says, his gaze lowering to the floor. "But I don't see why it's important."

"Because you're an amazing photographer," I say, sniffing — the onion I'm chopping is searing my eyes. "And I know Frédéric will really appreciate your work." A few tears drop into the onions. *Extra sodium.*

Sometimes Nobuaki is tough to read — like, how much of his self-deprecation is culturally specific and how much is a genuine lack of confidence? It's my custom now to counteract such comments with enthusiastic optimism and hope that through some form of osmosis the positivity transfers, at least a little.

When Frédéric comes home from work, I introduce him to Nobuaki and set the two of them up with beers and a bowl of crackers in the living room. They both want to help, but I shoo them away. I need to concentrate. I can't stray from the recipes, even a touch. I learned that the hard way, when the hummus I made the other day had the consistency of clay.

As I study my recipe, I hear Frédéric ignite a discussion about Japanese film directors, and their conversation takes off. *Good.*

When the pancakes are finally ready, I usher the men to the table and say, *"Bon app!"* Though I've never spoken French with Nobuaki, he is fluent, and so it is our language of choice for the evening. The pancakes are a bit oily, but not a disaster. To go with them — or maybe to salvage them — Frédéric selects his favourite vintage, a St. Julien. It makes any meal a classy affair.

There is a celebratory buzz, as if it's someone's birthday or one of us has accomplished something remarkable. Maybe it's because this is our first time entertaining in our new place. Maybe it's because Nobuaki is healthy and appears in good spirits. This is my third time drinking wine with him, but tonight there are no tears or words of despair. There is no room for such sentiments. Joy powers through.

THE NIGHT STRETCHES ON. It's past 2 in the morning before we finally make our way to the couch, glass of port in hand, and open the photo albums. I sit between Nobuaki and Frédéric and turn the pages.

I've already seen these photos, but I want Frédéric to see what a gifted photographer Nobuaki is. I once described to Frédéric the fourteen different lenses, and how he knows exactly which one to use according to the light, distance and the detail he wants to capture.

After a few pages, Frédéric, who has an eye for art, says, *"C'est très très beau!"* And I know he means it. Like many French people, he doesn't give false compliments.

There are dozens of photos, each enlarged to take up a full page. One is of a scene just after the sun has set. The street lights have come on and are blurred from the long exposure, making them shine like jewels: the stop lights in the distance are emerald and ruby, and the street lights along the Seine and stretching across the bridge to the left bank are gold. The water is a turbulent swirl of soft blues, purples and pinks. Along the quay is a man, his solitary figure backlit by a street lamp. The scene conjures an ache of loneliness. Perhaps it's a form of self-portrait. The next photo is taken through a window. A young woman is playing the piano. Her long hair is tied back and she's wearing a black tank top and jeans. Her image is centred and crisp, but around her is a myriad of abstract converging reflections. One of them is Nobuaki with his camera held up to his eye. Beside him is another man's face, small and slightly blurred. There are a few outlines of cars and some signs from across the street. The vague shapes form a curtain that appears to open to reveal the girl, her head lowered and her hands spread over the keys.

"I was walking on *Ile Saint-Louis* when I heard the music," Nobuaki says. "And there she was, playing in a chocolate shop. She knew I was there, but she kept playing, and I just listened. I took only one picture. It was a beautiful moment."

This is a beautiful moment. Do I say this or think it? The port is getting to me. And the fatigue. But for an instant, I feel it, the constant stream of moments, with no beginning or end. And as I sit nestled between friend and lover, even the boundary of where I end and they begin is blurred. The moment stretches out forever. The Now? *Stay like this,* I think.

ENCORE!

IT'S SNOWING AGAIN. FROM MY APARTMENT WINDOW IN MONTreal I watch the flakes flit down from the sky, shimmering in the muted sun. It's -19°C with the wind-chill. You could comfortably skate or ski on a day like today. Many people are. Winter, though, is my time for hibernation. It's my excuse to wear fleece suits and drink consecutive pots of tea and hot chocolate and, when need be, hot toddies. My violin is silent in its case these days, also in a state of dormancy. In Paris it's only 0°C, but with a relative humidity of 93 percent. I much prefer Montreal's windchill. At least here it's socially acceptable to be bundled nearly to the point of androgyny.

It's too cold to busk, of course, but there is a Metro system and a collection of characters who play there. I interviewed a few of them recently for an article in a local magazine. Some were foreigners, from Mali, China, Ecuador and Russia. Some were 50-year-old men with out-of-tune guitars, down on their luck without many other options to meet their basic needs. And some were young, in their early twenties, around the same age I was when I moved to Paris. I saw in them the same spark, the same innocence and joy and wide-open heart I had then. Ready for anything.

Yeah, so after a couple of years living together in Paris, Frédéric and I moved to Montreal. At first, we lived in a succession of different apartments, which we furnished through Craigslist ads. We went jogging in the park. We went camping, canoeing, and hiking. We got a cat. Then a dog. Eventually we bought a place together, a small triplex in the north end of the Plateau. With two tenants in the above apartments, we moved into the bottom floor. We were going to have kids and continue along the course that people naturally do. And then we didn't.

Our separation happened suddenly. We flung apart seemingly as quickly as we had flung into each other when we met six years before. One day we were together, and then we weren't.

when numbers are crashing   and prevent development
now, is the time to be cautious. If a herd disappears, that's it.
In sensitive calving ground

252 | BUSKER

Of course, the break had been slowly growing. Frédéric was increasingly invested in his work and had less energy at home. I worked mostly from home, translating and writing, and spent a great deal of time waiting for him to come home. Neither of us were happy.

The split was Frédéric's idea. Logic and rationale were always his forte. He thought we'd be able to evolve better on our own. Apart.

I would have fought fiercely for us, because that's what I do, but I couldn't fight all on my own. Part of me also knows he is right. As perfect as we were for each other when we met, we had become imperfect for each other over time — unintentionally stifling the other. Neither of us could breathe. We needed space. We needed *distance*. To find our selves again.

So, when one of our tenants moved out, I took the apartment upstairs. Now our beds are superimposed. We have separate lives, or we try to, but sometimes at night I lie awake, thinking of him below me and wondering how it is that one of us doesn't race up or down the flight of stairs that separates us and crawl into the other's arms.

"I can't live without you," we'd sob, and hold each other.

But we can. I mean, we are.

Sometimes I imagine us regaining our passion for one another. We'll build an inside staircase linking the two apartments. We'll keep our separate living spaces, but have a communal area, where we will meet for meals and discussion and movies and cuddling. I imagine us building a big solarium for all our books. We could meet there in the evenings and light candles, drink port and read and read and read.

OTHER TIMES I IMAGINE our lives drifting further apart. I imagine travelling again. To India. Or to Japan, where both Kosuke and Nobuaki are living now. I imagine meeting a thousand other people. And Frédéric meeting a thousand other people. And one day maybe we'll live so far from each other, in different countries or continents, that we might not even think about the other often, maybe only once in a while, and when we do, it won't be with a harsh pang of missing. It will simply be wondering how the other person was. A little blip and then life will resume.

WHEN I MOVED UPSTAIRS, I brought all my things with me, except for one: my violin. I still can't bear to take it. It was the object of our meeting and the centre of our union — a symbol of our love. Taking it would be too final. Too *over*. I like to think of my violin in his space, its case closed but full of potential. I long to play for him again, like I did the day we met, to have him watch me with those kind, attentive eyes, sitting on the staircase as if time did not exist. How strange that we met on a staircase, and now a staircase is what separates us.

I was having coffee at my neighbours' recently, a friendly couple I met walking my dog, and I was telling them that I've been miserable lately, due to the recent break-up. I told them that my future was a terrifying uncertain void.

"You should read this book I'm reading," my neighbour said. "It's by Eckhart Tolle. He says the present moment is what is important."

I put my coffee down and stared at him.

"It's just a matter of shutting off your conscious mind. Of living in the Now," he said.

I THINK I'LL LEAVE MY VIOLIN downstairs for a while yet. I don't have the heart to play, and nothing to prepare for. But in the spring, when the sun returns and the sound of dripping resonates through the streets, and soccer balls are blown up and people start wearing T-shirts even though it's still too cold, when windows crack open after a long season of immobility and the sweet spring air swallows the staleness and light is radiant on the faces of Montrealers for having survived another winter, that's when my fingers will start to itch. It happens every year. Melody will fill my heart again. That's when I will go downstairs and get my violin. I will tune the strings and play a gigue. Then I'll call my friend Jessie. She's a cellist and only lives a few blocks away. We'll meet on the street and walk together to our usual spot by the park in front of the grocery store. There we will set up our stands and open our cases.

Damn it. I am projecting into the future again when I'm supposed to be in the Now. Why is it so hard?

"*T'ES FRANÇAISE?*" people here often ask. I haven't picked up a Quebecois accent yet, and my anglo background is often concealed by my Parisian pronunciation and intonation.

"*Non,*" I say. "*Mais j'ai habité à Paris pendant quelques temps.*"

I often think about that city, my old love. Paris remains embedded in my psyche and in my heart. How could it not? Paris was so many things: an adventure, a challenge and, especially, a teacher. She taught me abandonment — first the abandonment of projected futures, when I let go of Pierre and what I thought life in Paris would be, then the abandonment of my past and its old pains and old sorrows. In Paris, playing on the streets, I just *was*. In Paris. Playing on the streets.

Stop. I'm getting distracted by the past. It's Now that matters.

MAYBE I'LL GO DOWNSTAIRS and get my violin after all. I could use a little Bach in my life. Yes, I'll go and get it. I'll put my shoulder rest on and tighten my bow. I'll tuck the violin under my chin as close to Tim's centre positioning as I can. I'll close my eyes, bring my bow to the strings and play the first piece that comes. I won't think about bowing or intonation. I won't think about anything. I will just play and maybe, if I'm lucky, despite it all I will remember how to resonate my inner string.

ACKNOWLEDGEMENTS

There were many times during the writing of this book that I stopped believing in myself. When that happened, there was a whole safety net of people there waiting, believing in me until I could pick up the reins again. Those I want to thank are many — more than could fit on this page. Here are just a few: Frédéric, who read countless drafts and whose enthusiasm never waned. My sister Ephie and my brother Simon for their steady support. My dear Auntie Jo, for our precious midnight talks. Jessie, for providing comic relief and for patiently enduring years of ranting. Kate and Merino, who read early versions and pushed me forward. Brendan, Mel, Brigitte, Jody, Amanda, Ting, Sophie, Lesley, and Karl, who were a constant choir of positivity. Linda, who first taught me the magic of the violin and of the metaphysical. Anne and René for the tea and talks. Pierre, Kosuke, Nobuaki, Jérémie, Tim, George, Monsieur Mystique, and Maâmar for adding beauty and colour to the city of light. Brigitte, Jean-Pierre, and Cathy Bourrely for their stunning generosity and for accepting me into their family. Isabel, Dimitri, Claire, Adam, and Alayna for showing me the way of words. Lily, my guardian angel dog. Jérôme, my weirdness equal, for loving all of me. Harold, my editor, for his extraordinary wizardry. Hagios Press, for taking a chance on me. My father, who taught me to read. My mother for her unconditional love and for accepting all my life choices, no matter what. To the people of Paris, for their generosity and for teaching me to speak French. And to everyone who put a coin in my case and encouraged me along the way. Thank you, thank you, thank you. Merci, merci, merci.

Nisha Coleman was born and continues to live in Montreal, where she writes, translates, and plays violin. Her work has appeared in publications such as *Every Day Fiction*, *Pif Magazine*, and *Road Junky*, and has been broadcast on the CBC (*WireTap*). She is a regular storyteller at Yarn and Confabulation. *Busker: Stories from the Streets of Paris* is Nisha Coleman's first book.